ASTON VILLA
FRIENDLIES, TOURS & TESTIMONIALS

By Bryan Sheppard

Published by:
Yore Publications
12 The Furrows, Harefield,
Middx. UB9 6AT

© Bryan Sheppard 2012

....

All rights reserved.
No part of this publication may be reproduced
or copied in any manner without the prior permission
in writing of the copyright holder.

British Library Cataloguing-in-Publication Data.
A catalogue record for this book
is available from the British Library.

ISBN 978-0-9569848-7-6

Managed and manufactured by:
Jellyfish Solutions Limited

About the Author

I was born into a divided household in the early years of the 1950's. My mother Alice was a devoted West Bromwich Albion supporter whilst Cyril my dad was Villa through and through. Keen to see his son supporting his beloved Villans he regaled me with stories of Villa's former glories and the exploits of players like Frank Barson, Billy Walker, Pongo Waring and of course the Gibson, Talbot and Tate half back line. Once dad realised that by the age of seven my indoctrination was complete, he took me to my first game.

I can recall the whole experience as though it was yesterday. It was a sunny day in 1960 and the Villa were playing Chelsea. Sporting my new claret and blue bobble hat and matching scarf, which my Albion supporting mother had reluctantly knitted for me, we caught the bus from town to Villa Park and were dropped off opposite the church. I can remember how excited people seemed and how dark their clothes were but the first thing that really struck me was the colourful rosettes and star badges that the street vendors were touting. Of course I had to have a rosette! My dad on the other hand seemed more concerned to make sure he got a programme for the game but that didn't interest me at all as a seven year old.

We walked up Trinity Road past the Holte Hotel and then the back of the massive Holte End came into view. I remember my dad telling me that it was the biggest end in the country. This meant nothing to me until I saw it from my seat in the Trinity Road stand, but more of that in a moment. As our walk towards the ground continued I was full of questions; I remember my dad pointing out Aston Hall and asking him if that was where the players lived! As we reached the ground the next job was to get a ticket for a seat in the Trinity Road stand and I can recall him grumbling that there were no reductions for children in those days.

Once through the turnstiles I was awestruck by the concourse which to me, at that time, reminded me of a cathedral. We made our way up the stairs which seemed very steep and quite dark until you looked up and saw the sun streaming through the beautiful stained glass windows. It felt like these steps were going on for ever, well I was only seven, but then we reached the top and entered the seating area. I was immediately struck by the beautiful green pitch laid out before and me how it contrasted with dark wooden seats and floorboards.

Once the game began the first thing that surprised me was watching grown men shouting and cheering, I assumed they would be a lot more conservative and it was only children who behaved like that! I never thought for one moment that the Villa would lose as they hung on to their 3-2 lead and was proved correct. I just knew we were going to win – THIS WAS THE VILLA!

Oh yes by the way, I still have both the programme and the rosette! Sadly I lost the ticket.

FOREWORD

By Graham Taylor

If you are an Aston Villa fan at heart you will take this book with you wherever you go!

It is about the games that nearly everyone forgets. Friendlies, Testimonials and Tour games, included within where former players, managers and staff reminisce about these games and tell stories that more than bring a smile to your face. In addition it is packed with photographs that many will not have seen before, which have been kindly lent by both fans and players. It really is an Aston Villa read, put together by Bryan Sheppard an avid Villa fan.

I have been both proud and fortunate to be an Aston Villa manager and am aware of how much the club means to its faithful supporters and I am sure that this book will be well received by them, especially those who remember these games, having in many cases travelled many miles to watch them.

What I call the heartbeat of the club is more than apparent in the stories that are told, and the memories that are brought to light are both fascinating and humorous. On many of the tours supporters and players mixed and socialized with each other, something that tends not to happen now.

I hope you all enjoy reading this book. It is different from the normal football book. It records many games that were played when football was a sport and not a business, when football was fun and both the players and supporters fought for the same cause.

Happy, happy memories!

Graham Taylor – former Villa Manager

ACKNOWLEDGEMENTS

I would like to officially thank, in no particular order, the following people without whose help I would not have completed this project.

Rob Bishop:- The editor of the Aston Villa News and Record who suggested that because I was collecting so much information about Villa's Friendlies, Testimonials and Tours that I should turn the hobby into a book. Rob has helped me in so many ways throughout the project it would take at least a page to list all the support he has provided.

Laura Brett:- The hard working archivist at the Villa with a "can do" attitude who has been unbelievably helpful. On numerous occasions she has "gone that extra mile" to make sure I was able to access vital information from the Villa archives.

Jon Farrelly:- A loyal Villa supporter who follows the team home and away in competitive games, friendlies and tours wherever they might be. Jon has been a brilliant help in identifying the early games which have never been properly recorded. As mentioned Jon has been on many Villa tours as a fan over the years, he has been crucial in correcting and supplying key information. He also has loaned numerous unique photographs for this project and many of them are included in this book.

Dave Bridgewater:- Another lifelong Villa fan and up until this year a regular contributor to the Villa programme. Dave helped so much in the earlier stages of this project by sharing key information both from his excellent memory and his personal collection.

Andy Hooper:- Andy, like most of us has been supporting the club all his life and is blessed with an encyclopaedic memory of Villa since the war. This combined with his large Villa related collection of memorabilia, which he shared with me for this publication, has been extremely helpful.

Reg Thacker:- A well-known and respected former Aston Villa employee whose knowledge was extremely valuable in the early stages of the project. His encouragement throughout the life of the project helped me enormously.

Barry Swash:- For so much on-going help, support and encouragement. In addition, his kindness in allowing me to plunder his massive collection of old newspapers, programmes, books and magazines for all the West Midlands clubs was invaluable.

Steve Stride:- Former Deputy CEO at the Villa; Steve shared so many memories, stories and photographs with me.

Graham Taylor:- For his memories and continued enthusiasm for this project.

Neil Rioch:- For giving the project his backing, sharing ex-players' contact details and making them aware that the Aston Villa Former Players Association supported the project.

Liz Bridgewater:- No relation to Dave Bridgewater, Liz my PA has helped with the proof reading of this book in her own time! Thanks Liz.

Hilary Roberts:- For her amazing patience and photographic skills in turning memorabilia; faded, torn and creased into amazing pictures for this publication.

John Russell:- Another lifelong Villa supporter who generously shared his extensive research of Villa's early games.

The Staff:- Birmingham Evening Mail.

Former Aston Villa Players:- Peter McParland, Harry Burrows, Jimmy MacEwan, Alan O'Neill, Alan Deakin, Bobby Thomson, Mike Tindall, Ron Wylie, Nigel Sims, Charlie Aitken, Lew Chatterley, Neil Rioch, Jimmy Brown, Ray Graydon, Brian Little, Chris Nichol, Jim Cumbes, Colin Gibson and Gordon Cowans for generously sharing their memories, photographs, films, cuttings and souvenirs.

The Staff of Birmingham Central Library - Archives Section.

Club Historians from a number of both league and non-league clubs, that between them have filled in many vital gaps in the research.

Thank you also to Gail my wife for her help with the vagaries of personal computers along with her constant encouragement when at times it looked like I would never get the book finished!

COPYRIGHT NOTICE

Many of the pictures in this book originated from scrapbooks and photograph albums belonging to former Villa players and supporters, and it has not been possible to establish clear copyright on evey item. Therefore apologies are offered should copyright have inadvertantly been infringed.

INTRODUCTION

Since their formation in 1874 Aston Villa have played over 1,300 so called friendly games. Indeed their first ever match, probably against either Aston Brook St. Mary's or Aston Park Unity, was such a game. Prior to the founding of the Football League, almost fifteen years later, the majority of the games played by most clubs were either cup ties, friendlies or benefit matches.

During the 19th Century in addition to the FA Cup, Aston Villa entered many similar local competitions such as The Birmingham Senior Cup, The Staffordshire Cup and The Lord Mayor of Birmingham's Cup. Whilst these games were keenly contested and played by the club's strongest teams, over the years they became less important and were subsequently contested by the reserve teams or occasionally by members of the first team squad. These games are not included in this work.

To use the word friendly, especially in the early days of football, was something of a misnomer as many games were full blooded affairs especially when local pride was at stake. Today most football clubs play the majority of their friendly games before the start of a new season. These are generally used to help players reach the necessary level of fitness and to sort out the tactics that the team are likely to employ for the coming season. However increasingly, with the financial pressures on clubs, there is now a tendency for many teams to take part in short tournaments which involve lucrative sponsorship deals. Neil Rioch summed it up, "The pre-season friendly was an integral part of your preparation for the new season and was treated exactly the same as an ordinary match."

Looking back it is interesting to note that mid-season friendlies for Villa were quite common and they seem to be played for a variety of reasons. Sometimes they were part of a transfer agreement; for example when a club bought a player from a less wealthy team they would sometimes agree to play a friendly game at the selling club's ground with the gate receipts going to the home team. A typical example of this was when Aston Villa bought Neil and Bruce Rioch from Luton Town in the late 1960's.

There were also the mid-season "money spinners" such as Villa's game against Santos in 1972 organised to raise funds for the club. A further reason for these matches was when a team had been knocked out of the FA Cup and subsequently had a free week-end as Villa did when they played the ill-fated match against Rangers in 1976.

Testimonial matches or "testimonials" as they are normally known were granted to players with ten years' service at a club. These games were frequently played against prestigious opposition or local rivals to ensure a reasonable crowd and the money raised from the game went to the player. The practice began when players, even those at top clubs, were paid far less in real terms than they are today. For example up until 1961 there was a salary cap for professional footballers in England of £20 per week which was strictly adhered to by clubs and monitored by the Football League. The testimonial game therefore often drew a respectable attendance to reward a player's loyalty.

Unfortunately in later years they were not afforded the support of fans that perhaps the players deserved. For example Gordon 'Sid' Cowans was granted a testimonial and for obvious reasons he tried to arrange a game against local rivals Birmingham City. Gordon takes up the story, "I wanted to play the Blues but the police wouldn't allow it. I then tried to get Celtic or Rangers but I couldn't persuade them to come down." By this time the powers at Aston Villa were putting 'Sid' under pressure to get a game played. Eventually Stoke City agreed to play but only around 4,500 people turned up and according to Gordon 2,000 of those came from Stoke!

This example was not untypical of games such as these around that time and was probably the beginning of the decline in testimonials. The continued fall off in recent years is probably in some way due to the salaries earned by professional footballers coupled with the diminishing number of players who remain at one club for ten years. Similar to the testimonial, a benefit game is normally arranged to support a deserving cause or appeal for example Villa played West Bromwich Albion in 1985 and all the proceeds from that game went towards the Bradford City Fire Appeal.

One final area that needs to be highlighted here are tours. These have become more popular amongst clubs since the end of the Second World War. However, they were not unheard of in earlier times, the most famous being Villa's pre-war visit to Nazi Germany which is featured later in this book. More recently the purpose of the end of season tour was described by Ron Wylie as, "…a bit of a break…a holiday…a reward for the players…" Then again the reason may not be that simple because even in the 1970's they generated income for the club and helped pay for the trip but these were not, "…the money spinners they are today" according to Colin Gibson.

Whereas there were clear rules determining the payers' behaviour on tour much of "what went on tour stayed on tour" and perhaps the following quote from Brian Little sums this up. "Over the years I learnt that taking a group of lads away on tour and locking them up together is not the greatest thing in the world so I tried to arrange home friendlies or games away to British clubs."

1884   CASTLE BLUES

September 27th

Castle Blues 1   Aston Villa 1

During the pre-league days it happened from time to time that Aston Villa fielded two different teams playing on the same day. The 27th September 1884 was such an occasion when one side entertained Aston Unity at Perry Barr whilst the other made the trip over to Shrewsbury to play the infamous Castle Blues. Whilst the two games were not billed as first and reserve team matches the Birmingham Post pointed out at the time that Villa fielded a "good representative side" against the Shrewsbury based club. However further research would suggest that the stronger of the two Villa sides were playing at Perry Barr.

The Castle Blues club had a fierce reputation and often employed unorthodox tactics in the course of their games. A typical example of this was when a match against their local rivals Wellington Town had to be abandoned early in the second half because of the Castle Blues "violent and unorthodox tackling" which left the opposition with just six outfield players on the pitch! Interestingly the hooliganism was not merely confined to the players, contemporary reports suggested that their supporters were even more aggressive than the Castle Blues team!

The Villa team selected to take on the infamous Castle Blues at the Underdale Recreation Grounds were:-

The notorious Castle Blues and their disreputable supporters.

Archie Vale; Simmonds, Foster; Burton, Horton, Fisher; W.Vale, Mitton, Hibbett, Lodge, Hodgetts.

The 27th September 1884 was a sunny day in Shrewsbury and this, coupled with a visit from Aston Villa, attracted a large crowd for the match. The first half went by without any untoward incidents and the two teams were level at the interval having scored a goal apiece.

The second period however was more eventful. Aston Villa took control of the game and looked the more likely to add to their tally, when a curious incident occurred. The ball mysteriously burst and although it was quickly replaced, that too soon met the same fate. Given the reputation of the "Blues" players and supporters suspicion fell on them once it was discovered that there were no more footballs available; leaving the referee with no alternative other than to abandon the game with the scores level.

In conclusion it is worth mentioning that the Castle Blues club went into decline not long after this game due to their disreputable behaviour on and off the field which hindered their progress. They finally disbanded in 1886 yet from their ashes Shrewsbury Town was born with the aim of equalling "The Blues" successes without their notoriety!

1885 PRESTON NORTH END

May 29th

Aston Villa 1   Preston North End 5

In 1884 Preston North End played an FA Cup tie against the now defunct Upton Park Football Club from London. At that time all soccer was amateur however the Upton Park officials felt that Preston were flouting this rule and reported them to the Football Association. When challenged Preston's Secretary William Sudell confirmed that the club's players were being remunerated, arguing that this did not breach the FA's regulations as it was common practice amongst the top clubs in England. The officials at the Football Association did not agree and Preston North End were thrown out of the competition. This was the catalyst which led to the professional game being recognised.

Sudell kept up the pressure, continuing to frustrate the FA by importing better players from all over Britain. In addition to paying these new players Sudell also found them good jobs in the town to supplement their income. Clearly the matter of professionalism was not going away as more clubs followed Preston's example, and in October that year when Preston and a number of other leading clubs met and threatened to break-away from the Football Association, matters came to a head.

The FA responded by setting up a committee, which included Preston's Sudell, to try and resolve the matter amicably. Whatever went on behind the locked doors of the smoke filled rooms, it transpired that the professional clubs got their own way. It was then on 20th July 1885, the FA announced "in the interests of Association Football, to legalise the employment of professional players but only under certain restrictions".

These conditions included a rule that clubs were only permitted to pay players who had either been "born or had lived for two years within a six-mile radius of the ground."

However this was ignored and it seems unlikely that any clubs were ever punished for not adhering to this rule.

Villa fans' involved in an early instance of football hooliganism.

In the midst of all the wrangling football continued to grow in popularity with gates improving all over the country. This was reflected at Perry Barr where over 5,000 turned up to watch the Villa take on the mighty Preston North End with their host of Scottish stars! The Villa put out a strong team to try and match the Lancastrians and lined up thus:- Harvey; Riddell, Simmonds; Dawson, Burton; Albert Brown, Whateley, Hunter, Arthur Brown, Houghton, Davies.

Archie Hunter lost the toss and the Preston captain asked Aston Villa to kick up the famous Perry Barr slope, into a strong wind with the sun in their eyes. Preston capitalised on their advantage immediately with a sustained period of pressure however Villa seemed unfazed by this and appeared happy to concede a number of corners which they managed to deal without too much trouble. Unfortunately for the home team the respite was temporary as Preston came roaring back with waves of pressure and believed on one occasion that they had scored but fortunately for the home team the effort was ruled off-side. Villa eventually pulled themselves together and came more into the game but sadly on the few occasions they breached the Preston defence Rose, in the visitors' goal and in great form, made a number of first class saves.

It was from one of Rose's long clearances that Preston took the lead. The ball was fed out to the wing and a pinpoint cross delivered which was met perfectly by Gordon who made no mistake with a powerful header, giving Harvey in the Villa goal no chance.

Once the game restarted some players began to put in some heavy tackles and the game got a little ugly culminating in the Preston centre forward, Dewhurst, clashing with Villa's half back Fred Dawson which, according to the Birmingham Post, almost ended in a "bout of fisticuffs." The resulting Preston free kick was laid off to the dangerous Dewhurst, who immediately hit a ferocious shot which easily beat Harvey and doubled Preston's lead. Spurred on by their success the away team laid siege on the Villa goal but thanks to some heroics by their defence, spectacular saves from Walter Harvey and some poor finishing by the North End forwards, they somehow managed to hold on until half time without conceding a third goal.

The second half began with the home team taking advantage of the slope and seeking a way back into the game, unfortunately when opportunities to score occasionally arose, the excellent Rose in the Preston goal appeared impregnable. However Villa persisted and were rewarded in the 52nd minute when Howard Vaughn hit a venomous shot, which the North End keeper managed to punch out back and into play.

Albert Brown, Villa's Goalscorer.

The ball fell at the feet of Villa's right winger Albert Brown whose well-directed effort sailed past the talented Preston goal keeper into the roof of the net.

This goal encouraged the Villans and they pushed forward at every opportunity but the North End backs Ross and Suter kept the home team at bay. With Villa well on top it was a "bit of a blow" when the visitors broke away and scored through Ross with a simple tap in from close range. Within five minutes a stunned Villa defence looked on as Preston increased their lead further with a neatly taken goal by Thomson but worse was still to come. With just minutes remaining Preston's wing half Russell put matters completely out of Villa's reach when he headed home their fifth goal. The Birmingham Post reported that, "This reverse seemed to wholly demoralise the Villa, the visitors having the game all their own way." Fortunately the Aston Villa players managed to hold out without conceding further but when the full time whistle blew things "got nasty."

The Villa supporters, who were not used to losing games by such a margin especially at home, invaded the pitch and attacked the Preston players. Pelted with stones, bottles and sticks, the Preston lads fled from the pitch pursued by the Villa "roughs" who quickly caught up with them and attacked them with "boots and fists". The visitors only managed to escape from the mob and take refuge in the dressing rooms when the Aston Villa players and "some of the more respectable onlookers" stepped in to help them.

1888 THE CANADIANS

October 24th

Aston Villa 4   The Canadians 2

In the autumn of 1888 a party of seventeen players from Ontario, Canada toured the British Isles taking in games against Rangers, Hearts, Sunderland, Middlesbrough, Blackburn Rovers, Notts. County, Newton Heath (Manchester United), West Bromwich Albion, Aston Villa and many others. The match against Villa was towards the end of the tour and the North American team had taken some notable scalps thus far during their twenty games. They now faced an Aston Villa side who were riding high in the inaugural Football League having won all of their home fixtures. The Villa officials were clearly taking no chances against their Canadian cousins and included a significant number of experienced players, lining up thus:- Warner; Cox, Coulton; Barton, Devey, Yates; Green, Brown, Hunter Hodgetts, Allen. The game evidently appealed to the local populous with over 4,000 people turning out to watch the spectacle on a drizzly Monday afternoon at Perry Barr.

The first fifteen minutes saw the Canadian team being outclassed and completely overrun by a rampant Villa side and the inevitable opening goal soon arrived via the boot of speedy winger Albert Allen. Then shortly afterwards the majestic Scot, Archie Hunter added a second with a dipping shot from twenty yards. Aston Villa were clearly trying to put the game beyond their "colonial cousins" as soon as possible and just a few minutes later they were three goals to the good when tricky inside forward Dennis Hodgetts finished a clever move with some style.

It would have been expected at this point that the shocked Canadians, losing 3-0 after just fifteen minutes would have buckled but evidently quite the reverse happened. The plucky North American team regrouped and attacked with a mixture of speed and clever football that surprised the Villa players and put them on the back foot.

Villa's first game against opposition from outside the British Isles.

The concerted pressure eventually paid off when centre half Carl Kranz sped down the wing and crossed to Dr. Harry Pirie, who turned the low centre accurately into the goal from close range. With the game swinging from end to end it was always likely that there would be another goal before the break and the home team didn't let their supporters down. An intricate passing move that involved a number of players ended with Hunter hitting a stunning effort from inside the box which gave the goalkeeper no chance and sent the home team in 4-1 up at half time.

The second half began with Villa seeking more goals but the visitors' defence held firm. Once the Canadians had weathered the storm they began to get control of midfield, dominate the game and were desperately unfortunate not to reduce their deficit when Walter Bowman's effort ricocheted off the woodwork. This slice of bad luck spurred the opposition on and resulted in a sustained period of problems for the Villa defence that only dissipated after full back Gershom Cox desperately cleared the ball out for a corner. The resulting cross caused more confusion in the Villans' goalmouth and was eventually scrambled away by a relieved Frank Coulton. Still the Canadians pressed and in the final minutes their incessant pressure was rewarded. This time it was another doctor, Walter Thomson, who seized on some confusion between the Villa defenders and grabbed a much deserved second goal.

The Canadian Team

1891 SMALL HEATH

February 14th

Aston Villa 3   Small Heath 0

Whilst research would suggest that the first player to be sent off in a football match was a certain John Lile in 1856 it was still a relatively unusual occurrence during the 19th century. As far as Aston Villa were concerned it seems likely that the dubious honour of being the first Villan dismissed from the field goes to one Dennis Hodgetts who was sent off for punching an opponent in 1888. Following hot on the heels of Dennis came Lichfield born Thomas "Surefoot" McKnight, who had signed from Burton Swifts at the beginning of the 1890-91 season.

> *An early report of a Villa player being sent off.*

Whilst he only made thirteen league and cup games, his name does crop up in some friendly games including the match at Perry Barr against Villa's neighbours Small Heath. Even without a number of experienced players such as the afore mentioned Dennis Hodgetts along with John Devey and Albert Brown the Villa side appeared strong enough to see off their non-league visitors from across the city. The full Aston Villa line-up read:- Warner; Cox, Evans; J. Campbell, Brown, H. Devey; L. Campbell, Graham, McKnight, F. Burton, Athersmith.

Centre forward Tom McKnight kicked off in front of the 4,000 fans and immediately the home team were in the ascendancy, putting their visitors under tremendous pressure and forcing Small Heath goalkeeper, Charsley into a number of top-class saves. The pressure continued unabated and it seemed only a matter of time before Aston Villa went ahead, however the Small Heath defence weathered the storm and managed a couple of attacks on the Villa goal themselves which tested keeper Jimmy Warner. This fired up the home team and they began to push forward once again. During this period of Villa pressure, the Birmingham Daily Post reported that an, "...altercation took place between Jenkins and McKnight, in which blows were exchanged..." The fracas led to the referee sending both off.

Once the two players were off the pitch and the game restarted the Villa mounted a series of attacks on the Small Heath goal and this pressure resulted in a corner which caused the alarm bells to ring in the visitors' box. The ensuing scramble eventually saw the ball fall to the feet of Villa's unmarked inside-forward Jack Graham who couldn't believe his luck as he efficiently dispatched the ball into the net to put Aston Villa ahead. Small Heath responded positively and threw caution to the wind in an attempt to get back on level terms. As a result the game became very exciting, swinging from end to end culminating in a fine header from the Heathens' left winger Hands that shaved the post. Spurred on by the near miss the non-leaguers began to dominate proceedings pinning their more famous opponents in their own half for long periods.

The home team managed to hang on, thanks to a couple of slices of luck and eventually broke away but unfortunately William Devey squandered a straightforward opportunity to double Villa's lead. Apparently, unmarked and just six yards out, he received a near perfect pass then somehow contrived to loft the ball over the bar when it would have been far simpler to score.

Unperturbed Small Heath continued to pull out all the stops and just before the interval Hallam missed a magnificent chance to level the score. Finding himself alone in the area with an open goal gaping in front of him he tried to pass the ball into the corner of the net only to see his weak shot cleared off the line by Villa's centre-half James Brown.

The subsequent corner was easily dealt with by the home team's defenders and the Villa went into the break with their 1-0 lead intact.

The second half continued much in the same vein as the first had ended with the underdogs pushing for an equaliser. Time and time again the Villa defence stood firm, making last ditch tackles and aimless clearances up field, then against the run of play the home team doubled their advantage. The move began in Villa's half of the field and some neat passing amongst the forwards saw Scottish right-half George "Monkey Brand" Campbell gain possession and according to the Birmingham Post "...put a finish to a smart run with a grand goal." This second goal seemed to knock the visitors' confidence and Aston Villa were suddenly head and shoulders above the Heathens pinning them in the final third of the pitch with a series of penetrating attacks.

The pressure seemed to have paid off when the crowd witnessed Jack Graham celebrating what he thought was a perfectly good goal, unfortunately the referee had different ideas and disallowed his first-rate effort.

The incident didn't deter Aston Villa and before long they were 3-0 ahead. This time it was Charlie Athersmith who described as "one of the fleetest right-wingers of his time," raced down the wing and delivered a textbook cross for "Monkey Brand" Campbell to score with a near post volley. From the restart the visitors took the game to their distinguished opponents once more and were considered very unlucky not to reduce the deficit when centre forward Shot's simple six yard header struck the crossbar and went over. Still the non-leaguers pushed forward but to no avail as the Aston Villa defenders had the upper hand and ensured the home team ran out winners.

Goalkeeper Warner

1896   DERBY COUNTY

October 5th

Aston Villa   2   Derby County   1

Born in the Newtown area of Aston during 1866, John Devey was first noticed by the Villa as a sixteen year old prolific goal scorer playing centre forward for local Birmingham team Mitchell St. George's. He signed for Aston Villa in 1891 and soon rose through the ranks eventually becoming captain of the club and subsequently leading them through the most successful period of their history. Under his guidance they won two FA Cups and five First Division titles, including a league and cup double in the 1896-97 season. Unfortunately Devey's inter-national career was not as impressive as that with his club side. The reason for this being that his career ran alongside two other great centre forwards of the time, Preston's John Goodall and Steve Bloomer of Derby, and so the great man unluckily gained just two England caps.

In 1896, as a reward for his loyalty and contribution to the club's success over the years, thirty year old John Devey was granted a benefit match to be played at Villa Park against Derby County. John gathered together a committee of friends to help him raise as much money as possible. According to the Aston Villa Committee's Minute Book it would appear that his benefit committee approached the Villa directors to ascertain whether it would be possible to collect money at the game to boost his funds. The Villa board rejected the request as they thought it would be "infra dig" i.e. beneath his dignity!

Regrettably Monday afternoon on the 5th October 1896, the day of the testimonial game was somewhat cold and wet, as a consequence only about 1,500 people braved the elements to pay their respects to the great man. The Villa lined up thus:- Whitehouse; Spencer, Evans; Chatt, James Cowan, Burton; Athersmith, Wheldon, Devey, John Cowan, Smith.

It had been announced prior to the game that Jimmy Crabtree would be playing sadly he had not recovered from an injury sustained against Sheffield United the previous Saturday in time for the Benefit Match for John Devey

According to newspapers at the time the meagre but enthusiastic crowd got behind the Villa from the start and cheered loudly every time Devey had the ball at his feet. The local press reported that Aston Villa were on top from the start and, kicking down the famous Perry Barr slope in the first half, were soon in front through none other than John Devey himself.

John Devey's Testimonial

Unluckily for the visitors shortly after this opening goal they were reduced to ten men when full back Jonathon Staley had to leave the field with a "severe strain." Aston Villa immediately capitalised on County's ill fortune when Fred Wheldon, a £350 signing from neighbours Small Heath, put Villa two goals to the good, nodding the ball past the stranded Derby County goalkeeper.

The second half saw a different attitude from the Rams, playing with the advantage of the slope, they went on the offensive and this soon paid benefits when Stephenson scored an exceptional goal. Oddly, rather than driving Derby on in search of an equaliser, the goal galvanised Villa who upped their game, took control and although they failed to add to their goal tally, they finished the game much the stronger team.

The takings for the game were £34.16s.9d (£34.84p) in gate money and £55 in advance tickets. The Villa directors made this up to £100 which would probably be worth almost £10,000 today. The club presented John with his cheque along with an illuminated certificate which read in part, "………

Under your judicious, kindly and firm captaincy the club has more than maintained the prominent position it attained under the leadership of your predecessor the ever to be remembered and beloved Archie Hunter......" Great praise indeed.

On his retirement from football in 1901 John coached at the club until 1903 whilst continuing his first class cricket career with Warwickshire where he notched up over 6,500 first class runs. During his later years with the "Bears" he established a thriving sports outfitters shop in Lozells and also served as a director of Aston Villa until his retirement in 1934. John Devey died six years later in Birmingham aged 73.

Perhaps the following taken from the Villa News and record in 1906 best sums up this Villa great, "For one so skilful, thorough and effective, his merits when in his prime were inexplicably overlooked by the (England) Selection Committee. He could play in most positions in the forward line, and was for many years one of the very best pivots in England. A close dribbler, with good pace, he was alive to every movement on the field, and possessing the rare gift of `intelligent anticipation`, made a splendid leader. He knew the game really well.....(and was) exceptionally clever with head and feet in front of goal; a prolific scorer."

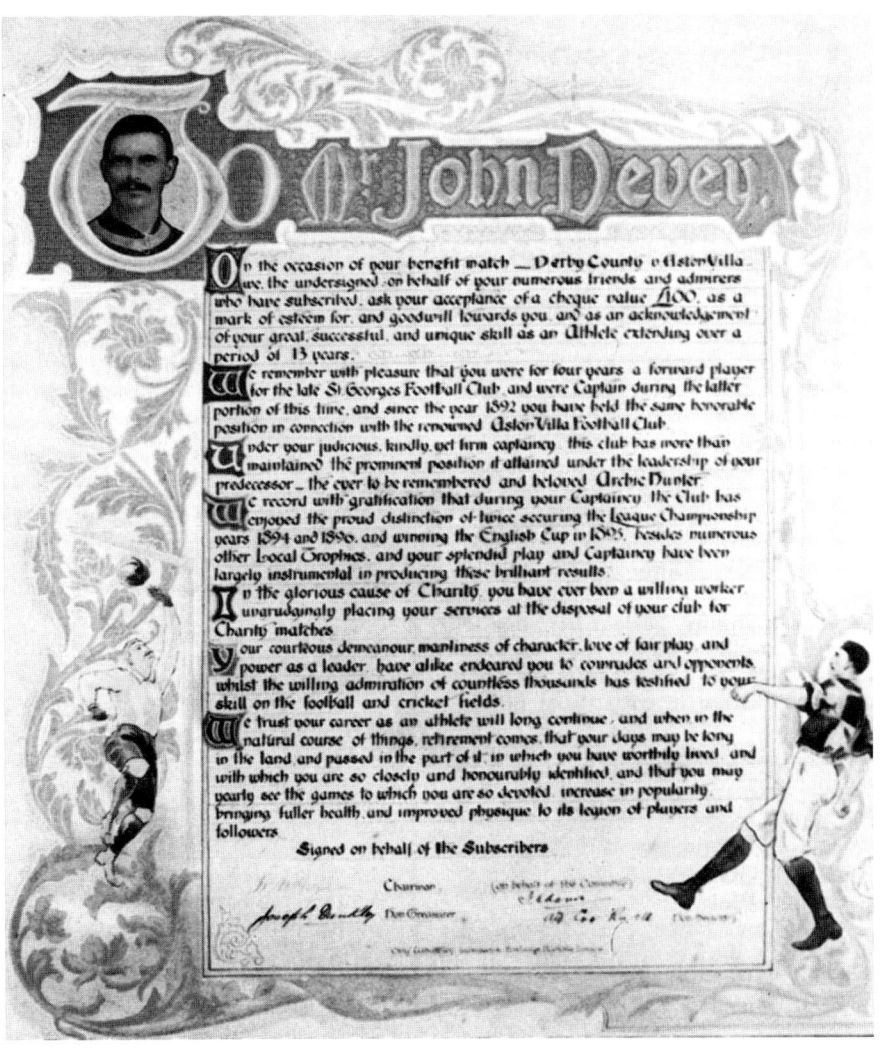

1898   THE CASUALS
February 23rd

The Casuals   1   Aston Villa   6

Founded in or around 1878 The Casuals were an amateur club who in their early days only signed players from the Charterhouse, Eton, and Winchester Schools. However in later years they opened this up to include all public school and university old boys. Between 1885 and 1898 Aston Villa played the Casuals on seven occasions in friendly games. Villa won all of these bar one, scoring twenty nine goals in the process, whilst only conceding eleven.

In terms of the FA Cup the Casuals' record was very poor having never successfully negotiated the first round. They faced Villa in just one of these cup matches and that was back in the 1890-91 season. Interestingly the game still features in the Aston Villa records because the 13-1 thrashing Villa dished out in first round of the competition still stands as the record aggregate score in a cup tie involving Aston Villa.

Some seven years later Villa travelled to Tufnell Park in London to play a friendly match against the Casuals. Over 3,000 spectators packed into a ground which also catered for athletics, on an overcast Wednesday afternoon, to witness the spectacle. The large crowd was probably attracted not only by the fame and quality of the opposition but more probably because the Villa had won the F.A. Cup and League double the previous season.

The London press suggested that the Casuals had fielded a weakened team and if they had played their best team then Villa would have "been obliged to go all the way to beat them."

It is interesting to compare and contrast that with the report in the Birmingham Post from the same week where they make it clear that Villa were fielding a number of reserves with no mention of the strength of the Casuals line-up.

As far as the game was concerned; the Birmingham Daily Post reported that the Villa had the "best of the opening play" and the London report grudgingly agreed that Villa "had it all their own way" in the first half. With this in mind, the first goal which was scored by the home team must have been against the run of play. However this didn't seem to faze the visitors who equalised on the half hour through Middlesbrough born inside forward Jimmy Suddick. Collecting the ball just inside the Casuals' half of the pitch Jimmy dribbled the ball a full thirty yards before unleashing a ferocious shot which soared into the top of the net. There were no further goals in the first half but whatever was said in the Villa dressing room during the interval clearly had the desired effect.

The London press report suggested that the visitors quickly put "matters beyond doubt when they chose to exert themselves..." in the second half. Exert themselves they certainly did and piled up five more goals before the final whistle. Fred Wheldon, whose record reveals that he averaged a goal every other game during his time with Aston Villa, lead the way with a hat-trick, whilst Bob Chatt and nineteen year old Malta born Cornellius Hogan weighed in with one apiece. The London press concluded that hat trick hero, "Wheldon was certainly the best forward on the field."

Villa's last ever game against The Casuals 1898

ASTON VILLA v. CASUALS: A Run Down the Wing.

1899 THE KAFFIRS

November 20th

Aston Villa 7   The Kaffirs 4

During 1897 Corinthian F.C, one of the top amateur football teams of the day, made a very successful tour of South Africa. This resulted; two years later, in the first ever Association Football team from Africa touring England. The team comprised mainly of Sotho, or as they were described at the time by the press, "pure blooded Basuto," players from Orange Free State who collectively played under name of "The Kaffirs."

One could imagine then that back in the 19th century the word "Kaffir" did not seem to have the same connotations as it has today. It has been argued that the origins of the word probably came from the Arabic word "gafir" meaning, among other things, "non believer". It could therefore be argued that this may have been taken up by early British missionaries who used the term to mean "heathen" when describing native South African people. Interestingly the word "Kaffir" does not seem to have become a wide spread abusive term until the 1930's.

The South African tourists or to give them their correct name, The Orange Free State "Kaffir" Football Club, arrived in Southampton in early September 1899. Here, according to Johnson, Holmes and Vasili in their informative paper "South African Footballers in Britain" the South Africans were greeted with a front page cartoon in a local Southampton sports newspaper declaring, "'Up come Eleven Little Nigger Boys from Savage South Africa." Another sporting journal printed something similar. This time the cartoon featured a black man in football kit, wearing just one boot, holding a spear in one hand and a tomahawk in the other, with feathers in his hair and a ring through his nose. Underneath the caption declares, "Jeeohsmiffikato, the crack Kaffir centre forward thirsting for gore and goals."

Leaving Southampton behind the Orange Free State team embarked on their mammoth forty nine match tour against first class opposition mainly from England but there is evidence to suggest that they also played some games in France, Ireland, Scotland and Wales. First stop for the South African party was the North East of England where on 5th September they played Newcastle United. Here the tourists were soundly beaten 6-3 in front of 6,000 "curious" Geordies. They next moved on to Sunderland where sadly they didn't fare much better losing 5-3 and then made the comparatively short trip to Middlesbrough to receive another trouncing this time by seven goals to three.

At the suggestion of the South African club it was agreed that the "Kaffirs" game against the Villa would be used to raise funds for the Birmingham Daily Mail's "Reservists Fund". Essentially any money raised from this appeal went towards supporting the Second Boer War in South Africa which had broken out after the tourists' arrival in the UK. With the game being played on a Monday afternoon in inclement weather, the game was poorly supported with around 3,500 turning out however this still raised well over £60 (worth around £5,500 in 2011) for the fund.

The first African team to play at Villa Park

Having noted the oppositions results around the country prior to the game the Aston Villa selection committee clearly decided it would be a "bit of a cake walk" and so named a few reserves; lining up as follows:- George; Noon, Evans; Bowman, Mann, Wilkes; Garfield, Leigh, Garratty, Wheldon, Smith. They also appointed Aston Villa first teamer Charlie Athersmith, who was coming towards the end of his career, as a guest referee. The Villa players emerged from the dressing rooms into a dank Autumnal afternoon, shortly followed by the black South African side who had pinned red white and blue ribbons to their navy blue shirts apparently to signify their loyalty to Queen Victoria.

Once the game had started it became immediately obvious to everyone in the ground that the tourists were out of their depth. This was illustrated when the Villa hit two goals in the first three minutes of the game. The first followed a neat passing move which ended with wing half Tommy Bowman pushing the ball through the South African keeper's legs. The second came directly from the restart when Jim Garfield cut in from the right wing, dribbled the ball round the goalkeeper and rolled it into an empty net. The visitors reacted positively to the setback and their enthusiasm and commitment, which continued unabated throughout the entire game, endeared them to the inquisitive Villa crowd. The Orange Free State players' positive attitude was supported by a local paper which suggested that "whatever they lacked in skill they made up for in determination."

With the Villa 2-0 up in as many minutes, the players realising the poor standard of their opponents, decided to abandon serious football and provide as much entertainment for the crowd as possible. Whilst this may well have been seen as patronising by today's standards it was probably just seen as a "bit of a laugh" by footballers 100 years ago. Fred Wheldon started the "fun" when he collected the ball close to his own penalty area and dribbled it almost the length of the field before hitting his shot wide. Not to be outdone many other players began to emulate him including goalkeeper Billy George who came up-field and played in the forward line leaving his defenders to look after the Villa goal, an act that was "thoroughly enjoyed by the crowd."

Whilst Aston Villa's revised tactics had clearly been designed to entertain rather than score goals they still managed to finish off one move in style to make it 3-0. This time it was the turn of full back Albert Evans, who had joined his forwards and scored with a delicate near post chip into the top corner of the net. With the majority of the Villa team still playing exhibition football in the opposition's half of the field it was no surprise when, just before the interval, the tourists took advantage of a rare Villa error. A misplaced pass fell at the feet of a South African forward who punished Villa with a powerful shot to reduce the deficit and send the visitors in at half time 3-1 down. The second half continued much the same way as the first, until a rare attack from the visitors resulted in a dubious penalty awarded by referee Athersmith who was clearly enjoying himself. Twayi hammered home the spot kick and Villa responded immediately, upped their game and scored three goals in quick succession to put the game beyond the visitors.

First on the mark was centre forward Billy Garratty whose speculative effort evaded everyone and nestled in the bottom corner of the net. This was followed shortly afterwards by his understudy the amateur Walter "Swappy" Leigh whose headed goal went in off the post. Then Fred "Diamond" Wheldon added a third a few minutes later cleverly deflecting in a cross from right winger Jimmy Garfield. Following this goal feast which put the game beyond the South African team the Aston Villa players returned to what the local Birmingham newspaper described as "the fun and games." During this period the visitors rarely had possession however they did surprise the hosts with a third goal when centre forward Twayi netted his second.

Goalscorer, half back Bowman

With the Aston Villa goalkeeper Billy George still playing up front with the forward line, his day was made when he scored Villa's seventh. It has to be said however that the final result could have been many more in Villa's favour had it not been for the athletic exploits of the South African goalkeeper Adolph who won many friends in the crowd as result. With Villa 7-3 to the good they began to sit back and pass the ball around whilst the final minutes ticked down, then totally against the run of play their visitors seized on a rare bad Villa pass and grabbed a fourth goal for themselves.

The next day the South Africans continued the English leg of their tour without exactly covering themselves in glory in terms of results. They lost all but one of their thirty seven games in England and drew the other one. It has not been recorded how many goals they actually scored themselves but they apparently conceded 235 at an average of six goals per game!

1901   BERLIN SELECT XI

January 7th

Aston Villa 6   Berlin Combined XI 2

Association football was beginning to take off in Germany during the early 20th century and Berlin appeared to be at the heart of the new pastime. It was reported at the time that there were over forty clubs playing the game in Berlin alone and crowds of around 4,000 regularly turned up to watch the "new" sport. To develop the game further the newly formed Deutscher Fussball Bund (German FA) selected a squad from their best players in Berlin to tour England and they began on Saturday 5th January 1901 at Southampton where they were soundly beaten 5-1.

Two days later, on a bitterly cold afternoon in January, Aston Villa welcomed the first ever association football team from outside the British Empire to play at Villa Park. An interested crowd of around 3,000 braved the weather to see the "foreigners" perform, against their beloved Aston Villa, on a rock-hard frozen pitch. The Villa selected a solid team for the match that comprised of, Whiteley; Spencer, Evans; Wilkes, Cowan, Crabtree; Templeton, Brown, Johnson, Bache, Smith. The Berlin team, wearing red white and blue armbands on their white shirts received a rousing welcome from the Villa faithful as they ran onto the Villa Park pitch.

The home team kicked off and for most of the early play passed the ball so effectively that the Germans were chasing shadows whilst the Villa forwards "camped" in the visitors' half of the pitch for long periods. With so much domination it was inevitable that the home team opened the scoring. The move was started and finished by Joe Bache. He collected the ball just inside the Villa half and after five intricate passes between his team mates Joe continued his run into the box unmarked and finished off a breathtaking move with a perfectly timed shot that flew in off the inside of the post.

Villa's first game against a team from the European mainland

Following the restart the Villa midfield were soon back in control and within a matter of minutes left-half Jimmy Crabtree doubled their lead with a 25 yard effort that deceived the keeper and nestled in the back of the net.

The second goal roused the visitors and they mounted a series of attacks culminating in an excellent effort from Zierold which flew just a few inches over the bar. Spurred on by the near miss the Berliners gained confidence and the speed of their players, coupled with their astute passing, was beginning to cause Villa some problems. This was perfectly illustrated when winger Gruechwitz raced past Villa's full back Howard Spencer with ease and laid on an inch perfect ball for Glasow to hit a thunderous shot, which flew just wide with Whiteley well beaten. It was an outstanding effort and was much appreciated by the Villa faithful. There were no further chances from either side in the first half but the second half turned out to be an example of exhibition football from the home team.

Directly from the kick off it was clear that the Villa meant business as they mounted a series of attacks on the Berlin goal, nevertheless the Germans defended resolutely and hung on, making last ditch tackles and clearing the ball upfield as best as they could. When the home team eventually broke through the Germans' well organised defence, they found the diminutive figure of goalkeeper Eichelmann "displaying wonderful agility between the posts" and keeping the home team at bay. The Germans' resistance eventually cracked and Jimmy Crabtree scored his second goal with a speculative shot from long range that deceived the otherwise faultless keeper with its bounce.

This third goal however still failed to break the spirit of the tourists and they continued to play positive football which eventually got the desired effect. Winger Kralle broke down the Villa left, leaving full back Albert Evans in his wake and sent in a hard, low cross that Wernicke, racing into the Villa penalty area, met perfectly and smashed into the net without a moment's hesitation. Villa, clearly stung by the goal, mounted a series of attacks forcing a series of corners. Unfortunately they failed to take advantage of their dominance, then with ten minutes remaining the Villa players began to notice that the opposition were tiring.

Full back Albert Evans

With the clock ticking down Villa appeared to have settled for a 5-2 victory and were passing the ball around confidently, when in the dying minutes a speculative effort from a Villa forward was handled in the area and they were awarded a penalty. Jimmy Crabtree stepped up and clinically placed the ball into the corner of the net to complete his hat-trick. The Berlin team barely had time to restart the game before the referee blew his whistle signalling the end of the match and Aston Villa had made history once again, this time by beating a German team at the first time of asking.

This was the signal for the hosts to up their game and benefit from the situation. As a result the next Villa attack of note saw inside right Brown race through the Berlin defence, wrong foot the goalkeeper and neatly slot the ball into the Germans' net. This was swiftly followed with another stunning long range effort from Johnson which easily beat Eichelmann in the Berlin goal.

At 5-1 to the good the Villa players thought that the visitors looked beaten but still the Germans wouldn't lie down and pushed forward whenever the opportunity arose. It was no shock to most people inside the ground when the visitors' positive attitude was eventually rewarded with their second goal.

Following the match the players and officials made their way to the Holte Hotel for an evening meal. In his after dinner speech Aston Villa's chairman Fredrick Rinder explained how pleasantly surprised the Villa officials were at the quality of the football played by the Berlin team. He went on to highlight the excellent contribution made by the German goalkeeper along with his captain Schricker. The Berlin team manager responded saying that the Germans decided to tour England because they were still learning the game and that the match against Aston Villa had taught them a great deal. He then invited Aston Villa to play in Germany but felt it would be four or five years before they would be able to give the Villa a decent game. The captain of the German side concluded the speeches by saying that games between clubs from England and Germany would "help to remove many of the misunderstandings that existed between the two nations."

1905 IRISH TOUR

Having won the FA Cup for the fourth time and aiming for a top four finish in the league the Aston Villa directors decided that this would be an ideal time to make their first trip overseas. So on the evening of 22nd April 1905, directly following their 3-2 victory at Bury in the First Division, they travelled to Fleetwood and caught the overnight ferry to Belfast. On arrival they checked into their central Belfast hotel and then made the short journey to Bangor where they spent the day sight-seeing. That evening they were the dinner guests of the Irish whiskey distillers Dunville and Co.

April 24th

Belfast Distillery 1 Aston Villa 1

The next day over 10,000 spectators crammed into Grosvenor Park and whilst keen to welcome the English Cup winners they were hoping Distillery would inflict an unlikely victory over their illustrious visitors. The Aston Villa team that ran out onto the superb playing surface was greeted noisily by the tightly packed capacity crowd. Aston Villa sportingly fielded their cup winning team comprising of:- George; Spencer, Miles; Windmill, Leake, Pearson; Brawn, Garratty, Hampton, Bache, Hall.

Distillery kicked off with a slight breeze blowing across the pitch. Keen to prove themselves against the FA Cup winners the Irish pressed the visitors from the outset and were unlucky not to take the lead early on when a golden opportunity went begging. A cross came in from the left which "Billy" George in the visitors' goal failed to collect; fortunately for the Villa, full back Alf Miles was on hand to head away the danger. The move gave the Irish lads confidence and they laid siege on the Villa goal for long periods with Magill and Murray creating havoc down the left wing. The tourists weathered the storm and slowly began to take the game to the Irish and were very disappointed to see centre forward Billy Garatty miss an absolute sitter. Unmarked and no more than eight yards out Billy blasted the ball over the bar when it looked easier to score. This miss proved costly for Aston Villa because just prior to the interval Distillery took the lead.

Unfortunately the second half was not widely reported nonetheless somehow Villa managed to grab an equaliser to ensure they moved on to Dublin, undefeated.

April 25th

Bohemian FC 1 Aston Villa 3

The following day was a Wednesday and the Aston Villa contingent was in Dublin. The opponents this time were the Irish Football League side, The Bohemian FC and the game was played at their home ground, Dalymount Park, in front of a full house numbering in excess of 5,000 people.

The English cup holders had much the better of the first half but were unable to score owing to the fine defensive showing by the Bohemians. The home team did most of the attacking in the second half but near the end the tourists improved significantly. Harris scored for the Dublin team whilst Harry Hampton weighed in with two for the Villa with Joe Bache adding the third.

Villa's first games played "over water."

The next day the Villa party set sail for England to fulfil a league fixture with their Black Country neighbours Wolverhampton Wanderers. A tired Villa side somehow managed to dig deep and beat the Wolves 3-0. However one could easily imagine that after the game it was an exhausted group of players that reflected upon playing a tiring four games in just six days with two ferry journeys across the infamous Irish Sea thrown in for good measure.

The teams line up before the Distillery match..

1924 SOUTH AFRICA

October 15th

Aston Villa 0   South Africa 3

The autumn of 1924 saw the first official tour of Great Britain and Ireland by an international South African football team and what an impact they made! They won over half of their 22 matches, scoring 73 goals in the process and all this against high quality opposition Amongst their standout performances were a 2-1 victory over the Irish national team, the 3-2 defeat of Everton and a 5-2 trouncing of Liverpool. Add to this their performance at Villa Park against an Aston Villa team who a few months earlier were contesting the FA Cup final against Newcastle United and it was clear that many of their players could easily earn a living playing professional football in the UK.

The South Africans arrived in Birmingham with a strong reputation following a string of positive results against some of Britain's top teams. A crowd in the region of 6,000 turned out at Villa Park on a pleasant Monday afternoon full of expectation that Villa would beat these "upstarts" from the Southern Hemisphere. However for all their positive rhetoric the home club were taking no chances with the fixture and fielded an experienced team; Spiers; Smart, Bowen; Moss, Milne, Blackburn; York, Kirton, Varco, Walker, Dorrell.

According to a report in the Villa News and Record at the time the home team made a "cautious start.........believing that there was no immediate need to over-exert themselves." They were soon to find out the folly of their ways as the visitors played fast pass-and-move football and whilst no individual stood out their teamwork soon bore fruit as the South Africans took the lead which they held until the interval. The general consensus at half-time was that Villa would come out in the second half and give the visitors a lesson in the art of football.

The first official tour of the UK by a South Africa representative team.

Unfortunately this was not to be as the home side were unable to settle into any sort of rhythm. The South Africans took full advantage of their hosts' unease and increased their efforts, upped their speed around the pitch and with fifteen minutes to go were three goals to the good. Villa certainly had their chances but failed time and time again to turn these opportunities into goals. A typical example of this was Villa left winger Arthur Dorrell. He hit five outstanding shots all of which swerved menacingly round the post with the goalkeeper grasping fresh air. Add to this Billy Walker's uncharacteristic squandering of a number of superb opportunities and rookie centre forward "Saccho" Varco failing to find the net after being presented with numerous straightforward chances, it was hardly surprising that Villa lost a game that they really ought to have won.

After the match the teams and officials were entertained to dinner by the Villa directors in the Pavilion (Trinity Road Stand) at Villa Park. Frederick Rinder, Chairman of Aston Villa, said that they had witnessed a very interesting display of football and he was sure that the Villa players would be the first to congratulate the visitors on the well-deserved victory. He went on to say that the South Africans played "cleverly and keenly in a sportsman like spirit." Next he congratulated the referee for permitting "vigorous, honest charging" commenting that "Football was a man's game and was never meant to be a namby-pamby game!" The response came from the South Africans who amongst other things explained that the name Aston Villa was probably as well known in the wilds of Rhodesia as in Birmingham. Once the dinner was over the entire party visited the Grand Theatre in Birmingham's Corporation Street to watch a variety show.

1926   SCANDINAVIA

By 1926 Aston Villa had accomplished most things in football but numerous invitations to undertake foreign tours had not previously appealed to them sufficiently and therefore were turned down for a variety of reasons. Towards the end of the 1925-26 season the Aston Villa directors were approached once again, this time by the Scandinavians, to undertake a six game tour with matches scheduled for Oslo, Stockholm, Gothenburg and Copenhagen. At the time of the offer Villa were having a reasonable season, aiming for another top six finish in the league and a decent cup run. Perhaps this in part influenced the directors to decide that the time was right for Aston Villa to play football on foreign soil for the first time.

Villa's first ever games on the European mainland.

The Villa players and officials gathered at New Street Station on Friday May 21st in preparation to catch the 4.50pm train to London. Unfortunately one of the newer additions to the Villa squad Joe Nicholson failed to join the party apparently due to the disruption caused by a recent railway workers strike. However it was an excited bunch of young men that embarked on the clubs first ever continental tour and a large crowd of Villa supporters gathered at the station to see Tommy Jackson, Tommy Mort, Teddy Bowen, Jock Johnstone, Jack Yates, Joe Corbett, Len Capewell, Tommy Muldoon, Billy Walker, Arthur Dorrell, Fred Norris, Billy Armfield, Billy Kirton, Alex Talbott, Billy Kingdon and George Stephenson leave Birmingham bound for their Scandinavian adventure.

That night the party stayed in the capital and by noon the next day were at Tilbury to board the Swedish Lloyd boat "Patricia" bound for Gothenburg. The ship set sail at 1 p.m., steamed down the Thames and out to sea. Thankfully the crossing was calm and most players occupied themselves on board by playing deck quoits and in the evening by making their own entertainment. The star of the Villa night-time show was Jock Johnstone who turned out to be the life and soul of the party with his accomplished piano playing. The next morning Gothenburg was in sight and the ship docked at 8.30a.m. There to greet the boys from Birmingham was a large crowd of fans who had been waiting for hours just to catch a glimpse of the Villa players. Accompanied by a band playing "God Save the King," the Aston Villa party made their way safely down the gangway and onto dry land. Their next potential obstacle was clearing customs because many of the players had brought whisky and other spirits along with them. When the contents of their bags were inspected and the spirits located the Customs Officers demanded answers. The players explained with smiles on their faces that the various spirits were in fact essential medicines for footballers and thankfully the Customs Officers saw the joke, turned a blind eye and wished them the best of luck with the tour.

Once through customs they were transported to their base, the finely appointed Grand Hotel Haglund. On arrival they discovered that the Derby County players, who were nearing the end of a similar tour, were staying at the Palace Hotel opposite. The Villa lads made their way across the road and soon got in conversation with County boys asking them all manner of questions about football in Scandinavia and no doubt a number of other subjects cropped up as is the norm when footballers meet. As the chat developed it became apparent that the Derby boys were due to play a friendly against a local side that afternoon. Immediately the Derby officials made special arrangements for the Villa party to attend the game. The match, which Derby won comfortably, was played in pouring rain in front of around 8,000 enthusiastic spectators.

The following day the Villa contingent was taken by charabanc to Kungalv, a local beauty spot. They visited the ruins of a castle and a church with some fine brass work which the Swedes had captured from the Germans at the Battle of Prague back in 1757.

Players and officials on board ship.

May 26th
Orgryte Idrott Sallskap 5 Aston Villa 2

The next day the players rested prior to the evening kick-off in the 20,000 capacity municipal stadium against one of the oldest football clubs in Sweden, Orgryte Idrott Sallskap. With the ground surprisingly only half full and a cinder running track surrounding the pitch, the players expected that the atmosphere might be seriously affected. However they need not have worried as contemporary reports explained that the enthusiasm of the home crowd was something to be remembered. The team selected to represent Aston Villa in their first ever game on foreign soil was:- Jackson; Bowen, Mort; Johnstone, Talbott, Muldoon; Stephenson, Kirton, Capewell, Walker, Dorrell.

Villa took to the field in confident mood and having seen their Derby County colleagues wipe the floor with a Swedish side the previous day, probably didn't take the opposition too seriously. The Swedes were clearly up for the game and playing rapid and forceful football soon put the Villa on the back foot. It really was no shock then when the visitors found themselves a goal behind but when the Swedes added a second the Villa lads decided that enough was enough.

Spurred into action at last the tourists laid siege on the home team's goalmouth for long periods and were harshly denied a number of clear penalty appeals for hand-ball.

The Birmingham Daily Mail reported, "The referee had little notion of the penalty rule and constantly ignored handling in the penalty area." The Aston Villa players were obviously upset by the poor refereeing this was probably a contributory factor to their below par showing in the first half.

Behind at the break Villa came out in the second period determined to put things right. They heaped the pressure on the opposition's goal but chance after chance went begging. Then following more appeals for hand ball in the box the referee at last awarded them a penalty. Billy Walker made no mistake from the spot however rather than inspiring Villa it was the Scandinavians who hit back in style with a fifteen minute blitz when they netted three times. The tourists managed to reduce the deficit with two minutes remaining when Billy Kirton at last turned a period of Villa pressure into a goal. When the final whistle blew it was greeted fervently by the local supporters who never imagined in their wildest dreams that their little team would ever beat the mighty Aston Villa at all, let alone by five goals to two!

Thursday found a very tired and somewhat dejected Villa squad either trying their hand at golf like Billy Kirton, Tommy Mort, Len Capewell and Tommy Jackson on the Gothenburg nine hole course or taking it easy and fishing in the waters next to a hospitable country mansion.

May 29th
Kombineral Gotesburgslag 2
Aston Villa 1

Friday soon came round and the Villa were once again in the Gothenburg Municipal Stadium this time for a 7.15pm kick-off against a local team playing under the name of Kombineral Gotesburgslag (Gothenburg Combined). In contrast to Villa's previous visit to the stadium, this time it was sold out with hundreds locked outside trying to watch the game from trees and other vantage points.

Actual reports of the game are superficial but in summary it seemed that Villa were by far the better team and deserved their victory. They were evidently playing good football but appeared over eager in front of goal, squandering numerous chances including a shocking penalty miss by Billy Walker. Although two goals behind, the visitors kept plugging away and were eventually rewarded with a well taken goal by Len Capewell. Unfortunately it was, as in the previous game, a case of too little too late and a very frustrated Villa team trudged into the dressing room leaving the Swedes on the pitch to celebrate another victory with their jubilant supporters.

That evening a very downcast touring group were wined and dined at the Tradgardsforeningens restaurant which was mysteriously described at the time as a "typically continental amusement place, the like of which is not to be found in England." There were over 100 people at the event and the usual speeches and presentations took place with Villa taking home a silver plate from Gothenburg Alliansen and an embroidered flag from the ladies of the city.

The next morning the players were afforded some free time before they embarked on the seven and a half hour journey to Oslo. The train was painfully slow and there were long animated conversations between the players regarding their need to significantly improve the level of their performance when they played their next match, which was scheduled for the following day in the Norwegian capital. Very late that evening and after a tiring journey the Villa contingent eventually checked into the centrally located Bristol Hotel had supper and went straight to bed.

May 30th
Lyn og Frig 2   Aston Villa 11

The players arose refreshed after a good night's sleep but with a tiring journey and two defeats behind them and facing an early afternoon kick off one could imagine that they were not best prepared for the game. Their opponents were another combined team, chosen from the Frigg Oslo and FK Lyn clubs and although the ground was some distance from the city centre the Aston Villa players were pleased to see a large crowd waiting to greet them.

Lyn og Frig kicked off and the Norwegians flew out of the traps and took the game to the Villa however the experienced English First Division team used their heads and made the ball do the work with some thrilling exhibition football. With the game even at half time the superior fitness of the visitors began to tell in the second period when the opposition ran out of ideas, tired and spent their time chasing shadows. Villa took full advantage of this and hammered home eleven goals. On the mark were Len Capewell who scored four, Billy Walker with a hat trick, Arthur Dorrell managed a brace, whilst George Stephenson and Tommy Muldoon weighed in with one apiece. With twenty minutes remaining and the game won Villa changed it around slightly in an attempt to get Tommy Mort on the score sheet. He switched positions with Billy Walker and led the line but unfortunately he was unable to break his duck.

Following the game it was generally agreed that Tommy Muldoon's effort was the goal of the game. He had collected the ball on the halfway line and sent a speculative shot from just inside the Lyn og Frig half and much to the surprise of everyone, including Tommy himself, it sailed over the goalkeeper's head and into the net. It was a jubilant Villa team that returned to hotel and one can imagine that a few drinks were had by all.

The day after the game the Villa contingent embarked on a scenic railway trip to Holmenkollen situated high in the mountains to see the newly built world class ski jump. Unfortunately the outstanding view that the tourists had been promised was somewhat limited due to the dense fog.

The next leg of the tour involved yet another protracted train journey, this time it was a fourteen hour trip to Stockholm. The train left Oslo very early in the morning and A.E. Machin who was travelling with the team summed the journey up, "This sort of travelling is no joke. We were glad to arrive and get to bed as quickly as possible." The Villa party stayed at the luxurious Grand Hotel Royal situated close to the river and the Royal Palace. One member of the touring party who found the city familiar was Billy Walker. He recalled scoring for his country three years earlier in an international match which had taken place in the same arena that Villa were scheduled to play their game the next day.

June 2nd
Stockholm (Combined XI)   4   Aston Villa   5

The fourth match of the tour was played in the Olympic Stadium where once again the pitch was surrounded by the obligatory 400 metre cinder running track. The opposition this time was another combined team comprising of players from the four main football clubs in the city. It seemed as though the game had captured the imagination of local football fans, selling out long before match day and setting a new attendance record in the process.

The two teams emerged from the dressing rooms in pouring rain and were enthusiastically welcomed by a partisan crowd that were "packed-in to suffocation." The pitch was reported as being quite uneven in places and when coupled with the greasy surface it must have made the bounce of the ball difficult to read. The Norwegian team were clearly up for the game which they saw as an opportunity to claim a famous scalp and played as though it was a local derby. Machin commented that there was a "verve and abandon about the Norwegians' general play."

From all accounts the match was hard but very exciting and swung from end to end from start to finish. Such was the intensity that both Len Capewell and Joe Corbett received heavy knocks early on and were little more than passengers for the rest of the game. The away team's first goal came courtesy of a Stockholm full back. Billy Kirton sent in a vicious shot which the Norwegian defender tried to head away but only succeeded in directing it over his goalkeepers' head and into the gaping net.

Other highlights from the game included a brace from Billy Walker which included a penalty and a goal apiece for Arthur Dorrell and Len Capewell.

This saw Villa stretch their lead to 5-3 and they were playing down the clock when in the last minute the home team reduced their arrears leaving Villa the winners but only by a very narrow margin. The game was followed with the obligatory grand dinner in honour of Aston Villa and there were of course the usual speeches and presentations followed afterwards by some good natured merry making which went on until the early hours of the morning.

The next day saw a tired out and somewhat hung over Villa party make the best of a hectic day visiting the sights of the city, of which A.E. Machin enthused thus, "...we shall never forget what a beautiful city Stockholm is..." The tourists had lunch at a celebrated underground restaurant and that evening were driven a few miles out of town to Restaurang Foresta, Lindigo for dinner. Here some of the players became a little "refreshed" and decided to give an impromptu concert. Jock Johnstone, Villa's virtuoso on the piano, provided the musical accompaniment whilst Billy Kirton and George Stephenson performed a "Spanish" dance. On completion of their act they received flowers from some of the lady diners who also called for more. Machin concluded thus, "We would have stayed longer had we not been due back to prepare for another long train journey the following morning."

Thankfully for the Aston Villa players the final part of the tour was broken into two legs which would see them stay in Malmo overnight before taking the ferry to Copenhagen. They were seen off at the central station by a large group of well-wishers as they boarded the 10.15a.m train for the eleven and a half hour journey to the south of the country.

Following the overnight stay in Malmo, "an old fashioned place" according to Machin, the team and officials boarded a steam ship at 11.30 a.m. which ferried them in bright sunshine across the Baltic Sea to Copenhagen.

Once back on dry land in the Danish capital the players and officials were driven to their base for the final part of the tour; the luxurious Phoenix Hotel which dated back to the 17th century. Sadly the Villa boys did not have much time for unpacking, let alone sight-seeing as they were scheduled to kick off in their first game that afternoon at half past one, against a strong team made up from the best players in the area.

June 5th

Copenhagen (Combined XI)   1   Aston Villa   4

Prior to the match there had been some disquiet in the city because admission prices had been increased for the visit of the "famous English football team" conversely this didn't affect the gate and over 22,000 excited fans squeezed into the tiny Municipal Stadium.

The Aston Villa players were extremely impressed with the compact ground which was rectangular and clearly built with football in mind. The changing rooms were a revelation in comparison to what they had experienced thus far in Sweden and Norway. The most welcome sight in the dressing room was the bathing facilities which were similar to or perhaps even an improvement on what they were used to back in England. Machin enthused, "There was a large plunge bath and spacious individual showers."

The Aston Villa team for that day included a few squad players as some of the regulars were carrying knocks and therefore lined up thus:- Jackson; Bowen, Muldoon; Kingdon, Talbott, Yates; Kirton, Stephenson, Norris, Walker, Dorrell. Even with the changes, those players chosen to represent the tourists were considered to be more than capable of winning the game. The players pulled on the famous claret and blue shirts, ran out enthusiastically onto the pitch and made history once again by being the first Aston Villa team to play on Danish soil.

Whether it was over confidence, tiredness or a combination of the two that affected the team one cannot be certain but inside ten minutes the Villa were a goal behind with the partisan crowd celebrating wildly in disbelief.

The local supporters continued to play their part jeering what they considered to be poor refereeing decisions and blowing whistles throughout the game which the away team found somewhat distracting. Eventually the Villa boys settled down and came more into the game resulting in Aston born centre forward Fred Norris hitting the back of the net on two occasions. He scored his first after a shot from Billy Walker rebounded off the woodwork and then bagged a second with a drive that flew into the net with the goalkeeper grasping at thin air. Both of these goals were received in total silence by the Danish crowd. Fred's brace certainly settled the visitors down and it was not unexpected when George Stephenson hit home the third with a powerful shot to send the visitors in 3-1 up at half time.

Whilst substitutes were not allowed in the UK at that time, it was quite normal on the continent to replace an injured player with a reserve. Villa took advantage of this rule early in the second half when Alex Talbott took a knock and was substituted. By this time the tourists were playing "keep ball" of the sort that today would be greeted with shouts of "Ole!....Ole!..." Late on in the second half, following a long period of Villa possession, the final goal of the game arrived. A cross came in from Kirton on the right and an unmarked Billy Walker darted in to head the ball powerfully past the outstretched arms of the Danish goalkeeper. The goal, like the previous three, was received once more in complete silence!

June 6th
Copenhagen (Combined XI) 2   Aston Villa 5

That evening the Villa management declined all invitations to socialise as they needed an early night in order to prepare properly for their final game the following day.

The Copenhagen side for this game was considered to be much stronger than the team that Villa had dismissed without too much trouble the previous day. The spectators turned up again in their thousands and it was a capacity crowd that enthusiastically welcomed the Villa team as they emerged from the dressing rooms and into the stifling heat of the Municipal Stadium. The tourists began to warm up, passing the balls around and hitting shots and crosses at Jackson in the Villa goal. Their warm up went on for much longer than anticipated because the opposition failed to materialise. The crowd became restless and when their team eventually emerged from the dressing room, over ten minutes late they were roundly jeered by their own supporters.

The formalities complete the Copenhagen team set about avenging the defeat of their colleagues the previous day. However whatever had gone on in their dressing room before the game began seemed to have affected them because after just two minutes they were a goal behind. That man Fred Norris helped himself to the opener when he rose to steer the ball home with a fine header. Late on in the half George Stephenson, Billy Walker and Billy Kirton each added a goal and it looked as though they had put the game out of the Danes' reach by the time the referee blew up for half time. The club officials at the ground appeared to agree with the local supporters' verdict and they lowered the numerous Danish flags that surrounded the ground to half-mast to indicate that, as far as they were concerned, the "worst had happened."

Back in the Villa dressing room the magic sponge was working overtime as a number of players were carrying leg injuries. However all eleven emerged for the second half feeling confident with their four goal cushion; a lead they couldn't possibly throw away or could they?

Within five minutes of the restart Jock Johnstone, who had been limping badly, had to be replaced by Jack Yates and this seemed to disrupt Villa's flow. The grateful Danes seized the opportunity with both hands as they saw a way back into the game. Their pressure quickly bore fruit when Villa's keeper Tommy Jackson uncharacteristically fumbled a fierce shot and then looked on in horror as the ball squirmed out of his reach and trickled into the net. This spurred on the Copenhagen crowd and their players responded accordingly.

With Tommy Mort, Teddy Bowen, Tommy Muldoon and Jack Yates no more than passengers due to their various injuries it seemed only a matter of time before the rampant Danes would reduce their deficit further. However, against the run of play, it was the home team that found themselves on the back foot and defending desperately. A clever move involving an intricate exchange of passes resulted in George Stephenson sliding in to toe poke home his second goal of the game and restore the visitors' four goal advantage. The goal quietened the partisan crowd and Villa responded by passing the ball around with a degree of swagger to try and run down the clock. Everything was going well until a misplaced pass in the 88th minute by the injured passenger Jack Yates led to the Danes breaking away and scoring their second goal. However their effort was too little too late and Aston Villa ran out 5-2 victors.

After the match the Villa players and officials were taken to the races in Copenhagen and some of the players believed they were "set fair" when the English jockeys present at the event provided them with a series of tips. The Villa contingent responded by eagerly laying their bets on these "certs" unfortunately none of the horses won. That evening saw the usual dinner with speeches and presentations and once over the Villa contingent made their way to the massive fun fair in the Tivoli gardens. Here Billy Walker "proved himself to be the champion of the hammer swingers!"

Their final full day on the continent was spent shopping in Copenhagen for presents for their families and loved ones back home. Afterwards they had a sight-seeing bus trip which they enjoyed and then spent the evening in their hotel having a few drinks. The journey home began early in the morning on the 9th June with another long rail and ferry journey, eight hours this time, to the seaport town of Esbjerg. From there they set sail for Harwich and although the crossing took 24 hours, thankfully for everyone concerned, the sea was calm and they arrived in what they considered to be plenty of time to catch their connecting train to London. Unfortunately disaster stuck when they faced customs.

Many of the players had bought numerous items whilst away and now had to pay 33.3% import duty on what they thought had been bargains. This meant unpacking and repacking their luggage which caused them to miss their train to London and so it was the early hours of the following morning before they arrived back in Birmingham.

W.E.Machin summed the tour up, "It was a memorable trip, a lasting memory to all who took part in it. Our continental friends were delighted with the exhibitions of football the team gave and there can be no doubt that the reputation of the club was enhanced. The trip was a distinct financial and sporting success."

(Above) The players line-up...
(Below).... and action -
at the Gothenburg match.

1938 GERMANY

Aston Villa in Nazi Germany

By March 1938 Nazi Germany had developed into a formidable footballing nation due in part to the occupation and annexation of Austria whose national football team at that time was considered to be one of the strongest in the world. The Austrians had performed exceptionally well at the 1934 World Cup in Italy and two years later, under Jimmy Hogan, had reached the final at the Olympics. By 1938 they were looking forward to the World Cup which was scheduled to take place in France that summer. Unfortunately, as result of becoming part of Greater Germany, they were obliged to withdraw from the competition because Austria no longer existed as a country in its own right.

During autumn 1937 it had been arranged for the England football team to play an international friendly against Germany in May the following year. To add to the spectacle Aston Villa were contacted in December 1937 to play three games in Germany around the same time. Villa's invitation came from a Dr. Otto Nerz a Nazi party member and former head coach of the German national football team.

Although not stated in Nerz's letter it seems likely the reason that Aston Villa had been selected for the tour in front of other famous English football teams was due to the high regard in which their manager was held in Germany following his successful period coaching the Austrians. Nerz offered to pay all Villa's expenses for the tour and in addition a £350 match fee for each of their three games. The Villa directors responded favourably to the invitation but did not consider the match fees suitable and suggested that the two parties share equally the receipts from each of the games. This proposal was agreed by the Germans who wasted no time in forwarding a proposed itinerary to the club.

Meanwhile as May approached the England officials were becoming anxious that the Germans could gain an unfair advantage in their international match by selecting the best players from Austria to bolster their team. In view of this they contacted the German FA and requested that no Austrian players be selected for the game.

The Germans reluctantly accepted the proposal providing Aston Villa played a friendly match the following day against a combined German and Austrian team. The Villa directors agreed to the request and the tour arrangements were finalised.

The Aston Villa directors selected a resilient squad for the tour comprising of:- Jimmy Allen, Frank Biddlestone, Ernie Callaghan, George Cummings, Alex Massie, Bob Iverson, Frank Broome, Freddie Haycock, Frank Shell, Ronnie Starling, Eric Houghton, Bill Carey, Bill Cobley, George Pritty, Len Latham, Jackie Maund and Andy Kerr.

At 5.20pm on Saturday 7th May, following their last game of the season, the newly crowned Second Division champions left Villa Park by coach bound for Birmingham's Snow Hill station and the 6.00pm express train to Southampton. The jubilant party arrived on the south coast at around 10.30pm and checked in at the South Western Hotel. After breakfast the players had a little free time prior to boarding the SS Europa at noon bound for Bremerhaven. The sea journey to the continent was apparently trouble free and they arrived in Nazi Germany at 9.00.a.m. on Monday 9th May. Once they had cleared customs the Villa contingent were transported by a plush special train the thirty or so miles to Bremen. Here they were met by a line of chauffeur driven cars which transported them in convoy to Hamburg where they booked into the Hotel Atlantic, a luxury hotel built in 1909 and situated on the shores of Lake Alster. The next day their hosts ensured that the city was shown off to its best with sight-seeing trips that included a visit to the Zoological Gardens in Stellingen and an evening visit to the famous Reeperbahn where they took in a cabaret show.

On Wednesday 11th May, the Aston Villa players and officials were on the move again, this time there was a three and a half hour journey to Berlin ahead of them. On arrival they checked into the exclusive Hotel Bristol which was built in 1872 by a Jewish business man, Berthold Kempinski.

After acclimatising themselves during the evening the next morning they visited Postdam, the historic city that had been the residence of the Prussian kings and German Kaisers until 1918. Afterwards they enjoyed a boat trip through the series of interconnected lakes around the town.

The following day the players and officials visited the Olympic Stadium where their game against the German Select XI was due to be played on the Sunday. The players and officials were given a full tour of the ground and photographs taken at the time suggest that they were impressed with the set up. Back at the Bristol Hotel they had some free time before dinner and afterwards they attended a show at the famous Berlin Winter Gardens.

Saturday May 14th was the day of the infamous Germany v England international and after spending the early part of the day sight-seeing in the German capital the Villa players and officials took their seats in the packed Olympic Stadium as guests of the German FA. Also in attendance were a number of high ranking Nazi party members including Herman Göring, Joseph Goebbels, Rudolf Hess and Joachim von Ribbentrop, however contrary to popular belief they were not joined by Adolf Hitler.

Whilst the England team were preparing for the match the British Ambassador to Germany, Sir Neville Henderson, along with FA Secretary Stanley Rous went into the England dressing room and explained to the players that they would be expected, as part of the pre-match formalities, to join the German players in giving the Nazi salute during their hosts' national anthem. It has been argued in some accounts that the England team reluctantly went along with the directive.

Stanley Matthews on the other hand recalled later, "The dressing room erupted. There was bedlam. All the England players were livid and totally opposed to this, myself included. Everyone was shouting at once. Eddie Hapgood, normally a respectful and devoted captain, wagged his finger at the official and told him what he could do with the Nazi salute, which involved putting it where the sun doesn't shine.

Other reports have suggested that Matthews' version which was corroborated by many of his team mates, only materialised once the British press ran with the story about the England players' agreement to make the Nazi salute.

With the formalities over England lined up for the kick off with debutant Frank Broome on the right wing. England were immediately on top and the pressure soon paid off when, after sixteen minutes, left winger Cliff Bastin opened the scoring with a smartly taken goal. Whilst Germany soon hit back through Gellesh, Sheffield Wednesday's Robinson restored England's advantage driving the ball confidently past the German keeper from a corner.

With England in control and dictating the play Frank Broome latched onto a defence splitting ball from Welsh and fired home England's third goal much to the delight of his Villa team mates in the stand. With just a few minutes remaining before the half time interval two goals were scored in almost as many minutes. First Stanley Mathews crowned a wonderful "jinky" run to score England's fourth and then straight from the restart the Germans hit back through centre forward Gauchel.

Early in the second half, Robinson restored England's three-goal cushion with a low drive that evaded the German goalkeeper. Then Frank Broome who was clearly enjoying his debut had a great chance to double his tally when he left his marker "for dead" but hit his shot straight at Jakob in the German goal. With less than 15 minutes remaining, the hosts once more reduced the deficit but England were not to be denied their three-goal margin and with just a few minutes remaining, inside forward Len Goulden, scored and England ran out winners.

That evening the Aston Villa contingent donned their best bib and tuckers along with the English and German teams and attended an official banquet given by the German FA at the Esplanade Hotel, which at that time was considered to be one of the German capital's most luxurious and celebrated hotels.

May 15th

German Select XI 2   Aston Villa 3

The Villa players had the next morning free prior to making their way back to the Olympic stadium for their first match on German soil. On arrival they were surprised to discover that the so called German/Austrian combined team only contained one German player. Added to this, newspapers from the period make it clear that the Aston Villa players were told that they would be expected to line up with the opposition and give the Nazi salute both before and after the game. Contrary to the recollections of some players and various accounts in numerous articles and books, it is clear from contemporary newspaper reports that the Villa players did in fact line up in the middle of the pitch, with the "Germans" and give the Nazi salute before the game began. This was loudly applauded by over 100,000 enthusiastic German supporters at the end of their national anthem.

This was Villa's first game since winning the 2nd Division title and being against what seemed to be the majority of the recently defunct Austrian national team, manager Jimmy Hogan picked his strongest possible side which included Frank Broome playing his second game in twenty-four hours. The team in full comprised of:- Biddlestone; Callaghan, Cummings; Massie, Allen, Iverson; Broome, Haycock, Shell, Starling, and Houghton. Villa won the toss, played with the sun behind them and attacked the "Germans" from the outset.

With just seven minutes gone Freddie Haycock and Frank Broome cleverly worked the ball down the right wing and then Broome made a diagonal run into the box, sweeping past three defenders in the process and slotted the ball under the goalkeeper from close range.

The German combined team were clearly shocked by this early setback and responded with a number of concerted attacks on the Villa goal. Villa, pinned in their own half for long periods only managed to stay in front by a mixture of good fortune and poor finishing on the part of the opposition's forwards.

However although they were clearly "under the cosh" Aston Villa slowly came more into the game towards the end of the first period, then with just seven minutes remaining disaster struck. Left winger Leo Neumer, from the Austria Vienna club (SC Ostmark), sent a low cross into the box which was met by Camillo Jerusalem, Leo's club teammate. He quickly brought the ball under control and struck a fierce shot which Fred Biddlestone did well to beat out. Unfortunately the ball fell directly into the path of "Pepi" Stroh, yet another player form the SC Ostmark club, who wasted no time in steering it into the net for the equaliser.

Villa did have one more chance before the break to increase their lead. Ronnie Starling and Frank Shell cleverly exchanged passes resulting in Starling's tremendous shot crashing against the crossbar with the goalkeeper grasping at fresh air. During the first half the temperature had soared into the 90's and both sets of players were relieved to hear the whistle blow for half time. A report at the time suggested that, "The respite was a thankful one for the Villa lads, with tongues parched dry and shirts glued to their backs they were entitled to an Olympic reward for sheer guts and stamina alone."

Cleary encouraged by their late equaliser the "Germans" began the second half the stronger team and seemed intent on pressing home their advantage. Aston Villa did not seem fazed by the relentless pressure and dealt with each attack on its merit, often catching the Austro-Germans with their well-rehearsed off-side tactics. Whilst effective, these tactics were not appreciated by the majority of the crowd who began jeering and whistling every time the Villa full-backs, Callaghan and Cummings, moved out in unison and continually caught the opposition forwards in the trap. Eventually the home team sorted themselves out and came to terms with their opposition's plan and subsequently the Villa goal came under terrific pressure and only some heroic defending combined with poor finishing kept Villa in the game.

Very much on the back foot and relying on breakaways for respite, it was undoubtedly against the run of play when in the 70th minute the Brummie lads took the lead following one of their famous, "Shell switches with Broome" tricks. Alex Massie raced along the wing and then whipped in an excellent cross which Frank Shell met perfectly and blasted into the net. Leading 2-1 the Villa began to dominate the game although Neumer and Jerusalem were a pair of perpetual thorns in the visitors' side. It was during one of their attacks that Jerusalem was brought down by a Villa defender in the area and it looked to be a nailed on penalty. Luckily for Aston Villa the referee, ignored the pleas of the "German" players and amazingly waved play on.

This piece of good fortune gave the Villa a much needed lift and they went on the offensive in search of their third goal which would put the match beyond the Austro-German. Their increased pressure was rewarded with just thirteen minutes remaining. Frank Broome outpaced the "German" defence and from close range calmly placed the ball well out of keeper's reach, high into the top corner of the net.

Even 3-1 down the "Germans" didn't give up; instead they went searching for goals and began to dominate proceedings putting the visitors under severe pressure for long periods. The hosts' hard work eventually bore fruit in the dying embers of the game when Wilhelm Hahnemann drifted in from the right and scored with a low hard shot that was in the back of the net before Frank Biddlestone in the Villa goal hit the ground. Unfortunately for the home team it was too little too late and a few minutes after Villa had restarted the game the final whistle blew, Villa had won 3-2 and celebrated their victory whilst the crowd loudly barracked the referee.

At this point in proceedings both teams and officials were expected to line up once again in the middle of the pitch and give the Nazi salute. However, according to Edward Smith treasurer and member-in-charge of the Aston Villa Shareholders' Association, "When the game finished it happened that most of the Villa players were in the portion of the pitch near to their dressing-rooms and several of them immediately ran towards them, just as they do in any game in England. Jim Allen and one or two were farther away and when the German players lined up once again to give the salute he tried to call the other players back. By that time the others had practically got back to the tunnel leading off the field, and they started to come back but by then the Germans had given the salute and were themselves walking off the field. It was clearly a misunderstanding by the Villa players who thought the salute before the match was sufficient." In another interview he added, "The German people we spoke to after the match expressed the view that it had been a very good game and there no special comments about the salute and it must be remembered the Villa players joined in the Nazi salute before the match commenced."

Sir Patrick Hannon M.P. president of Aston Villa was also at the game and speaking to the Birmingham Mail commented, "The game was clean and undisturbed by any untoward incident from beginning to end. Such trouble as arose was due to the fact that something like 110,000 spectators were not accustomed to decisions arising from the offside rule. The referee gave perfectly impartial and correct decisions but these were misunderstood by the spectators. As a result there was some disturbance and noise but it certainly left no ill-feeling." He went on, "The incident at the end of the game when the Villa players did not stay behind to salute, was due entirely to a misunderstanding and I am satisfied that there was no want of courtesy on the part of the Aston Villa players."

Former Villa half back Alex Leake, who was a spectator at the game, commented, "When the match ended the Villa players started to troop from the field and Houghton was the first to enter the tunnel to the dressing rooms. Apparently he was told that he should have remained on the field but it was too late when he and several others returned (to the pitch). Meanwhile the Germans had lined up and given the Nazi salute to the two main sections of the crowd."

Commenting on the salute many years later George Cummings said in a radio broadcast during the 1950's, "It was about 100 degrees and over 100,000 spectators. Anyway we came out and the Germans stood in the centre giving the Nazi salute and (laughs) we wouldn't give the Nazi salute. We just cheered like we had scored a goal. The crowd started jeering and whistled at us but we still wouldn't do it. At the end of the match we were supposed to line up and give the Nazi salute but we just ran straight off the field. There was a terrible rumpus about the Villa players not giving the Nazi salute."

Eric Houghton who also played in the game commented in Rogan Taylor's 1995 book Kicking and Screaming, "Our manager Jimmy Hogan said, 'They'll expect you to perform the Nazi salute.' The fellow in charge of the England team had come to our manager and said, 'We've had a chat about it and we think it would be better if your players gave the Nazi salute to be really friendly.' We had a meeting about this and George Cummings and Alec Massie and the Scots lads said, 'There's no way we're giving the Nazi salute.' So we didn't give it. Our argument was that we were a club side and not an international side. Anyway, they treated us very well but it did leave a bit of a nasty taste in the mouth, us refusing to give the Nazi salute"

After the game the Villa players returned to their hotel and one might assume that a certain amount of celebrating ensued bearing in mind their superb result earlier in the day. The following morning the players, some with a foggy recollection of events the previous night, and officials boarded the 8.a.m. train for the six and half hour journey to Dusseldorf. Both breakfast and lunch were served on board and on arrival at Central Station the party were ferried the short distance to the City's "Old Town" where they stayed in the stunning Park Hotel, so named one might surmise, owing to its proximity in relation to "The Hofgarten" Düsseldorf's famous park. The following day, Tuesday May 17th, the Aston Villa touring party went on a day long sight-seeing trip to Cologne and also visited the famous Seven Mountains, a low mountain range which offered spectacular views. Lunch and tea was taken at the Petersberg Hotel nestling among the mountains and overlooking the impressive River Rhine.

After breakfast on the morning of their second game the players looked forward to a quiet day as the match was scheduled for an evening kick off and would be played in part under floodlights. Whilst that day's programme included a visit to a horticultural exhibition in Essen for the Aston Villa party, manager Jimmy Hogan insisted the players remained at the hotel complex and rested throughout the day. Whilst they relaxed Jimmy found time to carry out a telephone interview with Birmingham's Evening Despatch. Asked about the Nazi salute he commented, "The players will give the Nazi salute before and after the match tonight." He also confirmed that Frank Broome's place would go to either Albert Kerr or Jackie Maund.

One of the tour matches reported in the German Sporting Press.

May 18th

German Combined XI 2   Aston Villa 1

The Birmingham Evening Despatch began their report of the game thus, "After giving the Nazi salute before and after the match and refusing to exploit the offside game, Aston Villa were beaten by a combined German-Austrian team at Dusseldorf last night." The reported salute was captured on camera and the subsequent photograph used on the cover of the programme for Villa's match in Stuttgart later in the tour. Eric Houghton op cit, confirmed that they gave the Nazi salute thus, "The next time they said we'd got to give the Nazi salute, you see, so we had a meeting and said that, for peace and quietness we'd give the Nazi salute."

The game kicked off, in front of a partisan 60,000 crowd, with Villa playing towards a strong setting sun however this did not appear to distract them as they were soon on top. Contemporary newspaper reports suggested that Villa's "speedy and skilful forwards" made life difficult for the German defenders. The pressure soon translated into a goal in the fourteenth minute. Eric Houghton collected the ball just inside the German half, weaved his way through their defence, raced towards goal and drove a shot which flew into the net leaving Raftl the Rapid Vienna goalkeeper helpless. On the other hand the Birmingham Post reported that, "Villa took the lead after twenty minutes. Starling made a splendid opening for Frank Shell to put the ball into the net."

Whichever report is accurate they both agreed that the goal failed to spur the Villa on to put the game beyond the opposition. Instead the Austro-Germans "rolled up their sleeves" and within fifteen minutes they were ahead. The equaliser came following a surging run from the ever improving Rapid Vienna half back Franz Wagner who opened up the Villa defence with a near perfect through ball to Josef "Jupp" Gauchel. The stylish German forward gave Fred Biddlestone no chance, with his long range "thunderbolt."

This was followed five minutes with a hotly disputed goal which the Villa players felt was clearly off-side however it has to be said that it was a well worked move that put the opposition in front. It began once again with the Rapid Vienna half-back Franz Wagner who emerged from a midfield skirmish with the ball and then hit a glorious pass into the path of his Austrian team mate Hans Pesser. The Rapid Vienna star burst through the middle of the Villa defence and Fred Biddlestone, alert to the danger, rushed out of his goal to narrow the angle unfortunately the ball evaded him and rolled into the back of the goal leaving the Villa a goal behind at the break.

According to the Evening Despatch the Villa were on top for most of the second half as they searched for an equaliser. Alex Massie and Bob Iverson spent much of their time supporting the forwards but the "German" defence managed to hold on for a very professional victory.

One could imagine that it was a frustrated and somewhat dejected group of players that made their way back to the Park Hotel that evening however there was no time for reflection as they were back on the road the next morning for a 126 mile train and Rhine boat trip to Assmannshausen. On arrival in the tiny picturesque Rhine-side hamlet they checked in at the Hotel Krone situated in the centre of the village. The next day they were up early and after breakfast were taken to Frankfurt in a convoy of cars where they spent most of the day sight-seeing before moving on to Stuttgart.

Reaching Stuttgart at around 7.30pm they made their way to the Hotel Marquardt situated in the "Schlossplatz" a large square in the centre of the city. This was an excellent base for the Villa contingent and the following day many of them went shopping and visited places of interest around Stuttgart. During the evening the Villa party took in a variety show before retiring for the night.

May 22nd
Greater Germany XI 1   Aston Villa   2

Sunday 22nd May soon came around and this was the day of Villa's last match of the tour. The game was to be played at the imposing Adolf Hitler Kampfbahn (Stadium) which was designed by the German architect Paul Bonatz and built in 1933 for the National Gymnastics Festival. Interestingly the stadium, now renamed the Mercedes-Benz Arena, is used mainly for football as it is the home of Bundesliga side VfB Stuttgart.

The weather on the day of the game was, according to Jimmy Hogan, atrocious however it didn't seem to worry the manager too much who felt that the wet conditions would suit his Villa lads perfectly. The German management selected a strong team for the game and virtually the same that would go on to represent their country in the World championships in Paris the following month. Villa were forced into making a number of changes for the match having to play without Frank Shell, Fred Biddlestone who were injured and Frank Broome who was still away with the England party. When these changes were announced before the game, the large crowd of between 60,000 and 75,000 were clearly annoyed and "whistled derisively." The Villa starting line-up then comprised of:- Carey; Callaghan, Cummings; Massie, Allen Iverson; Kerr, Haycock, Pritty, Starling, Houghton.

Amazingly the issue regarding the Hitler salute was still rumbling on as Eric Houghton commented much later, "At the next place, I think it was Stuttgart, both teams gave the Nazi salute, so (afterwards) we went to the centre of the field and gave them the two finger salute and they cheered like mad. They thought it was all right. They didn't know what the two fingers meant." One has to mention here that unfortunately it has not been possible to find any newspaper reports that confirm Eric's lovely story.

It was almost half an hour before the game's first goal. Bob Iverson the Villa wing half delivered an excellent pass to inside-forward Ronnie Starling who worked hard to carry the ball through the heavy ground and then passed it out to Eric Houghton. The Villa winger scampered down the left flank close to the goal line and then crossed the ball. Bob Iverson, who had continued his run into the box from a deep position, met the ball perfectly and directed his firm header past the out stretched arms of the keeper. After the game manager Hogan commented that it, "was one of the best goals I have ever seen!" praise indeed from the maestro.

Villa's second goal came from a penalty shortly before half-time. Schnaus, the German full-back, brought down reserve striker George Pritty in the box. The ever reliable Eric Houghton takes up the story, "Billy Walker always told me never to get flurried when you are taking a penalty. I was taking my time and was putting the ball on the spot and the German goalkeeper came off his line. He said to me 'You Engleesh pig, you Engleesh pig.' He was trying to put me off you see and I said, 'Alright mate, you keep calm. You get back on your line and I'll endeavour to knock your square head into a round un. And it just missed his head going in, hit the stanchion, just missed his head coming out and he was on the floor." (Kicking and Screaming, Rogan Taylor and Andrew Ward)

The "Germans" began the second half with purpose and immediately put the Birmingham team's defence under extreme pressure. Centre forward Lenz was a particular thorn in Villa's side and he went close on a number of occasions with some forceful headers. Thankfully for the visitors their defence withstood the battering until the 75th minute when Jimmy Allen, the versatile half-back, took a heavy knock which robbed Villa of one of their most influential players. Aston Villa needed to reorganise and responded by moving Pritty to centre half but defending their two goal advantage for the rest of the game with ten men was very difficult.

Aston Villa's worst fears were realised just one minute after the match restarted when the home team went ahead.

A well worked move saw Lehner provide an almost perfect cross for the tireless Lenz to halve the deficit with a spectacular header that soared past rookie goalkeeper Bill Carey into the far corner of net. This was the signal for hosts to push for the equalizer and for Villa to mount a rear guard action that seemed to have paid off.

However, in the eightieth minute the "Germans" were handed a golden opportunity to pull level when the referee awarded them a penalty. Luckily from the Villa's point of view, the hosts squandered the chance but it didn't seem to deflect them from the job in hand task because they continued to attack persistently in search of the equalizer. The boys in claret and blue hung on for dear life with a mixture of skill and good fortune until 89th minute when it looked as though they had conceded a second penalty. Fortunately for the Villa, the referee waved play-on and a very disgruntled partisan crowd spent the final few minutes with a non-stop barrage of derisory whistling. Thankfully this didn't affect the Villa lads who hung on for a famous victory. As the final whistle blew the police completely surrounded the playing area to prevent the crowd, who were still angry at the referee's performance, from invading the pitch.

With the game over the Villa players shook hands with their opponents and then made their way to the centre of the pitch to give the Nazi salute however the "German" players were nowhere to be seen. The Villa lads and even the English press were somewhat mystified by this but eventually after some research the press reported that, "According to German football routine German teams only salute at the beginning of each match and not at the end." It must have been very difficult for the players and officials of Aston Villa to come to terms with this given the controversy they had caused in Berlin by leaving the field without giving the salute.

It's probably best to leave the final comments on this game to manager Jimmy Hogan, "In the whole of my experience on the continent I have never seen an English team play as well as they (Villa) did today!" he went on to tell everyone back home that "All the boys send their kindest regards to their friends in Birmingham. Tell the Birmingham people that we kept the Villa flag flying to the end."

The next day the Villa players and officials moved on to Baden-Baden where they stayed until the Wednesday morning when they visited Heidelbergen on the way to Wiesbaden where a banquet was given in their honour. The following day Thursday May 26th the touring party began their journey home on the Rheingold Express bound for the Hook of Holland. They set sail for England at just before midnight the same day and arrived safely in Harwich at six o'clock the next morning just in time to catch their train which arrived back in Birmingham at 1.00pm.

(Above) Match ticket from the May 15 game.
(Below) Action involving (left to right)
Allen, Cummings and Callaghan.

1944 EDINBURGH

August 5th

Edinburgh Select XI 3   Aston Villa 4

Aston Villa play a wartime charity game in Scotland.

Between 1941 and 1962 an Edinburgh Select XI side met a top English club to raise much needed funds for various charities such as The Red Cross Fund, whilst at the same time heralding in the new football season. Essentially the local team comprised of a combined team from Hearts and Hibs along with a few guests. These annual games were played alternately at Easter Road and Tynecastle. The first two years saw the local side lose to Arsenal and then beat a strong RAF team by the odd goal in five. In 1944 it was the turn of War Cup Finalists Aston Villa to take on Edinburgh's finest on a sunny afternoon in August at Tynecastle.

The Edinburgh team comprised almost entirely of players from the two main local clubs but there were a couple of exceptions one being Preston North End's famous wing-half and future Liverpool manager Bill Shankley. Aston Villa fielded their War Cup Final team of, Wakeman; Potts, Cummings; Massie, Callaghan, Starling; Broome, Edwards, Parkes, Iverson, Houghton and over 35,000 spectators welcomed the two sets of players onto the field on a warm August afternoon.

The first half was all Villa but it took over half an hour before they turned their dominance into a goal. Frank Broome received the ball just inside the Edinburgh team's half, beat four defenders and tucked the ball in the corner of the net giving Jimmy Brown the diminutive Hearts goalkeeper no chance at all. Following this reverse the home team began to fight back but sadly for the Scots just two minutes before the interval and it has to be said, against the run of play Villa struck again. This time it was Eric Houghton who took the credit with one of his trademark thunderbolts.

The second half began much as the first had ended with the visitors pushing for a third goal to secure a victory. The pressure soon told when inside forward Bob Iverson's well struck shot flew into the net and looked every inch the winner. Certainly the visitors thought so as they casually passed the ball around as though it was an exhibition match. Then with just a quarter of an hour left the home team's fight back began in earnest and Villa saw their three goal lead evaporate.

Walker was the first Edinburgh player on the score sheet and this was quickly added to by the future Manchester United winger Jimmy Delaney, who lobbed the ball over Wakeman in the Villa goal. Time was running out for the Scots but then from Aston Villa's perspective, who thought they had successfully battened down the hatches, the unthinkable happened when the Edinburgh team were awarded a penalty. Jimmy Walker smashed the ball into the roof of the net to bring the scores level.

'Guest' Bill Shankly

The Scots now smelt victory and pushed forward in numbers in search of a fourth and winning goal. Alas, in their eagerness the Edinburgh lads left gaps at the back and in the final minute of the game Frank Broome snatched a winner for Aston Villa.

With the game being played during the afternoon and Britain still at war the Aston Villa players and officials caught the train back to Birmingham straight after the game. Eric Houghton's journey back however was somewhat problematic. Eric had a reputation for being a joker and apparently on one trip back to Birmingham by train he waited until the players in his compartment were asleep and then shouted, "Ticket's please!" Eric then took great pleasure in watching his team mates wake up with a start and fumble through their pockets, half asleep, searching for their tickets.

On the way back from the Edinburgh game Eric recalled in Bernard Bale's book "Villa in the Blood" the tables being turned.

He recounted the story "We were on a train coming back from a friendly against Hearts in Edinburgh. I fell asleep and when the lads woke me they told me we were at Crewe. I had no reason to doubt it. I got off the train to get some tea from the kiosk when, to my horror, the train moved off with the lads waving cheerio to me." Eric was left on the platform in his shirt sleeves, without much money in his pockets and quickly discovered he was a long way north of Crewe in fact he was marooned on Preston station. Eric concluded ruefully, "It was three o'clock in the morning before I finally made it back to Birmingham!"

1946 NORWAY & EDINBURGH

Following the cessation of hostilities in Europe the 1945-46 season saw first class football return to England, initially in the form of the FA Cup and attendances boomed all over the country. Indeed Aston Villa recorded their largest ever crowd during this period with over 76,000 people packing out Villa Park for a sixth round tie against Derby County. The success of the competition led to an announ-cement that League Football would recommence at the beginning of the following season.

Villa's return to Norway

In preparation for the new campaign the Villa directors accepted an invitation from the Norwegian Football Association (NFA) to play three games against various mixed sides in their country. The reason for this was so that the NFA selectors could assess their players prior to choosing the Norwegian team to play two international games against Sweden and Denmark respectively during the following month.

Once the three Norwegian games were over the Aston Villa contingent was set to return to the UK via Tyneside and thence onto Edinburgh.

Here they were scheduled to play another charity game against an Edinburgh Select XI, this time at Easter Road, before returning home to the Midlands. The Villa squad selected to tour Norway included:- Joe Rutherford, Alan Wakeman, Vic Potts, George Cummings, Roy Gutteridge, "Mush" Callaghan, Eddie Lowe, Frank Moss, Harry Parkes, John Morby, Bob Iverson, Ronnie Starling, Eric Houghton, Billy Goffin, George Edwards, Les Smith and Frank Broome.

According to reports at the time it seemed the boat trip across the North Sea was expected to be smooth. Unfortunately Frank Broome was still recovering from gastric flu and the Villa management still had some concerns that he would not be well enough to make the journey irrespective of the weather conditions. Just to be on the safe side the Villa directors organised a last minute medical examination for Frank in Newcastle where thankfully he was given the all clear to join his team mates on the boat bound for Norway. So on Saturday May 25th a full strength Villa squad made their way to Tyneside docks where they boarded the S.S. Bretagne and set sail for Oslo.

The trip across the North Sea was a new experience for some of the players and thankfully the weather forecasters were accurate and sea was kind to them. Aston Villa's manager Alex Massie commented, "We had a grand sea trip, the sun shone brilliantly and the sea was not too bad at all. Notwithstanding the good behaviour of the North Sea however, we had a few of the customary casualties." Evidently Vic Potts, Eric Houghton and Frank Moss had decided to go up on deck following a large four course dinner on the Saturday evening. Vic was very sick but as Alex Massie saw the funny side commenting, "It was lucky for the other two that the wind was blowing in the right direction!"

Fortunately the next day brought much calmer waters but alas more players, including Ernie Callaghan, Eddie Lowe, Jack Morby and Les Smith were still under the weather. Thankfully there was no further illness amongst the squad and by the time SS Bretagne steamed proudly into Oslo at around 10.00a.m. on Monday the 27th May the players were ready for the task awaiting them. Once through customs the Villa contingent were transported to their hotel by coach and after unpacking they were taken to an exclusive mountain restaurant overlooking Oslo for lunch. The players returned to their hotel and spent the rest of the afternoon and early evening relaxing in the sunshine before their evening meal. The day culminated in the entire touring party being taken to a variety show in the heart of the capital which seemingly was enjoyed by all

May 28th
South Norway 2   Aston Villa 2

The next day Villa played their first game of the tour and the venue was Oslo's Ullevaal Stadium the home FK Lyn. The opposition, although including some Lyn players, was mainly selected from clubs all over the south of Norway. The visitors certainly didn't take their opposition lightly and manager Massie fielded a strong team consisting of Rutherford; Potts, Cummings; Iverson, Callaghan, Lowe; Goffin, Starling, Edwards, Smith, Houghton. Frank Broome was not included due to his illness.

Nevertheless he was with them in spirit apparently "kicking every ball" whilst watching from his seat in the main stand. A 27,000 crowd crammed the stadium to capacity and enthusiastically greeted their famous visitors from England onto the pitch. Perhaps unexpectedly the Villa players took some time to settle into the game which later they blamed on the unpredictable behaviour of the continental ball". With Villa far from their best it came as no great shock when the Norwegian's took the lead. Stunned, the visitors rolled up their sleeves and came more into the game once they began to fathom out the vagaries of the "continental" ball and finished the half the stronger team.

The beginning of the second period was delayed due to one of the linesmen mislaying his flag. Typical of the resourcefulness of the Scandinavians at that time he solved the problem by uprooting and utilising one of the half-way line flags! Once the second half eventually began the English First Division teams' class at last came to the fore and in due course they turned their domination into goals. The first, a crisp well taken effort, came from Herbert Smith and shortly after a second was added by Tamworth's favourite son William "Billy" Goffin. He collected the ball twenty five yards out, cleverly evaded two defenders and drove the ball confidently past the despairing Scandinavian goalkeeper.

Lifted by their control of the game the visitors looked confident and began to play some classy soccer. Their possession football was aimed at running down the clock and they looked to be coasting to victory when, with just a few minutes left on the clock, the Norwegians upset the apple cart and snatched an unexpected late equaliser from close range.

The next day was a scorcher weather wise and the players spent their time relaxing and sightseeing before making the relatively short trip to Sarpsborg to play Oestfold District in the local stadium. The opponents were reputed at the time to be much stronger opposition than those Villa had faced in the previous game and so leaving nothing to chance they insisted that the game was played with an English football!

May 30th
Oestfold District 2 Aston Villa 4

Aston Villa made one change from the team that drew two days earlier because Vic Potts had an injured knee so Ernie Callaghan moved to right-back and Frank Moss came in to fill the gap. The line-up therefore read:- Rutherford, Callaghan, Cummings, Iverson, Moss, Lowe, Goffin, Starling, Edwards, Smith, and Houghton. The first half was something of a goal feast with the two teams sharing four goals. On the mark for Aston Villa was Eric Houghton whose cannonball like shot beat the Norwegian's keeper with ease whilst George Edwards' effort was more mundane.

However it was another incident during the first period that caught the crowd's imagination. Evidently a wire haired terrier ran onto the field and decided to chase the ball. The referee had no alternative but to halt the game whilst the players tried in vain to capture the animal. After numerous failures by a variety of players George Edwards apparently made a magnificent rugby tackle to grab hold of the terrier. George carried the frightened animal off the pitch and as he crossed the touchline the crowd rose as one and loudly cheered his exploits.

The second half produced two more goals courtesy of the in-form "Billy" Goffin and his brace helped Villa secure their first victory of the tour by 4-2. His first effort was blocked by the goalkeeper however he was able to control the rebound and deftly place his shot just inside the post. His second goal had a touch of fortune about it. Billy received the ball no more than six yards out with his back to the goal. He skilfully turned and controlled the ball in one movement and then somehow miscued his shot. The ball completely deceived the home team's goalkeeper and fortunately for Billy it trickled into the corner of the net. Manager Alex Massie commented after the game, "We won much more comfortably than the score suggests."

Next stop was Stavanger which lay almost 200 miles from the tourists' base. When they arrived, following a very slow journey though torrential rain, they checked into their hotel and then made their way to the ground to have a look around.

They soon discovered that the heavy rain they had experienced throughout the latter part of their trip had reduced the pitch to a sea of mud. In fact the weather was still so bad was that three of the West Norway team, who were travelling by light aircraft to the game from Oslo, failed to arrive at the stadium because their plane was unable to land. Luckily three local players were able to step in at short notice.

June 5th
Combined West Norway XI 1 Aston Villa 9

The next day Aston Villa fielded the same side that beat Oestfold District and spent no time at all in putting their weakened West Norwegian opponents to the sword on the extremely heavy pitch. By the end of the first period "Billy" Goffin had put the game beyond the hosts netting no less than four times. Not to be outdone George Edwards weighed in with a brace giving Villa a 6-1 advantage by the interval. The second half went much the same way as the first this time however it was Edwards' turn to shine, adding three more goals to his tally, leaving Villa to run out 9-1 victors.

After the game the Villa players and officials were given a farewell dinner by the Norwegian FA where manager Alex Massie was asked to say a few words. According to Alex he, passed the buck and George Cummings was given the honour and according to reports at the time he coped superbly.

Just a few hours after the game the Villa party were on board the MS Astrea bound for the North East of England and from there on to Edinburgh for the charity match against a local Select XI at Easter Road. However before they could contemplate the game they had to face a rough voyage across the raging North Sea. Reports at the time suggested that the crossing resulted in all but two of the entire Villa contingent suffering severe sea sickness throughout the entire passage. Thankfully the boat docked safely on Tyneside early in the morning on June 7th and the weary party, which now included Johnny Dixon who had joined them on Tyneside, travelled by coach to Edinburgh to play the charity game at Easter Road, home of Hibernian.

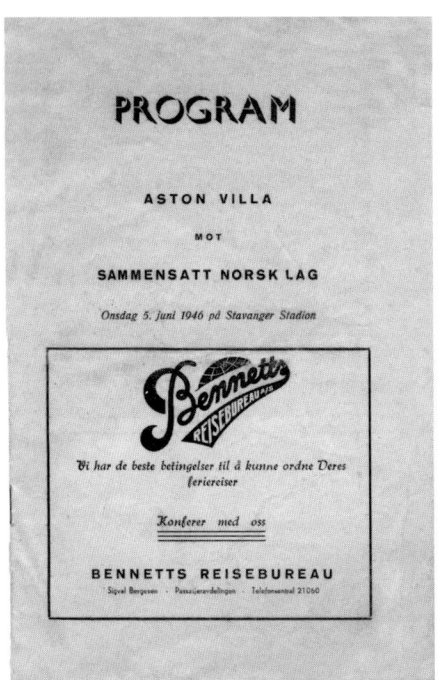

June 8th
Edinburgh Select XI   3   Aston Villa   3

Having won their previous game against the combined forces of the Edinburgh clubs two years earlier, the players were especially keen to end their tour on a high note, with another comfortable victory. The Villa put out a solid team in Rutherford; Potts, Cummings; Iverson, Callaghan, Lowe; Goffin, Dixon, Edwards, Starling, Smith.

The game itself was enorm-ously exciting as both clubs put on an entertaining show playing attacking football and squandering a number of gilt edged chances in the process. A typical example from Villa's point of view was when centre forward George Edwards managed to put his shot high over the bar from point blank range.

Shortly afterwards Edinburgh's centre forward John Aitken hit the post with the Villa keeper out of position and then Billy Goffin, with only Brown in the Scots' goal to beat, fired well wide.

The first goal eventually arrived on the half hour when Airdrie's John Aitken, who had been a perpetual thorn in Villa's side, took advantage of some confusion in the visitors' box and slid the ball into an empty net. Five minutes later Aitken added to his tally with a speculative shot from just outside the box to give the Scots a two goal advantage going into the break.

Whatever was said in the Villa dressing room at half time certainly had the desired effect, for within ten minutes of the restart Villa were level. First of all Billy Goffin scored his eighth goal of the tour when he placed a firm header into the corner of the net following Ronnie Starling's excellent cross. Then a speculative shot from left winger Les Smith was deflected past a stranded Brown and into the net by the Scots' full back Shaw. With just a few minutes left Edinburgh regained the lead through Walker and then, roared on by a fiercely partisan crowd, looked the more likely winners. However with the final minutes ticking away; up popped George Edwards to nod the ball past Brown in the Scots' goal.

The players and officials remained in Edinburgh overnight and returned to Birmingham the next day where undefeated manager Alex Massie told the awaiting press, "It was a most pleasant and enjoyable tour."

Far left Cummings, goalkeeper - Rutherford.

Match action in Norway.

1957   GERMANY & FRANCE

Having won the FA Cup, Aston Villa were invited to participate in a prestigious game with their French equivalents from Toulouse. The game was scheduled to take place at the end of May in 1957 at the Parc des Princes Stadium in Paris however we are jumping ahead. Before the "Battle of Paris" as it became known, the Villa boys had to complete a short end of season tour of West Germany. This involved a game against a combined team from Hamburg followed by a trip to Frankfurt to play FSV. It was hoped that they could field their FA Cup winning team for the latter game providing Pat Saward arrived in time. Pat had been selected to represent the Republic of Ireland in a World Cup qualifier against England in Dublin on the 19th May and so it would be "touch and go" as to whether or not he would manage to get to Germany in time for the Villa game.

The tourists had quite a hectic social schedule prior to playing the game in Hamburg, including a visit to Hagenbrook Zoo and a boat trip around the port, the latter being remembered fondly by Peter McParland.

May 18th
Combined Hamburg XI   1
Aston Villa   3

The Hamburg team comprised of the best players from the city's two premier teams at that time, Altona 93 and St.Pauli. The main concern of the local Hamburg press focussed on how the referee would perform. They all agreed that he would have a difficult job because there was a significant difference in the interpretation of the rules in the two countries.

Villa visit Germany and then do battle in Paris.

For all the anxiety shown by the media the game went off without a hitch. Villa raced into a 3-0 lead with Hamburg's only reply being through a converted penalty in the 77th minute which was conceded by centre-half Jimmy Dugdale. According to Peter McParland there was a great atmosphere inside the ground mainly because the attendance was swelled to over 20,000 by a large contingent of British servicemen who urged the Villa on by making a terrific noise with their rattles and trumpets.

Peter also remembers the game for the generous hospitality shown by the Hamburg clubs. After the match they invited the Villa players and officials into their social club and everyone had a thoroughly enjoyable evening. Peter also recollects meeting the Hamburg goalkeeper's wife that evening. She apparently had watched the 1957 FA Cup Final on television and was worried throughout the game that Peter was going to do the same to her husband as he had done to the Manchester United goalkeeper Ray Woods. Peter said, "She called me the 'goalkeeper killer' all night but it was all good natured banter."

May 21st
FSV Frankfurt 1 Aston Villa 3

The following day the team were up early to travel by rail to Frankfurt and straight into a controversy over floodlights. Evidently Villa manager Eric Houghton had made it crystal clear to the officials of both the Hamburg and FSV Frankfurt clubs, prior to the tour that his team were not prepared to play any games under lights until they were installed at Villa Park. When Villa reached Frankfurt they were shocked to discover that the game was not scheduled to kick off until 7.30p.m. and so the floodlights would be needed towards the end of the game. Houghton was not best pleased and insisted that the kick off time be brought forward otherwise the game would not go ahead. Eric being Eric he got his way.

Despite the dank evening and the rearranged kick off time there was still a large crowd inside the FSV ground to welcome Aston Villa's cup winning team (Pat Saward making it just in time). The keen interest in the game amongst the locals was probably because as mentioned earlier the recent FA Cup Final against Manchester United had been shown live on German television.

The Villa kicked off and the game was played throughout in the right spirit however with Villa leading 3-1 and ten minutes remaining, the light deteriorated and the floodlights were switched on. Manager Eric Houghton was not at all happy and told reporters after the final whistle that he had been asked before the game if the lights could be used, he explained that he had refused and made it very clear that he meant it. He went on to say that he was astonished when they came on, however as Villa were leading 3-1 and the night was drawing in he decided to be diplomatic and not lodge a complaint.

Villa had been travelling between games in Germany by train and now faced another gruelling journey home via what proved to be an extremely stormy crossing of the channel. Apparently the trip from Frankfurt to Birmingham had taken over twelve hours in all to complete and the players were adamant that they would never go through anything like it again. Peter McParland explained, "We told them (the directors) that if they wanted the game against Toulouse played then we fly to Paris – no more boats and trains!" The directors, after some deliberation, agreed with the players' request. So on Tuesday 28th May the Villa's 1957 FA Cup winning team, along with reserves Pace, Sabin and Birch and the rest of the party flew out of Elmdon Airport; destination Paris.

Everyone that was except manager Eric Houghton who had an agreement with his family that he would never travel by air until all of his three children had grown up. Eric went by boat and rail and said before he left, "We are hoping to do as well as we did on our recent trip to Germany. The lads played well in the two matches over there"

The two captains and officials meet in Paris.

May 29th   Toulouse 2 Aston Villa 1

The game against the French Cup Winners, Toulouse was played at the prestigious Parc des Princes Stadium on the evening of Wednesday 29th May. Peter McParland recalled that the pitch was surrounded by a cycle track and the crowd was, "packed in…there must have been over 30,000 people there".

The Birmingham Mail reported that following the formalities the game began with Villa adopting "some old fashioned English tackling which the French players (repeatedly) complained about." The French crowd constantly jeered the Villa players and this seemed to upset a few of them however Jimmy Dugdale, who was already having a great game, responded to the jeers in his own imitable way by bowing deeply towards them!

The game against the French Cup Winners, Toulouse was played at the prestigious Parc des Princes Stadium on the evening of Wednesday 29th May. Peter McParland recalled that the pitch was surrounded by a cycle track and the crowd was, "packed in…there must have been over 30,000 people there".

The Birmingham Mail reported that following the formalities the game began with Villa adopting "some old fashioned English tackling which the French players (repeatedly) complained about." The French crowd constantly jeered the Villa players and this seemed to upset a few of them however Jimmy Dugdale, who was already having a great game, responded to the jeers in his own imitable way by bowing deeply towards them!

Shortly after one of Jimmy's interactions with the crowd the Toulouse left-winger Bouchouk, who was beginning to look dangerous broke loose, evaded the close attentions of two Villa defenders and planted the ball confidently past Nigel Sims to record the opening goal. The French crowd were ecstatic however within three minutes their noise was silenced as the visitors equalised through captain Johnny Dixon. The goal came after a sustained period of Aston Villa pressure caused confusion in the Toulouse defence resulting in one of their full backs making a poor clearance. Johnny Dixon latched onto the ball, carried it forward and calmly swept it past the advancing French goalkeeper and into the net.

Following the equaliser the game swung back and forth until the half hour mark when according to Peter McParland, the game started getting a bit rough. He went on, "There was this Algerian 'fellah' playing for them. He had been causing a bit of trouble from the start and then he swung a punch a Johnny Dixon for some reason." Stan Crowther who was the nearest player to the incident went to Johnny's help and immediately the other players joined in. Fists flew in every direction and numerous blows were exchanged, even the Toulouse officials ran onto the pitch and joined in the mayhem. According to the Birmingham Mail the only player who didn't get involved was the French goalkeeper. The fighting continued unabated for almost five minutes before the Belgian referee Albert Alstern, aided by his linesmen and numerous gendarmes, regained control of the situation.

Amazingly there were no bookings or sending offs and eventually the match was restarted with a drop ball.

Within seven minutes Toulouse were back in front. Centre forward Eduardo Diloretto found himself in acres of space on the edge of the area and spotted that Nigel Sims was out of position. Without further ado he calmly placed the ball wide of the experienced Villa goalkeeper and into the corner of the unguarded net to send the French side in at half time 2-1 in front.

The second period was a much quieter affair, probably because the pitch had been completely surrounded by armed police officers, one of whom had been detailed specifically to sit next to the French manager Jules Bigot and keep him in order! As far as the actual game was concerned Aston Villa worked hard to draw level but sadly despite several promising attacks they failed to force an equaliser.

At the final whistle there were no handshakes or shirts exchanged as both sets of players quickly made their way towards the dressing rooms. Unfortunately once they were inside the tunnel and hidden from the crowd and gendarmes, the trouble erupted once more. Peter McParland remembered the situation clearly, "As soon as we got in the tunnel and out of sight of the police, the fighting started again. It was a real free for all and I can remember, which I laugh about now, Bill Moore, the Villa trainer being in the middle of it. He was stood on a chair with this heavy metal pump he used for inflating the balls and was whacking the French players with it. Well it eventually calmed down and the next thing we knew it was all over the English and French papers."

Indeed the French press were less than complimentary about the Villa's performance, "It has unfortunately become a regrettable tradition to see strong altercations happen when we receive British teams here in France. Too often they seem to leave their fair play at home" On hearing this for the first time from the author of this book, Peter responded by reiterating that it was the Algerian centre half that started the whole thing and added this interesting anecdote, "I met that Algerian player years later when I was playing for Northern Ireland. We got on great, even had a meal together and a good laugh about that Paris game!"

1958 G.A.I.S
(Gothenburg Athletics & Sports Association)
October 29th

Aston Villa 3   G.A.I.S. 0

On a dark, damp and drizzly Wednesday evening during October 1958, Aston Villa played host to Swedish side G.A.I.S (Gothenburg Athletics & Sports Association) to celebrate the opening of the newly installed Villa Park floodlights. It is interesting that whilst this was the official opening, the lights had in fact been utilised earlier in the season to illuminate some dank Saturday afternoon games.

The game against GAIS had been well publicised and the club were anticipating a large crowd to witness the official switch on. Unfortunately the weather had been poor all day and by the evening the smog was settling in Aston. This clearly deterred many supporters resulting in only 25,000 hardy souls braving the elements to witness the official opening of the floodlights, followed by a high profile game.

The Villa team selected a solid team for this prestigious game and lined up thus:- Sims; Lynn, Sharples; Lee, Dugdale, Crowe; Smith, Sewell, Myerscough, Burrows, McParland. The referee appointed for the occasion was none other than local M.P. and "First Class" referee Denis Howell.

Cheered on by the Villa faithful the home team laid siege on the Swedes' goal from the outset but due to some excellent defending by GAIS they only managed two shots in the first quarter of an hour and both were easily saved by goalkeeper Leif Andersson. First of all he dived full length to keep out Les Smith and then leapt across his goal in the opposite direction to punch away a Billy Myerscough effort. Two minutes later however Villa went ahead. Peter McParland had been lurking in the box and when Smith sent in a skidding cross Jackie Sewell stepped over the ball leaving McParland unmarked to smash it in off the post.

Official opening of the Villa Park floodlights.

Just two minutes later McParland was again on target but this time the busy Andersson managed to turn the ball around the post.

On the half hour Gothenburg at last posed some problems to the Villa defence. It all began with a great through ball from centre forward Andersson which put inside forward Jackobsson one on one with Sims in the Villa goal. The experienced Villa keeper rushed out to narrow the angle and was thankful to see the Swede's shot go inches wide. Determined to get back into the game and encouraged by Jackobsson's effort it was not long before Andersson was "at it again". This time with Sims out of position he found himself in front of an open goal but his weak shot was cleared off the line by the ever reliable Stan Lynn. Still the Swedes pushed forward and just before half time Nigel Sims pulled off a spectacular save by bravely diving at the feet of that man Andersson again when he looked odds on to level the scores.

The Villa emerged from the tunnel for the second half in determined mood following a half time roasting from manager Eric Houghton. Whatever he said to them appeared to do the trick because Villa scored two goals in quick succession. First rookie full back Gordon Lee drove the ball through a ruck of players that easily beat the unsighted Andersson and finished up in the back of the net. This was followed two minutes later when young debutant Harry Burrows, at that time still a part-time player with Villa's fourth team, scored Villa's third.

The Birmingham Post was cautious in their praise of the young inside left, "The opposition was hardly of a quality to give Burrows a fair test but the youth had opportunity enough to show that his powerful shooting alone would be a distinct asset to any Villa forward line." Harry

Burrows remembers this game very clearly, "It was the opening of the floodlights, Eric Houghton was the manager and he picked me to play inside left. I was surprised to be selected because I was just seventeen and only a part time player – I was working most of the week for my dad in his haulage business. I remember there was a great atmosphere inside the ground and I scored!"

The home team, now three goals to the good, eased off as it became increasingly apparent that the Gothenburg players did not have the quality in their ranks to get back into the game. When the final whistle blew the Swedes were loudly cheered by the Villa spectators however the Post commented that the cheer "must have been for their sporting approach to the game rather than for any prowess exercised during the preceding ninety minutes." Ouch!

The match....

The Ground....

The Floodlights

1960 SWEDEN & NORWAY

The 1959-60 season had been very successful for Aston Villa. Under Joe Mercer's management they had not only secured the Second Division title but also missed out by a whisker on another FA Cup Final appearance, losing narrowly to the eventual winners, Nottingham Forest, in a hard fought semi-final at Hillsborough. With this in mind the Aston Villa directors, along with Joe, decided that a six game tour of Scandinavia would be a nice way to reward the players for all their hard work over the previous season, whilst also helping to develop some of the more promising youngsters who would later become known as Mercer's Minors. In total there were seventeen players selected for the tour and the squad in full read:- Nigel Sims, Stan Lynn, John Neal, Doug Winton, Vic Crowe, Jimmy Dugdale, Pat Saward, Alan Deakin, Gordon Lee, Jimmy Adam, Ron Wylie, Jimmy MacEwan, Mike Tindall, Johnny Dixon, Bobby Thomson, Gerry Hitchens and Peter McParland.

The majority of the party flew out to Sweden on the Monday before the first game. The absentees were Ron Wylie and Pat Saward. Ron had a fear of flying and so left before the others and travelled on his own by train and boat to Helsingborg, whilst Pat Saward flew in a few days later following an international outing with the Republic of Ireland.

Scandinavia - Again!

Alan Deakin remembers the flight to Sweden as though it was yesterday, "I was only seventeen and it was the first time I had ever flown in a plane. I was sitting beside the window on my own and was feeling very anxious. Joe Mercer came along and settled down next to me. I wasn't sure if this was going to be helpful or not. Anyway every time the plane banked he leaned against me and kept taking the mickey out of me throughout the flight because he knew I was nervous."

May 10th   Gotenburgs Alliansen 2   Aston Villa 1

On their arrival in Gothenburg, the Villa party made their way to their hotel and didn't have long to wait for the first game of the tour which was against local side Gotenburgs Alliansen (Gothenburg Alliance), who included three internationals in their line-up. The Swedish supporters turned out in good numbers, around 15,000 in all, many coming just to see Peter McParland who had made such an impact for Northern Ireland during the 1958 World Cup in their country. In addition Aston Villa were also seen by local fans as old friends having played in the city three times previously. Interestingly Villa had lost each of these games and apparently some of the players began to look upon the fixture as being against a "bogey" team.

The Swedes included three international forwards in their side but Joe Mercer, true to his word, blooded youngsters and both Alan Deakin and Mike Tindall made the starting line-up. Mike said, "I was a bit nervous to be honest.

"I was only a youngster and in those days you didn't get into the first team until you were at least twenty. I looked around the changing room at our team. There was Vic Crowe who was hard as nails, with another tough player Stan Lynn behind him, as well as Peter McParland, Gerry Hitchens Jimmy Dugdale and Nigel (Sims) in goal. I thought to myself, what am I worrying about?"

Bobby Thomson remembers the game as being quite even for the first half hour with Jimmy Dugdale and Nigel Sims snuffing out any Gothenburg attacks. Unfortunately for the Villa on the half hour the Swedes took the lead through their inside forward Ove Olson. Shortly after the restart tragedy struck for young Alan Deakin when, following a heavy tackle he had to leave the field and be replaced by Jimmy Adam. This change required a reshuffle and so Bobby Thomson moved to wing-half whilst Jimmy Adam slotted into Bobby's position.

Meanwhile the other youngster, inside forward, Mike Tindall, was reportedly having a great game and with twenty minutes to go his firmly struck shot from inside the area nestled in the bottom corner of the net. Unfortunately for the tourists the goal spurred on the home team and their pressure was eventually rewarded, albeit in the last throws of the game, with a scrambled goal thereby making it four defeats in a row for Aston Villa in Gothenburg.

May 12th

Helsingborg 2   Aston Villa 3

The tourists had the next day off before their 130 mile trip to the Swedish sea port town of Helsingborg where they were due to play the local team. Peter McParland remembered this game as being the toughest of the tour. This time however Villa played some "attractive football that delighted the crowd" reported the Evening Mail and eventually emerged winners by the odd goal in five.

Aston Villa certainly didn't have the game all their way and with the Swede Karlson pulling the strings in midfield the home team were extremely unlucky not to be in front within the first ten minutes. Inside forward Ahlbergg latched onto a defence splitting pass from the stylish Karlson and raced towards an open goal but with only Sims to beat he somehow contrived to miss a straightforward chance. The blunder failed to dull the Swedes' enthusiasm and on fifteen minutes the inevitable goal arrived. Left winger Nordengren cleverly cut inside and hit a thunderous shot which left Nigel Sims in the Villa goal stationary.

The goal fired up the Aston Villa players and at last they started to show some of the form that made them Second Division champions. They gained control of midfield and began to put the home team under some serious pressure but the Swedes held out bravely. That was until, on the half hour, Gerry Hitchens latched on to an accurate pass from Bobby Thomson in midfield and equalised with a well taken goal that crept just inside the post. Now playing with a swagger in their step the away team laid siege on the Helsingborgs' goal and within five minutes the pressure paid off. Peter McParland collected the ball well outside the area, powered past two defenders and thundered in a typical cannon like shot which flew into the back of the net before the goalkeeper could move, to give Aston Villa a deserved 2-1 lead at the interval.

Within two minutes of the restart the outstanding Gerry Hitchens netted his second and Villa's third with a well worked goal. Following a series of passes in midfield Hitchens latched on to an inch perfect through ball and, following a determined burst through the middle, he unleashed a fierce shot from twelve yards out to put the away team 3-1 ahead. With the game all but won Aston Villa passed the ball around in a nonchalant manner and the Swedes spent much of the second half chasing shadows.

However with fifteen minutes to go the away team made one too many passes in midfield. The ball was neatly intercepted just inside the Villa half by the stylish Helsingborg inside left Ahlbergg who neatly created space for himself and surprised Villa's keeper Nigel Sims with a swerving effort that curled out of his considerable reach and into the top corner of the goal.

Villa responded positively to the setback and played some outstanding football during the final ten minutes and were extremely unlucky to see Hitchens' last minute volley skim the top of bar and fly out for a goal kick. There were no further goals and according to the Birmingham press "Hitchens and McParland were Villa's outstanding players."

Next up was a four hundred mile journey north to Norway and a game against Raufoss Idrettslag. On arriving in this beautiful little town, tucked away in the mountains, the players were surprised just how tiny the place was. Even today it only has a population of 6,000 and so for these young men representing Aston Villa back in 1960 it must have felt a long, long way from Birmingham.

From the tour.

(Above) The players come on to the pitch from the somewhat basic dressing rooms.
(Below) Team line-up before a match:
(Back) Lynn, Crowe, Sims, Neal, Dugdale, Thomson. (Front) MacEwan, Tindall, Hitchens, Dixon, McParland

May 17th

Raufoss Idrettslag 1
Aston Villa 13

The Raufoss Idrettslag club, known locally as Raufoss IL, at that time played in the Norwegian First Division. With this in mind Aston Villa were expecting another hard fought, tight game. How wrong could they be? The Villa team for this game was another strong one:- Sims, Lynn, Neal, Crowe, Dugdale, Thomson, MacEwan, Tindall, Hitchens, Wylie, and McParland.

Mike Tindall explained that although he was on the team sheet as an inside forward for the game, Joe Mercer told him to play a little deeper. He continued, "We soon realised that the opposition wasn't as good as we thought they were, so I started pushing forward." Mike eventually found himself unmarked in the penalty area and the ball dropped at his feet, he enthused, "I just hit it and it flew into the back of the net."

He then said that he had five more similar chances and scored on each occasion! "When I scored my sixth our players didn't bother coming to congratulate me – they were fed up with me scoring! So I played back in midfield after that." It wasn't just Mike Tindall who went on a goal scoring spree Gerry Hitchens bagged four and another three were spread around giving the visitors in a well-deserved 13-1 victory.

According to press reports at the time Villa outclassed Raufoss in every department throughout the entire game, running rings around the Norwegians' defence and splitting it wide open with their accurate passing. A comment from a local newspaper summed the whole game up, "It wasn't really a match, it was just a demonstration of first-class English football."

May 19th

Bollnas Sports Club 0 Aston Villa 6

The next morning the Villa party was on the move again with yet another long trip, 300 miles back into Sweden, in front of them. The opponents on this occasion were fourth division side Bollnas Sports Club. To be fair the press pointed out that Villa had little to beat and had it not been for the Swedish goal keeper Olsson, who had been borrowed from a nearby first division club, the result would have been even more embarrassing for the home team. In fact, according to Peter McParland, the majority of the first half had been played in the Swedes' half of the field as the Villa players passed the ball around at will and scored three goals in the process The first a rocket from Peter McParland and then a brace from the stylish Johnny Dixon.

During the half time interval Ron Wylie was shocked when Joe Mercer told the players that he had decided to play in the second half, however within ten minutes Ron realised that Joe was better than some of the others still on the pitch! Playing in the forward line Mercer in fact added to the goal tally with a tap-in whilst Gerry Hitchens poached two for himself. At the final whistle the local crowd of around 2,000 gave Villa a massive round of applause for what they considered to be a fine display of English football in winning the game 6-0.

Thankfully the players and officials were rewarded with a few days break before their penultimate game back in the mountains of Norway. It was a 320 mile journey to Trondheim but it was worth it, many of the players were stunned by the scenery. On arrival they found a thriving city with a population of over 150,000 people, the Villa contingent were based in a first class hotel, just outside the city, at the foot of the mountains. According to Peter McParland the weather was superb and everyone was sunbathing. Peter takes up the story, "

About fifty yards from the hotel was a beautiful lake so we all decided to cool off in it." Apparently it had been frozen over just two weeks earlier and irrespective of the sunshine that day, the lake was still bitterly cold. Nevertheless footballers on tour being an unusual breed decided that everyone had to take a dip. The entire party took up the challenge except manager Joe Mercer who steadfastly refused and trainer Ray Shaw who discreetly disappeared. Undeterred the players picked Joe up, carried him protesting to the lakeside and threw him into the ice cold waters.

What the players didn't realise was that back in 1954 when Mercer broke his right leg in two places he had metal plates inserted to aid his recovery. So when Joe began struggling and shouting for help, the players thought it was one of his "wind ups" and stood at the water's edge jeering at him. After a few minutes the players realised that Joe was genuinely in trouble and some of them had to jump in and rescue him. Peter continued, "We were all shook up when we realised what we had done. Apparently the cold water had attacked the metal plates and stopped him from being able to move his legs!"

May 24th

Trondheim 0   Aston Villa 6

The game against Trondheim was something of an anti-climax after this episode and Joe perhaps wisely chose not to play. The Villa ran out 6-0 winners with Gerry Hitchens scoring four of them. There was a good crowd of over 10,000 local supporters inside the ground to witness their team being pinned in their own half trying vainly to keep the score down. A newspaper report at the time suggested that, "...had Villa gone all out they might have repeated their 13-1 rout of Raufoss..."

The next stop on this protracted but enjoyable tour was Ostersund, a city 150 miles from Trondheim in Sweden with a population of around 50,000.

The party were based at a hotel on the shore of Sweden's fifth largest lake, Storsjön opposite the island of Frösön. Villa were not due to play Second Division team IFK Ostersund for a couple of days, consequently the players had a little free time to explore the delights of this beautiful Swedish city.

According to Bobby Thomson the only rules that Joe set rules on this tour were that he wanted all the players in their rooms from two o'clock to have a sleep for a couple of hours, before an evening game. Bobby takes up the tale, "What that meant to some of us was that we could be out all night if we liked, as long as we were in bed by two o'clock, the next afternoon!" Apparently on one occasion Bobby had been out all night and was walking back to the hotel with Jimmy Dugdale at about eight o'clock in the morning. Just before they reached their hotel they bumped into Joe Mercer and Ray Shaw. Joe asked them where they had been and Bobby's quick reply was that they were "having an early morning walk". Joe didn't believe a word of it and told the pair of them so but as it was nearing the end of the tour he didn't make a fuss about it.

May 26th

FK Ostersund 1   Aston Villa 7

So onto the game; According to the programme Villa fielded a very strong team:- Sims, Lynn, Neal, Crowe, Dugdale, Saward, MacEwan, Tindall, Hitchens, Thomson and McParland. The game was just as one-sided as the previous three with Villa rattling in seven goals whilst the hosts had to make do with a consolation goal.

Mike Tindall summed up the Scandinavian trip thus, "It was a great tour and we were up for every game" It certainly was and as Jimmy MacEwan pointed out, "You can only beat what's in front of you and we did that." The final stats for the tour were: - Played 6, Won 5, Drawn 0, Lost 1, Goals scored 36, Goals against 6.

1961 USSR

The 1960-61 season was Aston Villa's first back amongst the elite of English football. It was a mixed campaign with the Villa finishing a laudable ninth in the league and reaching the fifth round of the FA Cup only to lose 2-0 to the eventual winners Tottenham Hotspur at Villa Park in front of almost 70,000 spectators. 1960-61 was also the first season of the Football League Cup and by the beginning of May Aston Villa had reached the final. The game, which was to be a two legged affair against Rotherham United, had to be held over until the following season because Villa were off on tour behind the "Iron Curtain."

Gerry Hitchens, Villa's leading goal scorer for the previous season, was not selected for the tour of the Soviet Union. The reason for this was not, as many people thought at time, related to his proposed transfer to Internazionale (Inter-Milan). The explanation was much simpler. Hitchens had been selected to play for his country at Wembley against Mexico in a game which England won 8-0 and included an excellent goal from Gerry himself inside the first two minutes. Following his performance he was chosen to be part of the England party that toured Europe and so was not able to join up with his Villa team mates in Russia. Interestingly, according to an interview that Gerry gave back in 1962 to Topical Times the first approach from Inter-Milan to sign him was directly to the Aston Villa board following the Mexico game on May 10th. However Gerry himself was not made aware of this until much later because his team mates and management were away in the Soviet Union on tour.

So, bright and early on Monday 8th May 1961 the Villa party, without arguably their greatest asset at that time, embarked on their first tour of Eastern Europe with a direct flight from Heathrow to Moscow on a de Havilland DH 106 Comet. On board the plane in terms of playing staff were Nigel Sims, Geoff Sidebottom, Stan Lynn, Wilson Briggs, Alfie Hale, Gordon Lee, Vic Crowe, Jimmy Dugdale, Alan Deakin, Jimmy MacEwan, Harry Burrows, Alan O'Neill, Bobby Thomson, John Neal, Jimmy McMorran, and Alan Baker. Peter McParland made his own way to Moscow from Berlin a little later in the tour because he had been playing for Northern Ireland in Germany. Ron Wylie didn't make the trip at all because, as mentioned earlier in this book, he had a fear of flying whilst Vic Crowe was only available for the first two games as he was needed by the Wales national team for a World Cup qualifying game in Madrid.

On arrival in Moscow the party was taken by bus to their hotel which was located in the centre of the city near Red Square. Once their rooming arrangements had been organised, the players set about locating a suitable restaurant. Unfortunately this task wasn't as easy as they had anticipated due to the language differences. According to Harry Burrows the Villa group were assigned two interpreters however the players were fairly sure that one of these also worked for the KGB as he was constantly monitoring his colleague and so the players didn't trust them. In fact later in the tour this was confirmed when the "genuine" interpreter bought an English novel from Harry, "It was all very 'cloak and dagger and he didn't want anyone to see what we were up to. I had to give it to him vey discretely because western literature was banned in Russia at that time and you could get into terrible trouble if you were caught." Anyway let's get back to the story about the players search for somewhere to eat.

Alan O'Neill takes up the tale, "We eventually got to this restaurant that was recommended to us and settled down. There was nothing on the menu I fancied so I asked one of the interpreters to recommend something. He told me that the egg soup was very good in this particular restaurant so I took him at his word. I was a bit taken aback when they brought me this bowl of supposedly hot water with a raw egg still in its shell on a separate plate!" Apparently Alan was expected to place the egg in the bowl and let it slowly cook in the water.

Villa behind the Iron Curtain

When he tested the temperature of the liquid with his finger he found that it was tepid at best, and so not fancying a raw egg, he decided to give it a miss.

The next day the Villa players and officials were invited to the British Embassy. "When we got there we were absolutely starving...." commented Jimmy MacEwan "....because we had not had a proper meal since we left England." With this in mind one or two of the players got together and asked the embassy staff if they could provide them with some food to take back to the hotel. After much searching the staff located a large number of Heinz tinned soups which the players stashed into large sacks that the Embassy staff had found for them. Alan O'Neill recalls these sacks full of soup cans being extremely heavy and apparently it took three players to carry them back to their hotel.

Once back in their rooms Alan Baker was assigned the job of "Chef in Charge" unfortunately he had no way of heating the soup. According to Alan O'Neill, "Little Alan Baker was always sniffing about and after scouring the hotel he eventually got hold of a small electric fire from somewhere and he set about cooking the soup in his room." Alan O'Neill claims that they lived on this soup whilst in Moscow and quipped, "We trained on soup and played our matches on soup!" Harry Burrows added that, "Stan Lynn was a big lad but he ate hardly anything. He lived on Alan Baker's soup and lost over a stone in weight in the process."

With still another day to kill before the first game of the tour Harry Burrows remembers some of the players being taken to the Moscow State Circus and whilst Bobby Thomson has no recollection of this he does recall looking around the Kremlin and also visiting the Gorky Park Pleasure Garden. "I was really looking forward to going to Gorky Park because they told us there would be dancing there. Imagine how disappointed I was when we discovered that the only dancing was a display by a bunch of Cossacks. I was expecting a dance where there would be women to dance with!" laughed Bobby.

The following day the first match of the tour was scheduled to take place and during the morning the Villa players and officials visited the venue for the game and were impressed by the vast Central Lenin Stadium. Meanwhile over a thousand miles away in West Berlin Peter McParland was struggling. "I had been on tour with Northern Ireland playing games against Italy, Greece and then on May 10th, West Germany at the Olympic Stadium in Berlin before 90,000 people. The game was shown live on TV in both West and East Berlin. I got a nasty injury in that game against the Germans which required six stitches. Unfortunately the doctor who put the stitches in had had a drink or two and later on the wound started to go sceptic."

The morning after Northern Ireland's international game, it had been arranged for Peter to fly direct to Moscow, from an airport located in Berlin's communist sector, hopefully in time to play for the Villa against Moscow Dynamo. Picture the scene there was Peter, a young Irishman with a leg injury, alone in a strange divided city about to cross from West to East Berlin, via the Brandenburg Gate and Check Point Charlie. Fortunately for Peter he managed to limp across the border without too much difficulty however once in East Berlin he was immediately struck by the difference in the standard of living and commented that, "East Berlin was very poor."

Limping badly Peter pressed on eventually managing to find his way to the East Berlin Airport but once there he soon encountered problems. His passport and papers were taken from him by officials and he was sent to wait on the bus, which was used to take passengers out to the airliners, and was well past its sell by date. When he climbed aboard this bus there were the two Hungarian Airline pilots and about three other people inside. Peter continued, "We were sitting there in this bus for over half an hour and I was beginning to wonder what was going on."

Obviously the pilots were also concerned and got off the bus and went to try and find out what was causing the delay. They eventually returned to the bus and asked Peter to accompany them to a nearby office to meet with the East German officials. Peter was clearly becoming quite anxious, "I was getting a bit worried by this time but the Hungarian pilots came with me and that made me feel a bit better." When he got to the office he found the East Berlin officials, in Peter's words, ".....looking at my passport and papers trying to figure out what was what."

After what seemed an age to Peter one of the pilots turned to the East German officials and asked them in German (they interpreted it for Peter later) if they had seen the football match on television the previous evening.

They both said they had. To which the pilot replied that Peter was playing in the game. The East German officials looked Peter up and down and after a few moments recognised him, and in Peter's words, "I got the all clear!"

The aeroplane was very basic and passengers could sit where they liked. Peter remembers there only being about five people in total on board. The plane was late taking off due to the afore mentioned incident and it was going to be a very close call as to whether Peter would arrive in Moscow in time to play in Villa's game against the famous Dynamo Moscow. Unfortunately the old World War 2 plane wasn't able to make up the lost time and so sadly Peter missed the game, however he did watch the latter stages of the match on a small television in the foyer of the team's hotel.

The next day as far as can be remembered by those interviewed was spent shopping. Peter McParland recalls going into a store to buy some perfume for his wife. When he gave it to her on his return to the UK, she took one sniff of it and was horrified; Peter explained, apparently it smelt like cabbage water!

May 11th   Dynamo Moscow   2   Aston Villa   0

The Villa team for this first game of the tour was: - Sims; Lynn, Lee; Crowe, Dugdale, Deakin; MacEwan, O'Neill, Thomson, Hale and Burrows. When the Villa team ran out in front of over 75,000 spectators they were surprised to see a huge banner in the crowd declaring, "UP THE VILLA!" It turned out that it had been hoisted by a party of vociferous English fans who had been working on the exhibition buildings for the British Trade Fair, which was due to open in Moscow the following week.

As far as the actual game was concerned the first half saw Villa looking a little disorganised and lacking punch up front. According to press reports at the time they were clearly missing the "class of Hitchens and McParland". Dynamo Moscow took advantage of this and seized the initiative putting Villa under sustained pressure. Eventually their dominance paid off when in the 27th minute forward Chislenko, the Russian international striker, cut in from the wing and as Sims came out looking to smother his shot the Russian pushed the ball past him with embarrassing ease. Losing 1-0 at half time Villa came out fighting in the second half and according to reports should have scored on at least three occasions.

Their failure to do so was put down to indecisive work in front of goal coupled with inaccurate shooting and these misses were to eventually prove costly.

Following a further period of Villa pressure in the later stages of the game the Russians broke away and against the run of play, Igor Chislenko expertly took his second goal of the night. Shortly after Villa restarted the game the final whistle blew and the Moscow club had sealed their victory by two goals to nil.

After the match Villa manager Joe Mercer refuted suggestions that his team were too physical by saying, "It's the same old story - a different interpretation of the rules..." He continued, "We feel that we were entitled to play the ball wherever it was. The rules are clear. A player can charge a goalkeeper and that's what we did." When the players returned to the hotel they spotted Peter McParland in the foyer and one of them shouted to him, "Hey Peter how are you? Wait 'til you see what this place is like – you won't believe it!" and the rest of the players just laughed. Peter thought they were winding him up but he soon realised just how difficult things really were.

The next day as far as can be remembered by those interviewed was spent shopping. Peter McParland recalls going into a store to buy some perfume for his wife. When he gave it to her on his return to the UK, she took one sniff of it and was horrified; Peter explained, apparently it smelt like cabbage water! Harry Burrows and Jimmy MacEwan both purchased cameras, without thinking how they would get them through customs, but to be fair to them there wasn't much to else to buy. In fact the players sold more than they bought. Alan O'Neill tells the story about how while three of them were walking around the centre of Moscow someone tapped him on the shoulder and said very discretely "I buy, I buy!"

The Russian apparently took them to a house in a back street and bought most of their clothes from them. The word soon got round and a lot of the other players sold shirts, jackets, coats and shoes for what seemed like a considerable amount of money only to realise later that they would be prohibited from taking their accumulated roubles out of the Soviet Union.

To while away their boredom the players organised the inevitable card school and Alan Baker was in charge. They played mainly Brag and Alan who was still only sixteen at the time won, according to Jimmy MacEwan, "thousands of roubles from the others" and so they kidded him on that he was really wealthy and christened him "Bilko" after the Phil Silvers character in the TV series that was popular in the UK at the time. Bobby Thomson lost a lot of money in the card school and so decided to sell more of his clothes to pay off his gambling bills. He said that he was standing outside the hotel one morning waiting for the team bus – where they were off to he was unable to recall. He was looking in through the hotel window dressed in his club suit complete with the Aston Villa crest. Soon he was approached by a shady character asking him how much he wanted for the suit. Bobby was just doing the deal when a voice came from nowhere saying, "Oi! Thomson! Get in here, get on this bus now. You are not selling that suit!" it was Ray Shaw the Aston Villa trainer.

That evening Bobby, who had been to Moscow a few years earlier with the Wolves, knew that a good time could be had in the American Embassy but he couldn't remember exactly where it was. Unperturbed he jumped into a taxi with Jimmy Dugdale at his side and told the driver to take them to USA Embassy. When they arrived Bobby marched up to the door, told security who they were and the pair were admitted without any problems, just in time to watch a film show. Bobby remembers clearly that it was the 1958 movie, "The Naked and the Dead" staring Aldo Ray. The establishment apparently had a typical American bar and sold draft beer so the two of them spent an enjoyable evening with their American cousins, eventually leaving the embassy on foot a little worse for wear!

The next challenge for the pair was to find their way back to their hotel. All they could remember was that it was near the Kremlin which was in part visible in the far distance. However before they began their trek it was necessary for them to relieve themselves. It was a dark night with no one else around and they found just the spot, a nicely secluded area next to the steps that went down to the river.

Bobby takes up the story, "Before we had finished who should come round the corner but an armed policeman.....Jimmy and I started to run and we never looked back - we just kept running!" Bobby likened the whole fiasco to a scene from the Third Man film, "It was dark, we were next to the river, there were steps down from the road and dim lights shedding their glow over the water." They continued sprinting alongside each other in the general direction of the Kremlin never looking back. Bobby still wary of the armed policeman in pursuit recalls telling Jimmy, "Don't run alongside me keep a couple of feet away because if the policeman shoots, the bullet will go between us – we were definitely scared" Anyway the two lads eventually made it back to the hotel none the worse for wear, walked into bar and greeted the other players as if nothing had happened.

The next stop on the tour was T'bilisi over a thousand miles away and therefore required a lengthy flight down towards the Turkish border.

Whilst this would be quite a simple journey today it was considered somewhat hazardous back in 1961. According to both Harry Burrows and Peter McParland, there were no reserved seats. People got on the plane just like a bus and sat where they fancied, it was first come first served. "There was livestock too; chickens, ducks, small pigs allsorts – I'd never seen anything like it" added Alan O'Neill. He went on to say that he couldn't understand how the plane took off let alone stayed in the air. "It was an old World War 2 plane with propellers and the noise from the engines was deafening.....not just on take-off but all through the flight."

On arrival in T'bilisi they were transported directly to their hotel in a very old rickety bus. Alan remembers the poverty. Reflecting on this he said, "We were looking out of the bus windows and it was like a shanty town – real poverty. One thing that really surprised me was there were women working on the roads digging up cobble stones." The other thing that struck all the players was the heat. They came to Russia expecting it to be cold and were not disappointed whilst in Moscow, Georgia on the other hand was a different proposition. Here it was very hot with temperatures in the upper 90's Fahrenheit.

T'bilisi in 1961 was a complete contrast to Moscow and the players who had been warmly greeted by the friendly locals soon settled in to the more laid back Georgian culture. The hotel was more than acceptable but the thing all the players loved was the food. Here according to Peter McParland the Villa contingent ate meat for the first time since they had arrived in the USSR.

The match programme

In addition the beer was more akin to what they were used to back in the UK and apparently tasted much better than the local brew they had been reluctantly drinking in Moscow.

The day before the game against "FC Dynamo T'bilisi" the Villa party were taken to a large communist rally in the centre of the city. There were huge crowds and an enormous purpose built covered stage in the town square. The players were chaperoned by their interpreters and their "colleagues" who were "keeping an eye" on them. Only when the speeches began did the players realise that it was *Khrushchev,* the famous Russian leader, who was speaking. He was according to Bobby Thomson, "whipping up the audience" by extolling the feats of Yuri Gagarin, the Soviet cosmonaut and the first man in space. Gagarin had voyaged into space aboard Vostok One, a few weeks earlier, making the first ever orbit of the earth.

As the players watched the scene unfold, dark clouds moved in over the square accompanied by a strong wind and it looked as though a heavy storm was brewing. Peter McParland remembers witnessing the scene clearly, "Khrushchev was talking and we of course had the interpreters translating what he was saying for us. After a while the skies became gloomier and full of rain". Krushchev was not perturbed and according to Peter, told the massive crowd that, "It would not rain because Yuri Gagarin had been higher than god and that Yuri was the new god." At that moment a number of players can recall the wind blowing fiercely, thunder and lightning, a torrential storm, everyone running for cover and the event being called off. Peter wryly pointed out, "That's what god thought of *Khrushchev saying* Yuri Gagarin was the new god!"

May 14th Dynamo Tbilisi 2   Aston Villa 0

The next day Villa were due to play the local team during the afternoon but the kick-off had to be delayed until early evening because the temperature had soared to almost 100 degrees Fahrenheit. Even with the delayed kick off the players noticed the heat, which was still in the 90's, well before they reached the steps at the end of the tunnel.

The players selected for the game were: - Sidebottom; Lynn, Lee; Crowe, Dugdale, Deakin; MacEwan, O'Neill, Thomson, McMorran, Burrows; with Alan Baker named as the substitute. Peter McParland and Johnny Neal, who were still carrying injuries, took on the role of keeping the Villa players cool during the game by running around the pitch and providing ice cold sponges from their buckets. Villa had the better of the first half and were extremely unlucky to go behind in the 35th minute from a free kick which unfortunately Geoff Sidebottom only managed to push into the top of his net. There were no further goals in the first half and Villa went in at the break just the one goal behind.

Bobby Thomson recalls a tough second half but with Villa doing okay. He then described almost having his leg broken by a "big Cossack bloke" Bobby continued, "….that wasn't in the script so I was a bit naughty and gave him one back at the next opportunity. The referee tried to send me off but I told him I wasn't going. Joe Mercer backed me up saying 'If Bobby goes off then we all do' or words to that effect" and so Bobby remained on the pitch.

Villa continued to press but their dominance came to nothing and then to add insult to injury, with ten minutes to go Dynamo broke away and with goalkeeper Sidebottom seriously out of position the Georgian's winger stroked the ball into the net to make it 2-0. The tourists responded positively to this second setback and playing though the pain barrier in intense heat, they came close to getting a goal back when Bobby Thompson's header went slightly wide.

At the final whistle the 70,000 crowd were so impressed with Villa's "never say die" attitude that they loudly cheered their players as they walked from the pitch. Joe Mercer told the Birmingham Mail after the game, "The heat certainly bothered the Villa players and Dynamo were the better side in the first half but we were on top in the second…" The Russian press felt that Villa lacked speed against the Dynamo team but praised Mercer's men for their tackling, ball control, accurate passing and the way they utilised the open spaces on the field.

First thing the next day saw the Villa party back in the sky on another precarious flight bound for Moscow. The reason for catching this early flight was to ensure that the players had a couple of days to prepare for their final and probably toughest match of the tour. The opposition this time was a combined Russian team who were playing under the name of the Moscow Select XI. In reality they were more or less the Soviet Union team that reached the quarter finals of the World Cup in Chile the following year.

Aston Villa had a number of players carrying knocks including Jimmy MacEwan, Bobby Thomson and Geoff Sidebottom but probably the most worrying was Peter McParland, whose infected leg was becoming an increasing concern for the Villa management. Peter remembers this well, "My leg started to swell up and the Russian fellah who was looking after us said that I needed to get it looked at." Off Peter went to the Lenin Stadium and visited their medical department. Peter takes up the story, "I was taken into this big room with bare whitewashed walls, full of all sorts of medical equipment.

A big woman in a white coat examined my leg and told me that the stitches they had put in Germany, after the Northern Ireland game, were no good and needed removing"

Peter was told to return the next day and the medics would sort it out however they added if there was a problem then he would need to be admitted into the local hospital. Peter was not keen to return to the Russian Medical Centre and even less enthusiastic about spending time in a Russian hospital. It was a very worried Peter that returned to the hotel and met with manager Joe Mercer. He explained the situation and then asked Joe if there were any other options. Mercer took one look at his leg and escorted him to the British Embassy where they issued him with a course of penicillin tablets. The wound immediately began to heal but unfortunately not quickly enough to enable him to play in the final game of the tour.

The match programme.

On the morning of that remaining game Aston Villa were preparing to face, with a number of their key players carrying injuries, probably the strongest Russian football team any English club side had ever played. Jimmy MacEwan, Bobby Thomson and Geoff Sidebottom were all doubtful, Peter McParland was definitely out and Vic Crowe had left two days earlier to play in a World Cup Qualifying game for Wales in Spain. Consequently Joe Mercer asked the Russian officials if he could have three substitutes standing by in case any of the walking wounded broke down during the match and much to his surprise they agreed.

May 17th   Combined Russian XI   0   Aston Villa   1

Thankfully the three injured players made the starting line-up which therefore read: - Sidebottom; Lynn, Lee; McMorran, Dugdale, Deakin; MacEwan, O'Neill, Thomson, Hale, Burrows. The three named substitutes were Wilson Briggs, Alan Baker and Johnny Neal the latter was at last recovering from an injury which he sustained prior to leaving England. The Russian press on the morning of the match gave Villa absolutely no chance of getting any sort of result from the game. They explained that the Soviet Union Combined XI had been carefully groomed over the previous two years with the aim of representing their country at the World Cup Finals in South America the following year.

The Central Lenin Stadium was filled to capacity with over 70,000 spectators packed inside the intimidating arena. Prior to the game the excited crowd were entertained by the Argyll and Sutherland Highlanders Pipe Band who were in Moscow to support the British Trade Fair. The bagpipes were clearly heard in the Villa dressing room; Harry Burrows fondly recalled the moment their rousing pipe music infiltrated the changing rooms, "To hear those pipes made the hairs stand up on the back of your neck.

It was marvellous to hear them. It was a bit like we were going to war and it fired us all up! Then someone shouted 'come on let's get at them!' and we all cheered and were off up the tunnel"

The workers from the British exhibition who gave the Villa such magnificent support a week earlier were in great voice again urging the team on however the vast majority of the crowd could only see one winner and in their opinion that wasn't going to be Aston Villa. Following the away team's two previous defeats together with their injuries the Soviet Union team were confident of an easy ride culminating in a comfortable victory. However things don't always go according to plan and the Russians were shocked when according to the Birmingham Mail, on the half hour mark, "Jimmy MacEwan jinked his was down the right flank, whipped round two defenders and crashed the ball in for the only goal of the game." The goal shocked the home team who went in at half time looking downcast.

The second half was non-stop pressure from the Russians who had obviously been given a roasting by their management during the interval. Over and over again they attacked but the Villa clung on by the skin of their teeth and thankfully their defence stood firm. Shot after shot rained in on the Villa goal but through a mixture of good fortune, every player committed to the cause and some disciplined defending they hung on for a famous victory. When the referee eventually signalled time the Villa players celebrated whilst Russian team were, "...bitterly whistled and hooted back to the dressing rooms" by their supporters.

Players pose in front of the Tzar's Bell (The biggest bell in the world), Moscow.

Jimmy Dugdale was quoted after the game thus, "I have played in some Villa teams that have put up wonderful, incredible fights when the odds have been stacked against us but there was nothing like this!" Joe Mercer said, "This was probably the best performance I have seen our boys give. It was one of those times when British football was at its best." he continued, "Alan Deakin outshone them all. It was the best game I have ever seen him play."

The Russian team as one might expect got a right panning from the Soviet Press, "It is alarming that players from Russia's national clubs were considerably inferior to their rivals in the technique of playing the ball" was one of the more moderate comments.

After the game Alan Deakin remembers a banquet that was organised for the two teams, officials and dignitaries. It didn't go very well as the two sets of players were on opposite sides of the room and although there were interpreters available the Russians were forbidden to talk to the Villa players! Alan said that "we soon got fed up and went looking for somewhere to have a drink in the city". Unfortunately as usual the bottled beer and cheap champagne was not to the players' liking but there was nothing else on offer and who cared? It was their last night in Moscow and they had just beaten the Soviet Union's World Cup team!

1962 SWINDON

May 3rd   Swindon Town   1   Aston Villa   2

There have been many reasons for agreeing to friendly games but according to Harry Burrows, who occupied the left wing for Villa during the 1960's, manager Joe Mercer often used them to assess players that he was interested in signing. This particular testimonial game that was arranged for two Swindon stalwarts Arnold Darcy and Peter Chamberlain back in 1962 may have fallen into that category. As Harry continued, "We knew he must be interested in some of their players and we reckoned these were Summerbee and Ernie Hunt."

With Derek Dougan injured, Bobby Thomson led the attack and the line-up for the game read:- Sims; Lee, Aitken; Crowe, Sleeuwenhoek, Tindall; Ewing, Baker, Thomson, Wylie, Burrows. The game was taken seriously and the commitment of both teams contributed to a very exciting end to end match. Either side could have taken the lead but in the 39th minute it was the First Division team that broke the deadlock. Bobby Thomson collected the ball thirty yards out, made a diagonal run to the right hand edge of the area and hit a hard rising shot which Turner in the Swindon goal failed to hold on to. The ball spun cruelly from his hands and trickled into the unprotected goal to put Villa 1-0 to the good.

The Robins responded positively to the setback and within three minutes Ernie Hunt fired a bullet like effort which Nigel Sims failed to hold. A young Charlie Aitken valiantly attempted to clear the loose ball but sadly for the Villa he only helped it into the net. The goal spurred the home team on and they were extremely unfortunate just before half time when a shot from Mike Summerbee rattled the underside of the bar and bounced clear with Nigel Sims in the Villa goal AWOL. To the surprise and delight of the large crowd Aston Villa's popular manager Joe Mercer decided to play in the second half and replaced Alan Baker, at inside right. Joe's class immediately made a difference to Villa's game.

With their manager's presence on the field the visitors laid siege on the Robins' goal. First Joe Mercer hit a shot that looked goal bound from the moment it left his boot but somehow Turner in the Swindon goal tipped the ball over the bar. Harry Burrows sent in a pinpoint cross from the resulting corner which brought about a scramble in the Swindon penalty area. The ball eventually fell to Bobby Thomson who remembers scoring the winner with a "little tap in!"

After the game Joe followed up his interest in Ernie Hunt and Mike Summerbee by inviting them along to Villa to play in a practice game which Harry Burrows remembered well. "They both looked like useful players." Harry thought they would be joining him at Villa but "Nothing came of it. It may have been the way the club was at the time, they were not prepared to spend any money" lamented Harry.

Joe Mercer fails his quest to sign Summerbee & Hunt

Summerbee

At the end of 1964 Joe Mercer left Aston Villa on ill health grounds but he was not out of the game very long before being snapped up by Manchester City. One of his first signings for his new club was none other than Mike Summerbee for a fee of around £35,000. In his first season with Joe, Summerbee started every game and it could be argued that Mike went on to be one of the most influential players in that marvellous City side that won four trophies in three seasons between 1968 and 1970.

Swindon Town were relegated at the end of the 1964-65 campaign and Ernie Hunt left them to join Wolverhampton Wanderers in the September of the new season. The fee of £40,000 was at the time the most that Swindon had ever received for one of their players. Whilst with Wolves, Ernie was their leading scorer poaching twenty goals as they secured promotion to back to the First Division in 1967, ironically replacing Villa who went in the other direction.

1962 ITALY

May 18th FC Internazionale Milano 2 Aston Villa 4

Back in the summer of 1961, having returned from their successful tour of the Soviet Union, Aston Villa were contemplating life without their England international striker Gerry Hitchens. Gerry, a veritable goal machine, had signed for FC Internazionale Milano (Inter-Milan) in June for £85,000 which was a huge amount of money at that time and would probably be worth around £1.5 million at the time of writing. An additional element of the deal was an agreement that the two clubs would play each other in a friendly game, at the San Siro stadium in Milan, at the beginning of the 1961-62 season. Unfortunately this was not possible because it clashed with Villa's rearranged, two legged League Cup final, against Rotherham. Inter and Villa tried in vain to find a suitable date for the match but prior commitments continually got in the way. It was eventually agreed that the game would go ahead at the end of the 1961-62 season on 18th May in Milan.

Aston Villa's first ever game in Italy

So on Tuesday 15th May the party which included Sims, Sidebottom, Lee, Aitken, Tindall, MacEwan, Sleeuwenhoek, Deakin, Fencott, Ewing, Wylie, Baker, Dougan, Thomson, Neal, Burrows along with manager Joe Mercer and trainer Fred Archer, left Snow Hill station on the first leg of their journey. On arrival in London the Villa party made their way to the nearby Great Western Royal Hotel for an evening meal and an overnight stay in the capital. Everyone that was except Ron Wylie who, due to his fear of flying mentioned elsewhere in this book, took the boat train to Milan. The next morning the players and officials were up bright and early in order to make their way to Heathrow in good time to catch the 9.35.a.m flight to Milan's Linate Airport. The Villa group had a trouble free flight arriving in Milan on time and were taken by coach to the Hotel San Carlo which was and indeed still is, located in front of Milan Central Railway Station.

The next day the team utilised the local sports facilities to work out and this culminated in some five aside games. Bobby Thomson was playing with Joe Mercer's team which also included Ray Shaw. Bobby always enjoyed this because as he put it "I was expected to run-around like a lunatic as Joe and Ray didn't want to do any of the hard work!" One of these five-a-side matches, which was being played in the right spirit, was amazingly thrown into disarray following a moment of madness by Derek Dougan. According to Bobby Thomson, Derek kicked him completely out of the blue with real venom in the backside. Bobby described the scene, "...I turned round and saw it was Dougan and said to him, 'What's your game?' With that he punched me really hard on the nose making it bleed!" Thomson, living up to his tag as the fiery Scot, retaliated and grabbed the Doog by the neck and then, in Bobby's own words, "tried to bite his ears off!" By this time they were rolling around on the ground and the players had to pull them apart. Bobby's explanation for the Doog's behaviour was, "I can't really remember but I expect it was something to do with some bird!" That evening all was forgotten when the two of them went out drinking together and Derek apologised.

On Friday 18th May, the day of the game against Internazionale, the players were taken by coach to the San Siro stadium and were amazed at the size of the ground. Harry Burrows remembered that his first impression was one of shock at spotting a high concrete wall all the way around the pitch. He recalls saying to his colleagues at the time that, "If this ever came to England it would be ridiculous." Little did he realise that within 20 years fences would become common place in England and were not removed until after the Hillsborough tragedy in 1989. Bobby Thomson on the other hand remembered the luxurious changing rooms which were palatial when compared with those they experienced every Saturday afternoon in England.

May 18th   FC Internazionale Milano 2   Aston Villa 4

The Villa players were very excited at the prospect in playing in the famous stadium and those left out of the starting line-up of this historic match were clearly disappointed. The eventual team that took the field in Villa's first ever game in Italy comprised of:- Nigel Sims; Gordon Lee, Charlie Aitken; Mike Tindall, John Sleeuwenhoek, Alan Deakin; Tommy Ewing, Alan Baker, Derek Dougan, Bobby Thomson, Harry Burrows. Substitutes:- Jimmy MacEwan, Ken Fencott, Ron Wylie & Johnny Neal. Although the match was only a friendly and irrespective of the result the Villa party were scheduled to move on the next day for a three night break in Alassio on the Italian Riviera,; Joe Mercer had one more trick up his sleeve. Bobby Thomson remembers Joe ending his team talk by telling us, "Win this one boys and you won't have to buy any drinks in Alassio."

Internazionale took the opportunity to play a number of their new signings in the game including the Argentinean International forward Ribera. Unfortunately for the Villa lads they were not able to meet up with their old mate Gerry Hitchens who was unable to play because he was on duty with the England team that were playing a World Cup warm up game in Peru.

Aston Villa, perhaps spurred on by Joe's team talk, took a grip on the game from the outset and dictated the play throughout the first half. This pressure paid off as early as the 20th minute when left winger Harry Burrows hit one of his typical blistering shots that thundered into the back of the net leaving Bugatti the Inter goalkeeper helpless. It took the stunned Italians just four minutes to get back on even terms following a neat passage of play in which new boy Ribera capitalised on some poor Villa defending and guided a speculative effort into the net via the post. Ribera's goal turned out to be only a minor setback for Joe's boys who came storming back into the game, hitting a brace of goals in the last five minutes of the half. The first came from Derek Dougan after 40 minutes when he glanced a Tommy Ewing cross firmly into the net and the second, just two minutes later, was a close range effort from the diminutive Alan Baker. It must have been a very elated Villa team that went in at half time with an unexpected 3-1 lead.

The half time interval saw both teams make a number of changes to their line ups. Villa replaced Mike Tindall, Alan Deakin, Bobby Thomson and Derek Dougan with Jimmy MacEwan and Ken Fencott who took over as wing halves, whilst left back John Neal and Ron Wylie moved into the forward line. The key changes for Inter were the introduction of Masiera and Corso. The latter, nicknamed "Mariolino", was at that time a famous but somewhat inconsistent left winger. Bobby Thomson's view was more positive commenting "What a player he (Corso) was. No shin pads and his socks rolled down – he was some player" and it was his introduction into the fray that changed the game.

With the second half in its infancy the visitors soon realised that Internazionale meant business and subsequently became a much tougher proposition. Villa's defence doggedly held out until the 82nd minute when the constant Inter pressure eventually paid dividends for the Italians. Maseira collected the ball just inside the Villa half and after taking a few steps let fly with an effort that flew into the net off the woodwork leaving Nigel Sims stranded. Maseira's celebration was something clearly remembered by a number of Villa players but not reported at the time. Evidently he ran to where the Italian FA Selectors were seated, stood in front of them and made an offensive gesture in their direction. Apparently the reason for this somewhat controversial action was as a result of him not being selected for the Italian World Cup squad. Alan Deakin said, "We'd never seen anything like it. We just stood there and watched in amazement"

Maseira's goal led to a hectic final ten minutes with the Aston Villa players very much on the back foot as Inter pressed for an equaliser. The visitors hung on grimly but it looked to be only a matter of time before the hosts scored.

Then, with only a few minutes remaining, Villa broke away and 17 year old Alan Baker snatched his second goal of the game to give the visitors a famous, if some-what unexpected, 4-2 victory. At the final whistle the 10,000 Internaz-ionale supporters loudly barracked the Inter players and hurled cushions at them, saving their cheers for the Villa who they app-lauded all the way to the tunnel.

The celebrations by the Aston Villa party went on long into the night and a very weary group of players boarded the 9.20 a.m. train the next day at Milan Railway Station bound for the Italian Riviera resort of Alassio. On arrival they were driven to Hotel Rio where they stayed for a few days and enjoyed the relaxed atmos-phere which was in part created by the free drinks, courtesy of the club. The wea-ther was ext-remely hot; there were excellent sandy beaches and a beautiful blue sea. Bobby Thompson added,"...and some beautiful birds!"

The only players to miss out on the fun were Jimmy MacEwan and his room-mate Gordon Lee.

Apparently they overdid the sunbathing on the first day and spent the rest of their "holiday" in their room with sun-stroke. The players got up to all sorts of pranks whilst in the town and one member of the Villa contingent remem-bered that some of the players dec-ided to try out a Thai massage par-lour which had attracted their attention during the early part of their stay. The players who must remain anonymous egged each other on and entered the establishment looking forward to the supposed de-lights awaiting them inside. Imagine their surprise when they realised that their masseurs were very attractive but somewhat effeminate young men from Thailand. Apparently the testosterone fuelled players departed the establishment with some haste and took refuge in a nearby bar for a much needed drink!

The following day the Aston Villa contingent began their journey home. First up was a train ride to Milan and from there by coach to the airport. Here they caught the early afternoon flight to Heathrow and then back home by coach to the midlands.

Jimmy MacEwen, as captured by 'lon' during the tour.

1966 GERMANY & HOLLAND

Aston Villa's assistant manager Dick Taylor took over the managerial reigns on a temporary basis during the 1963-64 season following Joe Mercer's resignation due to ill-health. He succeeded in steering Villa clear of relegation and this resulted in him being handed the job on a full-time basis. Regrettably his appointment was not a success and the following two seasons saw little improvement in form as Villa struggled in the basement of the First Division.

In preparation for the 1966-67 season the Villa management arranged a week-long tour taking in games in both Holland and Germany. The Villa party flew out to West Germany on 29th July, just one day before the memorable 1966 World Cup Final and stayed in Westphalia. Once the players had settled into their accommodation it dawned on them that they were the only English people staying in the complex.

England win the World Cup but Willie Hamilton eats flowers!

However it didn't particularly bother them as they enjoyed a few after dinner drinks in the hotel bar before retiring to bed.

The next day was the World Cup Final and Lew Chatterley remembers the moment the penny dropped about them being the only English people in the hotel, "We were watching the game in the hotel's dining room surrounded by other guests who of course were rooting for the Germans. We were shouting and cheering throughout the match and when it was all over we realised that we were the only people in the hotel going berserk!"

The other guests had retired to their rooms, probably to make themselves scarce, leaving the Villa players to have a fabulous evening celebrating England's world cup victory over the old enemy.

July 31st   Schalke 04   2   Aston Villa   3

The next day a somewhat fragile group of players made the short coach journey to the Gluckhauf-Kampfbahn stadium in Gels-enkirchen. This ground was the home of Schalke 04 before they moved to their modern stadium in 1973. Lew remembers the game well because of the very noisy home crowd "baying for our blood" and seeking revenge for their country's defeat at the hands of the English the previous afternoon. Villa's manager Dick Taylor picked an experienced team for the game comprising of: - Colin Withers; Michael Wright, Charlie Aitken; Dave Poutney, John Sleeuwenhoek, Alan Deakin; Johnny Macleod, Willie Hamilton, Tony Hateley, Lew Chatterley, Tony Scott.

Aston Villa began the game positively mounting a number of attacks on the Schalke goal. Their best opportunity fell to the diminutive Johnny McLeod who struck a tremendous left footed shot which the German goalkeeper just managed to turn over the bar.

That opening fifteen minute spell was it as far Villa were concerned in the first half. From then on the home side, having taken the best that Villa could throw at them, took total command of the game and camped in the visitors half of the field. Villa were completely under the cosh and had a number of lucky escapes and one particular incident involved centre-half John "Slogger" Sleeuwenhoek to his mates. According to reports goalkeeper Colin Withers completely misjudged the bounce of the ball which looped over his head and was heading for the open goal when "Slogger" appeared from nowhere and blocked the goal-bound effort on the line.

Wave after wave of pressure ensued from the Shalke forwards and it was on the cards when, much to the delight of the home supporters, the Germans took the lead. The Schalke left winger cut inside, made his way into the area unhindered and hit a hard shot which Withers failed to take cleanly and watched in horror as the ball rolled gently into the empty net.

The Germans continued to dominate proceedings and a few minutes before the half time interval Schalke doubled their lead this time following some clever work by the diminutive Neuser. Collecting the ball just inside the visitors half he set off on a mazy run and then played a one two with a colleague before lashing an unstoppable shot into the bottom corner of the net. Lew Chatterley remembered that "we were relieved to hear the referee blow his whistle for half time."

Manager Dick Taylor was not best pleased with his charges and read the riot act to them during the interval. He was particularly critical of the contribution made by Scots Johnny MacLeod and Willie Hamilton and replaced both them with Bobby Park and Dave Roberts. The changes, coupled with the tongue lashing, clearly had the desired effect as a newly motivated Villa team tore into their opponents from the moment the second half began.

The newly vitalised Villa team had halved the deficit within five minutes. The ex West Ham United winger Tony Scott raced down the left touchline, sent in a fabulous cross that found the head of an unmarked Lew Chatterley, who directed the header firmly past Eiting in the Schalke goal. The goal visibly settled the visitors down and their newly found confidence soon lead to an equaliser.

This time it was Charlie Aitken's turn to break down the left wing and slide over a low centre which an unmarked Tony Hateley side footed home. With ten minutes remaining, following a concerted period of non-stop pressure, Villa scored what turned out to be the winning goal. Bobby Park and Dave Poutney combined to create yet another chance for man of the match Lew Chatterley who guided his effort into the bottom left-hand corner of the net to win the game and quieten the German crowd.

That evening the lads were in high spirits and had a few swift drinks to celebrate their victory before dinner. Willie Hamilton however was a little more "refreshed" than the others and was last to sit down for the evening meal. Even so the newly signed Scottish inside forward became increasingly frustrated at the time dinner was taking to be served. Charlie Aitken takes up the story, "There was big vase of flowers on our table and Willie said, 'Bloody hell I'm starving! Where's the food? I'm bloody hungry!' So I said to him, 'Well there's a lot of vitamins in those flowers.' Willie replied, 'I'll tell you what I'll eat them all for £20!' So we all threw a pound each into the kitty and he scoffed the lot stalks and everything!"

Willie Hamilton

August 3rd
Ajax 2   Aston Villa 0

Next on the tour itinerary was a game against AFC Ajax in Amsterdam so the party embarked on the 220 mile round trip to face the Dutch champions in the De Meer Stadion. Manager Dick Taylor selected the team that finished the game against Schalke in such a positive style and he wasn't disappointed by the start they made.

On the half hour Tony Hateley was convinced that he had put the Villa ahead with a well taken goal from a very difficult angle only to see the ball clawed back from behind the line by the Ajax keeper Bals. Unfortunately the only person in the ground who didn't see the ball cross the line was the referee who ignored the Villa players' protests and waved play on. There were two further incidents in the half when first of all Lew Chatterley and then David Roberts appeared to be obstructed when they were clean through the Ajax defence and about to shoot with only the goalkeeper to beat. These decisions visibly affected the visitors and Dick Taylor was relieved to get them in at half time without any further incidents. During the break the manager replaced Dave Roberts and Bobby Park with Johnny MacLeod and Willie Hamilton respectively. The Villa team clearly benefited from the introduction of the two Scots who added some much needed experience in the second half.

Within the first couple of minutes of the game restarting the Villa almost conceded a goal when Kelzer's rising shot seemed goal bound until the erratic Colin Withers pulled off a breath-taking save diving full length to his left and tipping the ball around the post for a corner. Ajax were definitely having the better of the exchanges in the early stages of the second period and in the 54th minute a teenager called Johan Cruyff found himself in space with just the Villa goalkeeper between him and the goal. The young maestro hit a firm shot from point blank range only to see Colin Withers pull off yet another astonishing save! Villa seemed to gain confidence from their goalkeeper's exploits and at last began to make inroads into the Dutchmen's defence.

Unfortunately following one of these raids Tony Hateley received his marching orders for tripping the Ajax left winger Piet Keizer. Hateley told the Birmingham press after the game, "I think it was a very harsh decision." Down to ten men and with over 35minutes still to play the visitors dug in and looked odds-on to hang on for a draw. That was until, with five minutes remaining, Ton Pronk headed a tremendous cross from the right wide of Colin Withers to take the lead. Villa threw everything at their opponents but unfortunately, as often happens on these occasions, they were caught on the break and Ajax sealed their victory when Henk Groot scored their second, with almost the last kick of the game, and Villa returned to West Westphalia with nothing to show from the game.

The next day the Villa contingent checked out of their hotel and boarded their coach for the long journey to Nuremberg. On arrival they settled into their rooms which Charlie Aitken remembered as being the first time he had ever seen a duvet, "I wasn't sure what to do with it!" commented Charlie. When dinner arrived Charlie was surprised at the enormous amount of food that the waiters brought to the table, "It was like a pyramid! It was full of calories and we just couldn't eat it" Charlie continued, "The body language of the other guests in the restaurant was saying, 'My god are they leaving all that food!"

After dinner some of the players went out to sample the Nuremberg night life and when they reached the city centre they discovered that there was a festival taking place. The three Scots; John Macleod, Willie Hamilton and Charlie Aitken decided to visit the fairground which was part of the festivities. Charlie remembers this clearly, "At the fair there was a stall where you shot pellets from a gun at ducks to win prizes. Amongst the prizes were a number of china monkeys which Willie thought were laughing at him!" Next, according to Charlie, Hamilton used up all of his pellets by shooting at and smashing the china monkeys to smithereens. "The chap that was running the stall went crazy. We literally ran for it with him fast on our tail." concluded Charlie.

August 6th

1FC Nurnberg 1   Aston Villa 2

The final game of the tour was against Nuremberg and a large crowd assembled in the hope of seeing their local heroes gain some revenge for their national team's recent defeat in the World Cup final at Wembley. Villa were unchanged from their previous game but played a more cautious style of football this time and limited the opposition to long range shooting. Following a typical attack the home side won a corner after Charlie Aitken had deflected the ball wide of the goal. The corner was delivered with German precision and Manfred Greif glanced the most delicate of headers into the roof of the net. 1FC Nurnburg retreated into their shell after the goal and were happy to reach half time ahead.

During the interval the Villa players felt the goal was against the run of play and emerged in the second half determined to finish the tour with a victory. With the Germans happy to defend, the Villa forwards laid siege on the Nurnberg goal and half way through the second period they were rewarded with two goals in quick succession. First Willie Hamilton cancelled out the Germans' lead with a professional finish from a Johnny Macleod centre and just two minutes later MacLeod was once again the provider. This time he collected the ball just inside the home team's half, scampered down the wing beating two players in the process and put in a an exceptional cross that Tony Hateley headed confidently into the Germans' goal.

Villa 2-1 up decided to shut up shop and defend their lead. Everything was going smoothly and the tourists were coasting until the 85th minute when one of the German forwards clashed with Colin Withers resulting in them both being sent to their respective dressing rooms. This inspired the home side, they took the bull by the horns and dominated proceedings but the Villa managed to hang on until the final whistle. This result meant that they ended their three match tour with a creditable two wins and just one defeat and were eagerly looking forward to the new season back home in Division One. Sadly things didn't pan out as they had hoped and the season ended with relegation to Division Two.

The Villa squad that travelled on the tour.

1968 BEDFORD

July 27th

Bedford Town 2   Aston Villa 0

Having failed in their quest to return to the top flight of English football at their first attempt Aston Villa manager Tommy Cummings was searching for new blood to help the Birmingham club make a concerted push for promotion. Having already signed the skilful Mike Ferguson from Blackburn Rovers for £55,000 he was struggling to find further suitable players within his limited budget, when out of the blue his next acquisition dropped in his lap.

Arriving in a blaze of publicity in July 1968 an Argentinian midfielder called Oscar Arce (real name Luis "Oscar" Fullone) arrived at Villa Park. According to the media at the time Oscar had been playing for South American giants Athletico Penerol and had bought himself out of his contract with the Uruguayan side two years earlier for around £5,000 because he was so keen to play football in the UK.

The excited British media were all over the story and amongst other things mentioned that Oscar had been out of football for two years running an Antiques shop in Glasgow with his British wife. The reason for the break from soccer the press announced was to enable him to complete his two years' residency in the UK which would allow him to play professional football in Britain.

The Birmingham Post informed eager Villa fans that his past clubs in addition to CA Penarol, included CA Boca Juniors and the French club FC Rouen. However despite significant research it has not been possible to find any evidence to support Oscar's claims that he played professional football anywhere in the world before moving to Scotland in 1966. Interestingly he did allege in 1968 that he had been approached by two Scottish clubs but turned them down because Argentinian international Antonio Rattin, who many people remember for his cynical tackles in the 1966 World Cup, recommended Aston Villa as being the team he should join.

The infamous Oscar Arce makes his one and only appearance for the Villa!

One interesting anecdote revealed by the Evening Mail at the time was that Oscar had actually played a game for Albion Rovers the previous year, under his real name of Louis Fullone. This game would have been well before he was eligible to play professional football in the UK however he assured the Albion Rovers' directors at the time that he had been playing regularly for Rouen in France – one could only speculate what difference this would have made. When questioned about his time in France by the Birmingham Mail Oscar replied that he had been "associated with Rouen" whatever that meant and went on to tell the reporter that whilst with Albion Rovers he had played in just two practice matches and had only joined them to get fit. Albion Rovers secretary at the time Richard Sands said of Oscar, "He just did not fit in with our style of play although as a ball player he was a delight to watch" In summary then Oscar who was not good enough for Albion Rovers, who at that time were a mid-table Scottish Second Division team, was about to sign full professional terms for Aston Villa.

So how on earth did Aston Villa come to offer Louis Fullone or "Oscar Arce" a contract in the first place? Evidently legend has it that his trial with Villa did not involve him playing in any practice matches or behind closed door friendlies at all. The story goes that Tommy Cummings discussed Oscar's footballing experience with him and then watched him practise his ball skills. The latter consisted of him flicking the ball onto his knee and then walking around the Villa Park pitch whilst juggling the ball from one foot to the other without letting it hit the ground.

This was followed by him lying flat on his back, propped up on his elbows, and "spinning the ball from foot to foot, onto his head and then back onto his knees."

That was enough for Tommy Cummings - the deal was on! It is hard to understand in hindsight why the Villa management at that time was so naive as to believe all the rhetoric without properly checking Oscar's credentials.

Perhaps the alarm bells should have rang when it was reported in a Villa magazine at the time that Oscar was "...hesitant to talk football..." and he was "...being excused from training with a cold..." or on another occasion that he joined Aston Villa because Tommy Cummings had apparently told him that he could take all the free kicks explaining that he also specialised in taking penalties and had only missed one spot kick in eight years of first class football. One wonders in hindsight how many he had actually taken - if any at all.

So let's get back to the friendly with Bedford Town and Louis "Oscar" Fullone's only appearance for Aston Villa. The Southern League opposition were highly regarded in non-league circles consequently they were distinctly up for the game and hoping to give their illustrious opponents a bloody nose. The programme for the game clearly lists Aston Villa's number ten as Arce however there were a number of team changes and Oscar along with his so called brother Hector were named as substitutes. The starting line-up was:- Withers; Edwards, Wright; Deakin, Chatterley, Chambers; Ferguson, Mitchinson, Greenhalgh, Rudge, Anderson. Brian Godfrey and Charlie Aitken were both injured.

Villa began the game with a new formation abandoning their out dated 2-3-5 model and switching to a more modern 4-3-3. Bedford opened in style and whilst the Villa were still struggling to come to terms with their new formation, their hosts gave them a lesson in direct football. Bedford always looked dangerous when they approached the Villa goal and on 34 minutes disaster struck for the boys in claret and blue.

In the words of the local Bedford paper at the time, "...Burridge swung a glorious cross-field pass into the path of (Laurie) Churchill...." who whipped an excellent ball into the penalty area. Colin Withers, the Villa goalkeeper came out to deal with it but unfortunately Lew Chatterley obstructed him, the ball rebounded off the centre back and into the open net giving Bedford Town a 1-0 advantage.

Villa were still struggling when just before half time, the moment the sparse travelling Villa support had been waiting for, at last arrived. Manager Tommy Cummings withdrew Mickey Wright and according to a local Bedford newspaper report, brought on, "Oscar Arce – the former Argentinian international" for his Villa debut. He was unable to make an immediate impact on the game as he was barely on the pitch for more than couple of minutes before the referee blew the half-time whistle.

If Oscar was unable to make his presence felt in the first half, this would change spectacularly in the second. During the next forty five minutes he made a lunging two footed, studs-up tackle on Peter Harris the Bedford substitute for which he was lucky not to be sent off. The resulting penalty was converted by Bedford Town's right winger Laurie Churchill and doubled their lead.

Within the next twenty minutes Oscar clashed with two other Bedford players on separate occasions. Then with minutes to go he brought more derisive cheers from the locals when he was involved in yet another unsavoury incident. This time it was a crude challenge on Bedford's Peter Harris which resulted in the pair grappling with each other on the ground.

The incident was not seen by the referee so it was left to Aston Villa's trainer Arthur Cox to rush onto the field without permission and drag Oscar away from the Bedford player. Towards the end of the game Oscar's brother Hector (it is not known if this was his real name or indeed if they were really brothers), came onto the field replacing David Rudge.

According to the Birmingham Mail he, "showed some nice touches" and Alan Deakin recalls him being "a much better footballer than Oscar."

The Villa party looked very dejected as they boarded their coach back to Birmingham. The Post reported that "Oscar Arce was glum and silent". Manager Cummings commented to the press, "The trouble is that Oscar is trying too hard. He is trying to do too much too quickly. The pressures on him are pretty severe."

The local Birmingham paper summed up the whole Oscar Arce situation thus, "Here was a player from Penerol, the former World Champion club, struggling to reproduce his best against a Southern League team and he didn't like it! Time and time again he was dispossessed by Bedford's tackling as he tried to bring the ball out of defence..." The piece concluded that Oscar's brother Hector, the Argentinean amateur over in the UK on a visit, had an altogether happier introduction to English football.

It seems that neither of the Arce/Fullone brothers ever played football for Aston Villa again.

However Oscar kept popping up over the next 40 years. For example during the 1978-79 season he was a coach at Sheffield United and then in the 80's got involved in "easing the transfers" of Argentinian international players into England. There is no further record of him then until the late 1990's where he was reported as being the manager of the Swiss club FC Sion under his real name Luis Fullone. His next move was to Africa where he appeared to have managed no less than fifteen different clubs between 2000 and 2011. His most recent appointment was with KAC Kenitra in Morocco, where he has been employed as head coach (manager). Luis Fullone is described as "being originally from Argentina and a former player at Independiente and Estudiantes." Independiente? There's another one to add to the impressive list of clubs that Oscar claimed to play for prior to joining the Villa.

Oscar Arce displaying pennants from two of his previous clubs!!

1969 UNITED STATES

Date	Home	Score	Away	Score
May 3rd	Aston Villa	2	Kilmarnock	1
May 9th	Aston Villa	2	Dundee United	2
May 10th	Dundee United	0	Aston Villa	2
May 14th	Aston Villa	1	Wolverhampton Wanderers	2
May 17th	Aston Villa	2	Tottenham Hotspur	2
May 19th	Aston Villa	2	West Ham United	2
May 24th	Wolverhampton Wanderers	5	Aston Villa	0
May 25th	Kilmarnock	2	Aston Villa	1
May 27th	West Ham United	2	Aston Villa	0
May 30th	Atlanta Chiefs	0	Aston Villa	2

Having appeared likely candidates for relegation to Division 3 earlier in the campaign, Aston Villa finished the 1968-69 season in a strong position. Back in the November however things were looking very gloomy indeed and half way through the month, following a run of one win in 13 games, the board responded to supporters' unrest by dismissing Tommy Cummings along with his deputy Malcolm Musgrove. Arthur Cox, Villa's trainer at the time, took over as caretaker boss however results did not improve and neither did the mood of the supporters.

In response to the directors' lack of investment in the club coupled with the blame of their predicament being heaped on the shoulders of Tommy Cummings, a well organised concerted campaign amongst the Villa supporters gathered momentum. This involved protest meetings and the boycotting of games, aimed solely at ridding the club of its "out of touch" directors.

Things came to head following a home game against Charlton Athletic when less than 13,000 people tuned up on 7th December. The gates had been steadily falling throughout the season but fans had actually been urged to stay away from the Charlton match in one final attempt to force the resignation of the Board. Shortly after the game, the directors announced that the club was in serious financial difficulties and explained that they were seeking new board members who were willing to inject some much needed finance into the ailing club. The Villa pressure group were having none of it.

Aston Villa's first time across the pond.

They wanted to sweep away the directors and replace them with a completely new regime. Under the weight of some intensive pressure from the Villa supporters the board of directors, admitting they were over half a million pounds in debt, agreed to sell the club. The first offer to take them over came from the USA in the form of the Atlanta Chiefs' owners but the Football League blocked their move and the Americans' attempts to purchase the club were quashed. This left the door open for wealthy financier and Chelsea supporter Pat Matthews to come to the rescue. He raised the necessary capital from a public share issue and appointed ex Birmingham City director Doug Ellis as chairman of the new board. The first job for the new regime was to find a manager and the fans were not disappointed with their choice when the charismatic Tommy Docherty was unveiled as the new man in the Villa hot seat. Once he was in post the clubs fortunes improved dramatically resulting in increased attendances, a good run in the FA Cup and a creditable lower mid-table finish to the season.

Around this time across the Atlantic in the USA things were getting tough for the executive director of the North American Soccer League; former Aston Villa play-maker Phil Woosnam. Unfortunately for Phil, the "new game" had not taken off in America as well as he had hoped and as a result attendances had fallen away alarmingly. He was now desperately trying to keep the NASL alive because it was obvious to everyone concerned with the game across the pond that soccer in the USA needed a shot in the arm.

Phil Woosnam's solution was to divide the football season into two halves. The first would consist of each of the five remaining NASL clubs being represented by a British football club. His hope was that the high quality football played by these teams would increase gate receipts and in his words "give fans a taste of soccer at its best." He truly believed that this would increase interest in association football amongst a largely indifferent American public and attract more spectators in the second half of the season, when the USA teams replaced those from the UK.

Aston Villa were one of the clubs selected to take part in this exciting adventure and based in Georgia they represented the local team Atlanta Chiefs in the round robin league. In addition to playing in the revamped American National Soccer League, the British clubs would be expected to take part in exhibition matches. Aston Villa's extra games were scheduled to be against Tottenham Hotspur and their hosts Atlanta Chiefs.

The Aston Villa squad who travelled to the USA for this exciting competition included John Dunn, Mick Wright, Charlie Aitken, Barrie Hole, Fred Turnbull, Dick Edwards, Brian Tiler, Alan Rudge, Peter Broadbent, Willie Anderson, Brian Godfrey, Lionel Martin, Alan Deakin, Barry Lynch and, Dave Simmons. Unfortunately Alan Deakin sustained a knee injury just prior to the party leaving, "I had my knee checked by the medical people and they told me it was my cartilage" so a bitterly disappointed Alan handed his suit over to Lew Chatterley who went in his place. Lew commented, "I wasn't a favourite of Tommy Docherty's and so wasn't expecting to go to America. I remember him casually coming over to me at the end of training and telling me to go and pack my bag as Alan was injured and I would be taking his place." Lew jumped at the chance to take part in the tour saying, "We were off to play football in America which was unheard of in those days."

May 3rd   Aston Villa 2   Kilmarnock 1

Aston Villa's first match on American soil was a "home" league game in Atlanta against Scottish First Division side Kilmarnock who were representing St. Louis. Charlie Aitken remembered the stadium clearly, "At one end of the ground there was a huge dais. On top of it was a massive wigwam and a Cherokee Indian who, when we scored, puffed clouds of smoke out of the top of the giant tepee." The reason for this link to Native Americans was most likely because Atlanta is in Georgia where over a quarter of a million residents are members of the Cherokee nation.

The Villa's team for this first game was: - Dunne, Wright, Aitken; Hole, Edwards, Lynch; Ferguson, Martin, Simmons, Tiler, and Anderson. Substitutes:- Rudge and Turnbull. Aston Villa began the game well and were cheered on by, what the Birmingham Post called, "a vociferously partisan" local crowd of around 8,000. They were clearly the better team in the first half which saw Lionel Martin and Brian Tiler squandering good opportunities to put Villa in front.

It was therefore against the run of play, when on the half hour Kilmarnock took the lead when, Jim McLean's powerful twenty five yarder found its way into the bottom corner of the Villa net. Following their goal Kilmarnock went into their shells, defended their lead and this strategy continued long into the second half.

The Villa boys continued to push forward in search of an equaliser and when it eventually came there was a huge slice of luck attached to it. Evidently Mike Ferguson sent in a high looping cross which went straight into the hands of Kilmarnock goalkeeper McLaughlin who, unfortunately for the Scots, fumbled the ball and an eager Barry Lynch rushed in to head the bouncing ball home. Less than two minutes later Villa were ahead when the burly ex Arsenal striker Dave Simmons scored the match winner. The goal came when Dave latched onto a through ball from midfield and hit his shot from point-blank range giving McLaughlin no chance.

May 8th
Aston Villa 2   Dundee United 2

Villa's next two games were both against Dundee United who were representing Dallas Tornado. The first was a "home" game in Atlanta which was played twenty four hours after the scheduled kick off time due to torrential rain. Although the next day was sunny and the pitch was in lovely condition the kick-off for the rearranged game had to be delayed for a further ninety minutes. The reason for the delay is probably unique in the history of Aston Villa. Evidently the local Boy Scouts Troupe had booked the ground, many months earlier, to rehearse their marching skills on the pitch in preparation for a forthcoming jamboree!

Once the youngsters had finished their rehearsal and left the ground the players made their way onto the field in front of a meagre crowd numbering barely 2,500. Tommy Docherty fielded the following team to represent the Villa:- Dunn; Wright, Aitken; Tiler, Edwards, Chatterley; Rudge, Martin, Simmonds, Ferguson, Anderson. Substitutes:- Turnbull and Godfrey.

Aston Villa kicked off and dominated play for the first twenty minutes or so. The pressure eventually paid off when eight minutes before half time Mike Ferguson broke out of defence and embarked on one of his mesmerising runs. After beating a number of players, some of them twice, he made it to the goal line and pulled back an inviting ball into the United box. Brian Tiler, who had galloped the length of the field, latched onto the ball and calmly slotted it home to put Aston Villa in front.

Eight minutes before the break the in-form Ferguson delighted the small crowd once again. This time he received the ball on the left wing, cut inside and then let rip with a drive that flew past the Scots' defenders in a flash and into the top corner of the net. The Villa pressure continued unabated unfortunately during this period Lionel Martin missed two golden chances to put the game well out of the reach of Dundee United. These misses spurred on the Scottish team and just before the break they clawed their way back into the match with a well taken goal by Cameron.

The second period saw Villa trying to play out the game and hang on to their one goal advantage. Unfortunately the few chances that the Villa managed to create were not capitalised on and in the 76th minute the Scots equalised once again when the prolific striker Kenny Cameron scored from close range. Manager Tommy Docherty immediately rang the changes bringing on Fred Turnbull and Brian Godfrey for Lew Chatterley and Dave Simmons and whilst this didn't bring any more goals it freshened up the Villa team and ensured they hung on for a well-earned draw.

May 10th
Dundee United 0   Aston Villa 2

The return match between the two clubs was played just a couple of days later in Dallas, Texas. Charlie Aitken clearly remembers being there because he visited the location of John F Kennedy's assassination commenting that it was a very sad experience. He chirped up however when he remembered the food, "They had the biggest steaks in Dallas you have ever seen in your life!"

Villa won the return encounter, in blistering heat, 2-0 with Brian Tiler heading both goals a result which left Villa top of the league. Their team for the game was: - Dunn, Wright, Aitken; Hole, Edwards, Tiler; Rudge, Martin, Godfrey, Broadbent, and Anderson. Substitute: - Chatterley.

According to various reports both teams seemed a little jaded having only played each other two days earlier. However Villa showed the greater aptitude for the task and almost went in front as early as the 11th minute when the United goalkeeper Don MacKay bravely dived at Brian Godfrey's feet to keep the ball out. Play was very even until the 20th minute when Brian Tiler broke the deadlock. The midfielder headed Aston Villa into the lead from close range following an expertly taken free kick by the diminutive Dave Rudge. Following the goal the Birmingham Post enthused that it, was "Villa all the way" up to the half time break.

The Birmingham team immediately took control of the game in the second half and sustained the pressure for long periods. Unfortunately often in games like this the team on the rack score against the run of play. This almost happened in the 80th minute when the Dundee United striker Ken Cameron, who had looked dangerous throughout the match, forced an excellent save from John Dunn. The Scot received the ball just inside the box and hit a low skidding shot so the Villa keeper had to dive full length to his left to tip the ball round the post.

The scare didn't deter the Villa and they were soon back on the attack. Their incessant pressure was finally rewarded in the 86th minute after Brian Godfrey had won a corner on the left. Willie Anderson's centre eluded United's keeper MacKay and there was none other than the reliable Brian Tiler, perfectly positioned, to head home his and Aston Villa's second goal to clinch the game.

May 14th
Aston Villa 1
Wolverhampton Wanderers 2

Back in Atlanta, Villa's next game was at "home" to an old enemy, Wolverhampton Wanderers who were representing Kansas City Spurs. Had the game been played between these two longstanding rivals back in the West Midlands it would have attracted a 40,000 plus gate however less than 2,000 turned up to watch the Wolves take the points with a 2-1 victory. The Villa put out an unchanged team for the game and therefore lined up thus:- Dunn; Wright, Aitken; Hole, Edwards, Tiler; Rudge, Martin, Godfrey, Broadbent, and Anderson. Substitutes:- Simmons and Fergusson.

The boys from the Black Country set out their stall early on in the game attacking their Birmingham opponents from the outset. The pressure soon paid dividends when Peter Knowles cleverly turned a cross from Wagstaffe into the net early in the first half. Aston Villa responded positively to the set back and soon pulled level however the goal owed a lot to a large slice of luck. Brian Tiler collected the ball in midfield and slotted an excellent pass through to centre forward Brian Godfrey.

The Welshman ran onto the ball, hit a speculative shot that was going well wide until it hit Wolves' full back Derek Parkin, eluded the Wolves keeper and nestled in the bottom corner of the net.

The two teams were level at half time but the second half belonged to the Wanderers. First Division Wolves took command from the restart and soon restored their lead through centre forward Derek Dougan. It was that man Wagstaffe again who supplied the cross, Dougan rose above the Villa defenders and steered the ball home with a superb header. Wolves kept up the pressure throughout the second half and by all accounts were unlucky not to win the game by a much bigger margin.

Following the Wolves defeat manager Tommy Docherty gave the players a two day break before Tottenham Hotspur came to town to play them in an exhibition in the Atlanta Stadium.

May 17th
Aston Villa 2
Tottenham Hotspur 2

The two day respite was appreciated by the players before their next game and it clearly motivated the team as they looked to get a result against one of the best teams in the tournament. Over 3,500 people turned out for the game and those who didn't bother to go missed a great advertisement for soccer. The Villa team, for this show piece occasion only, included Atlanta Chiefs' promising young striker Kaizer Mortaung as a guest centre forward.

Mortaung was born in South Africa and had been playing professionally for his local team Orlando Pirates in Soweto. In 1968 Phil Woosnam, Atlanata Chiefs' manager, was seeking new players and as part of his search he held a number of trials in Africa. At one of these sessions a 16 year old Kaiser caught Phil's eye and signed him for the newly formed Atlanta Chiefs team. Interestingly in 1970 Mortuang returned to his Soweto routes and founded a new football team which he named the Kaiser Chiefs by combining his name with that of his former club in Atlanta.

To accommodate Kaiser the Villa made a couple of changes in their team and lined up thus:- Dunn, Wright, Aitken; Broadbent, Edwards, Turnbull, Rudge, Ferguson, Mortaung, Martin, and Anderson. Substitute: - Godfrey

Villa kicked off in a game that was reportedly played in the right spirit by both teams. Spurs had the better of the first half and should have taken the lead after just fifteen minutes when a goal-bound Terry Venables effort was tipped round the post by John Dunn in the Villa goal. The Londoners continued to press but it was the Midlanders who took the lead on the twenty minute mark. The move was started in midfield by the cultured Peter Broadbent who laid a perfectly weighted ball out Willie Anderson. The left winger cut inside, carried the ball forward and drilled a ferocious shot towards the Tottenham goal. Pat Jennings, the Spurs goalkeeper, seemed to have it covered but unfortunately for the Londoners the ball struck either Cyril Knowles or Ray Evans (depending on which report you read) and a wicked deflection took the ball well out of the reach of Jennings and into the net.

The second half saw Villa in the ascendancy, constantly probing the Spurs' defence and going close to doubling their lead on a number of occasions. When on fifty minutes their second goal arrived the game seemed all over bar the shouting. Willie Anderson collected the ball on the left and sent in an early cross which caused some confusion in the Spurs box. Eventually the ball fell to Lionel Martin who kept a cool head and calmly side footed the ball home.

Aston Villa held their two goal lead until the 80th minute when a well-known goal poacher named Jimmy Greaves, who had been having a quiet game, decided to take it on himself to get Spurs back into the game. The goal was typical of the Tottenham striker. He pounced onto a loose ball and blazed it home from six yards. The goal didn't upset the Villa team who continued to pass the ball around in an effort to run down the clock. Everything was going fine until that man Greaves again latched onto a misplaced pass.

In almost one move he collected the ball, carried it forward a couple of paces and then rifled it past Dunn for a share the spoils.

After the game both sets of players were entertained at a ranch by a local businessman who was associated with the Atlanta Chiefs club. Lew Chatterley recollects the event well and said that he was amazed by the things he saw there that we now take for granted, "Well, if a barbeque in the garden in Brum at that time was unusual then cold beer in dustbins full of ice was unheard of and as for riding horses on a ranch....."

May 19th
Aston Villa 2   West Ham United 2

The following Monday saw Villa playing another "home" game in Atlanta. This time it was the turn of West Ham United representing Baltimore Bays. The Villa lined up:- Dunne, Wright, Aitken; Hole, Turnbull, Tiler; Rudge, Martin, Simmons, Ferguson, and Anderson. Regrettably the home team were without their regular centre half Dick Edwards who had returned to England to receive specialist treatment on a knee ligament injury sustained in the Spurs game. Dick's centre back role went to the reliable Fred Turnbull.

The Villa made a disappointing start to this game and conceded a goal, scored by 1966 World Cup hero Geoff Hurst and assisted by Harry Rednapp, in the first five minutes. Villa responded well to this setback and got back on equal terms through Dave Simmons, who scored a simple tap-in after Hammers' goalkeeper Ferguson fumbled a shot from his namesake Mike. The game was very exciting and lurched from end to end and more goals looked inevitable. The crowd were not disappointed when ten minutes after Simmons' equaliser, West Ham regained their lead. The goal once again was brought about by a goalkeeping error. This time it was Villa keeper John Dunne who failed to gather a back pass and left United's Trevor Hartley with the simple job of knocking the ball into an open goal.

Villa went into the dressing room at half time a little unlucky to be behind, nevertheless after 18 minutes of the second half they were level. Willie Anderson, Villa's mercurial left winger sent in an in swinging corner which eluded everyone including the Hammers' keeper and flew directly into the net. Willie subsequently reminded his fellow players that he had made a little bit of history because this was apparently the first ever goal scored direct from a corner in Atlanta. The match continued to ebb and flow but there were no further goals and both teams seemed content to share the points in what was by all accounts a very entertaining encounter.

Following the 2-2 draw with the Hammers, Villa found themselves third in the league and now faced an eight hundred mile flight to Kansas City where top of the table Wolves were waiting for them. Tommy Docherty in his wisdom decided it would be beneficial to leave for Kansas early the next day so that the players would have a few days to acclimatise themselves with the local conditions. Charlie Aitken remembers this part of trip very well, "When we got there it was pouring with rain and it never stopped; it absolutely threw it down." It transpired that this was only a minor distraction given what was to follow.

The next difficulty facing the management team was that when it was agreed to travel to Kansas a few days earlier than expected no one had taken it upon themselves to arrange somewhere for the team to train. On arrival an irate Tommy Docherty spent literally hours on the telephone trying to rectify the situation. Sadly, despite his best efforts, he was unable to locate anywhere suitable. With this in mind he called a team meeting in the hotel. Charlie Aitken, captain for this leg of trip, takes up the story and recalls "The Doc" saying, "Right lads, I want you to think about this. I reckon we should fly back to Atlanta because we can't just hang around here waiting for the game with nowhere to train." Evidently, according to Charlie, Tommy wanted the players to discuss it between themselves and feedback their feelings to him. However, just before he left the room he dropped a bombshell as far as the players were concerned adding, "Of course there's just one more thing lads, you will have to pay for the flights yourselves!"

The players unanimously decided to refuse the proposal of a return to Atlanta if it meant shelling out their own money for the flight.

After all they felt they were on a tour organised by the club and they thought that if it was necessary for them to return to Atlanta, then the club should at least pay the air fares. According to Charlie Aitkin, Tommy was not happy with the players' response but had no choice other than to remain with the squad in Kansas, with nowhere to train.

Without a training schedule the party had a lot of time to kill prior to the Wolves game. Some players did their own thing in the city; Charlie recalls going to the cinema, others going shopping but the majority just hung around the hotel. One story that Charlie tells about this hiatus is regarding the Doc. It seems that some of the Villa lads spent a lot of time in their rooms playing cards or chatting. Charlie was quietly reading in his room when he received a phone call from Willie Anderson asking him to come to, what Charlie thought was, Willie's bedroom. When he got there Willie and his room-mate Lew Chatterley were playing pop music on a record player which they had acquired from somewhere.

There was general chit chat amongst the three of them and then eventually one of them asked Charlie what he thought of Tommy Docherty. Charlie told them that he thought Docherty was a "bloody waste of time." There were a few seconds silence and then The Doc leapt from a wardrobe, where he had been secretly hiding, uttered a number of expletives and pushed Charlie onto the bed. Charlie's quick thinking got him out of trouble; he told Tommy that he knew that he was in the wardrobe all the time and thought he would have a laugh at the Doc's expense. Tommy apparently accepted this story and it was only then that Charlie realised that he was actually in Docherty's room rather than as he thought, Willie and Lew's.

Shortly after this incident there were knocks on the door as more players gradually joined the throng. After some banter The Doc sent Willie Anderson to the bathroom to collect a few bottles of Champagne which Tommy had been leaving to chill in a bath full of cold water. Charlie being tee total didn't drink alcohol preferring a soft drink but remembered the session going on for quite some time a some of the players got very drunk.

May 24th
Wolverhampton Wanderers 5
Aston Villa 0

Match day eventually rolled round and hardly any of the players, according to Charlie Aitken, were properly prepared for the game. The Villa team for the game was:- Dunn; Wright, Aitken; Broadbent, Turnbull Tiler; Rudge, Martin, Godfrey, Ferguson, Anderson. Aston Villa kicked off and matched Wolves for the first twenty minutes although it has to be said that their left winger Dave Wagstaffe who once was a Villa target, had been causing numerous problems down the flanks. It was therefore only a matter of time before Waggy sent in a perfectly flighted corner and ex-Villan Derek Dougan took great pleasure in flicking the ball in from underneath the crossbar with his head. Just six minutes later Aston Villa were two down, the enigmatic Wagstaffe was again the provider but it was Hugh Curran's turn to head in powerfully from point blank range.

The Villa players trudged off at half time 2-0 down and feeling sorry for themselves however worse was to come. Wolves began the second half relatively slowly and Villa responded by showing some signs of a recovery but any hopes of a comeback all but disappeared when Wolves scored two goals in a five minute spell. First of all Hugh Curran grabbed his second and Wolves' third and before the Villa defence had sorted themselves out following this setback Ted Knowles rubbed salt into their wounds with an excellent volley.

Unfortunately for the Villa team the agony was not yet over. In the dying embers of the game the Molineux men completed the rout by adding a fifth goal through Leamington Spa born Dave Woodfield. The Villa team trailed off the field looking very dejected but were given no time to recover from the thrashing by their black country neighbours because they were straight onto a plane, bound for St. Louis 250 miles away, where they were due to meet Kilmarnock the very next day.

Manager Tommy Docherty interviewed shortly after the game revealed that, "The defeat by Wolves hurt. It was the heaviest we have suffered since I became manager. We missed two or three chances and defensively we were very poor. Usually this is our strongest point. Sadly we were also lacking in work rate."

May 25th
Kilmarnock 2   Aston Villa 1

For this match Lew Chatterley replaced Fred Turnbull which meant that the team chosen to play against Kilmarnock was: - Dunn; Wright, Aitken; Hole, Chatterley, Tiler; Rudge, Godfrey, Martin, Ferguson, and Anderson. Substitute:- Broadbent. According to reports a somewhat lacklustre Aston Villa team took the field against their Scottish opposition but nevertheless played some good football for the first fifteen minutes, in an ill-tempered match, before leaking two quick goals that settled the game.

It took the Scots just ten minutes to show their superiority and it was not unexpected when Kilmarnock's Jim McLean, who later in his career went on to manage Dundee United, connected with a pin-point cross just a couple of yards out. He headed the ball down and although goalkeeper John Dunn had it covered the ball squirmed between the keeper's legs and into the net. A second blow came just a few minutes later when Kilmarnock increased their lead this time through the outstanding Gerry Queen, who would later move to Crystal Palace. Queen latched onto a through ball from Frank Beattie and hit a speculative shot from the edge of the area which Dunn only managed to push into the top of his net. The game ebbed and flowed throughout the remainder of the first half but there were no further goals and Villa went in at half-time with a two goal deficit.

A much more determined Villa team emerged for the second half probably due to a roasting from the Doc. Their new found enthusiasm paid dividends when following a concerted period of pressure they managed to halve the deficit through a Brian Godfrey goal. Collecting the ball just outside the box he exchanged passes with Ferguson and then hit a terrific shot which beat the outstretched arms of Mclaughlin.

Just after the goal Docherty brought on substitute Peter Broadbent and within five minutes he had scored what looked like a perfectly good goal. Sadly the players' celebrations were cut short once they realised that the "goal" had been disallowed by the rookie linesman for offside. English referee Norman Burtenshaw immediately ran over to the linesman and a long discussion ensued but the goal was disallowed.

It later came to light that the protracted conversation between the referee and linesman had nothing to do with the disputed goal but concerned Burtenshaw's need to get the airport in time for his flight. With this in mind at the end of their chat he handed his whistle to the linesman and then dashed from the ground to try and catch his flight back to the UK. There were no further incidents or goals and referee Burtenshaw just about made his flight, thanks to some help from the local police. Apparently they handcuffed him to make it look like an emergency case, sped him to the airport and through the various checks directly onto his plane!

Tommy Docherty speaking at his post-match press conference commented that, "Ferguson was the man of the match. He has been our best player in every game. In fact I would nominate him as the best player in the tournament. Although technically he is still for sale if he can play like this next season then money would not be able to buy him. I would be delighted to have a change of heart if he can continue playing like that."

The next day was scheduled as a rest day to be spent in St Louis. The team were staying in a relatively luxurious hotel overlooking a beautiful wooded area of what seemed to be a very large park. From the hotel's upper floors it was just possible to make out in the distance, beyond the woods, what looked like some amusements. Michael Wright and Charlie Aitken were bored and so decided to take a stroll in the park and investigate what lay beyond the trees. After walking some distance through the wood they came to a clearing where they discovered a huge open air roller rink packed with skaters.

The two of them stood and watched for a while as they were transfixed by the amazing skills displayed by the roller-skaters. After a few minutes however it suddenly dawned on the pair that they were the only white people in the vicinity. Charlie went on, "...remember this was the time, I think, of the black power movement...." So after a very brief discussion the two of them decided to get out of the area as quickly as possible.

They ran as fast as they could back to their hotel. Charlie commented, "When we got back and told people where we had been and we were shocked to discover that there had been numerous murders and muggings in this park!"

May 27th

West Ham United 2

Aston Villa 0

The next morning saw the Villa party back in the sky bound for Baltimore, 840 miles away and a date with West Ham United who were second in the league. The Villa side for this came was comprised thus:- Dunn; Bradley, Wright; Tiler, Lynch, Hole; Anderson, Ferguson, Martin, Broadbent, Godfrey. Substitute: - Rudge.

Although they lost, it was reported that the Villa played well in this game. Whilst starting poorly and finding themselves two goals behind by half time courtesy of the excellent Martin Peters, in the second half they rallied and more than held their own against their illustrious opponents.

That defeat for Villa was the last game of the tournament and the result meant that West Ham would be runners up to the eventual champions Wolverhampton Wanderers. Aston Villa finished second from bottom, rather than third from the top, due to a curious system of awarding bonus points which Villa failed to capitalise on.

May 30th   Atlanta Chiefs   0   Aston Villa   2

The Aston Villa players had just one more game to play before they returned home to the UK. This was an exhibition match back in Georgia against their hosts the Atlanta Chiefs. The Aston Villa team for this final game read:- Dunn; Bradley, Wright; Hole, Tiler, Lynch; Ferguson, Godfrey, Martin, Broadbent, and Anderson. There were some familiar faces in the Atlanta Chiefs line up which not only included ex-Villa player and future manager Vic Crowe along with substitute Norman Ashe but also two Zambians named Emment Kapengwe and Freddie Mwila and the afore mentioned South African Kaiser Motaung. The two Zambians must have caught Docherty's eye during this game because he signed them both for the Villa later that year. Kapengwe is often erroneously reported as being the first black player to represent Aston Villa in a competitive match however that record is most likely held by Stan Horne who was of mixed race origin and made his debut in 1963.

There was a good crowd of almost 6,000 in the Atlanta Stadium to see the local team take on the Villa. From the outset the visitors clearly meant business and pulled out all the stops to illustrate their difference in class. Following a series of attacks without scoring the Atlanta team believed they had weathered the storm and came back into the game. Aston Villa had different ideas however and threw caution to the wind and deservedly went ahead in the 36th minute through a stinging Barry Hole shot. There were no further goals in the first half but Villa dictated play from the outset of the second half with Peter Broadbent pulling the strings in midfield. It was from one of his cool through balls, latched onto by Willie Anderson, which doubled Villa's lead in the 59th minute.

Anderson weaved his way past three players and crashed home a terrific shot which flew past the Chiefs' keeper in a flash.

There were no more goals, although Altlanta went close on a couple of occasions, and so Aston Villa ran out 2-0 winners. After the game the players attended an end of tour party which continued into the early hours of the following morning. One can imagine therefore that it was a blurry eyed contingent of Villa players who climbed aboard their airliner bound for Heathrow airport in London.

Brian Tiler summed up the whole experience on his return to Britain, telling journalists that a lot of the Villa party were, "very choked" when they boarded their plane in Atlanta. He went on to say that this wasn't because they weren't looking forward to getting back to England and being with their friends and families but that they had experienced such wonderful hospitality whilst in the States. He said that none of the party had fallen out and the whole trip was a great bonding exercise making everyone keen for the new season to begin and make of a concerted push for promotion back to the First Division.

AS far as the team's performances were concerned he felt that the star player of the trip was Mike Ferguson. Tiler continued, "He really played some great stuff and has settled into his midfield role well." The consensus of opinion was that although Aston Villa didn't win the mini-league; the tour was more than worthwhile for both the friendships that were forged and the team building that took place amongst the players.

FINAL N.A.S.L. STANDING

Team	W	L	T	F	A	Bonus Pts	Pts
Wolves	6	2	0	25	13	21	57
West Ham	5	2	1	23	13	19	52
Dundee United	2	4	2	13	22	13	31
Aston Villa	2	4	2	10	16	10	28
Kilmarnock	2	5	1	11	18	11	26

VILLA IN AMERICA:
Match-by-Match Analysis

ASTON VILLA 2, KILMARNOCK 1
At Atlanta Stadium. *Att.* 8,171
Scorers—Villa: LYNCH (60), SIMMONS (62). *Kilmarnock:* QUEEN (31)

Aston Villa	Kilmarnock
DUNN	MCLAUGHLIN
WRIGHT	KING
AITKEN	DICKSON
HOLE	WADDELL
EDWARDS	MCGRORY
LYNCH	BEATTIE
FERGUSON	MCLEAN (J.)
MARTIN	QUEEN
SIMMONS	MORRISON
TILER	EVANS
ANDERSON	MCILROY
Subs.: RUDGE, TURNBULL	*Sub.:* RODMAN

ASTON VILLA 2, DUNDEE UNITED 2
At Atlanta Stadium. *Att.:* 2,543
Scorers—Villa: TILER (18), FERGUSON (32). *Dundee Utd.:* K. CAMERON (40 and 66).

Aston Villa	Dundee Utd.
DUNN	MACKAY
WRIGHT	ROLLAND
AITKEN	CAMERON (J.)
TILER	GILLESPIE
EDWARDS	SMITH
CHATTERLEY	WOOD
RUDGE	HOGG
MARTIN	REID
SIMMONS	CAMERON (K.)
FERGUSON	GORDON
ANDERSON	WILSON
Subs.: TURNBULL, GODFREY	*Subs.:* SCOTT, MARLAND

DUNDEE UNITED 0, ASTON VILLA 2
At Dallas
Scorers—Villa: TILER (25 and 74)

Dundee Utd.	Aston Villa
MACKAY	DUNN
ROLLAND	WRIGHT
GILLESPIE	AITKEN
WOOD	HOLE
SMITH	EDWARDS
MARLAND	TILER
BRIGGS	RUDGE
GORDON	BROADBENT
CAMERON (K.)	ANDERSON
SCOTT	GODFREY
WILSON	MARTIN
Sub.: REID	*Sub.:* CHATTERLEY

EDWARDS

TURNBULL

WOLVES 5, ASTON VILLA 0
At Kansas City.
Scorers—Wolves: DOUGAN (23), CURRAN (28 and 67), KNOWLES (73), WOODFIELD (89).

Wolves	Aston Villa
PARKES	DUNN
WILSON	WRIGHT
PARKIN	AITKEN
BAILEY	BROADBENT
HOLSGROVE	TURNBULL
MCALLE	TILER
KNOWLES	RUDGE
MUNRO	MARTIN
DOUGAN	GODFREY
CURRAN	FERGUSON
WAGSTAFFE	ANDERSON
Subs: WALKER, WOODFIELD	

TILER

AITKEN

ASTON VILLA 1, WOLVES 2
At Atlanta Stadium. *Att.:* 1,869
Scorers—Villa: PARKIN (own goal, 59). *Wolves:* KNOWLES (20). DOUGAN (64).

Aston Villa	Wolves
DUNN	PARKES
WRIGHT	WILSON
AITKEN	PARKIN
HOLE	BAILEY
EDWARDS	HOLSGROVE
TILER	MCALLE
RUDGE	KNOWLES
MARTIN	MUNRO
GODFREY	DOUGAN
BROADBENT	CURRAN
ANDERSON	WAGSTAFFE
Subs.: SIMMONS, FERGUSON	*Subs.:* WALKER, WOODFIELD

ASTON VILLA 2, WEST HAM UNITED 2
At Atlanta Stadium. *Att.:* 3,520
Scorers—Villa: SIMMONS (21,) ANDERSON (64). *West Ham:* HURST (5), HARTLEY (33).

Aston Villa	West Ham
DUNN	FERGUSON
WRIGHT	BONDS
AITKEN	CHARLES
HOLE	PETERS
TURNBULL	STEPHENSON
TILER	MOORE
RUDGE	REDKNAPP
MARTIN	BOYCE
SIMMONS	BROOKING
FERGUSON	HURST
ANDERSON	HARTLEY
	Subs.: LINDSEY, BENNETT

KILMARNOCK 2, ASTON VILLA 1
At St. Louis.
Scorers—Villa: GODFREY (67). *Kilmarnock:* MCLEAN (J) (14), QUEEN (23).

Kilmarnock	Aston Villa
MCLAUGHLIN	DUNN
ARTHUR	WRIGHT
DICKSON	AITKEN
GILMOUR	HOLE
MCGRORY	CHATTERLEY
BEATTIE	TILER
MCLEAN (T)	RUDGE
QUEEN	GODFREY
MORRISON	MARTIN
MCLEAN (J)	FERGUSON
MCILROY	ANDERSON
Sub: RODMAN	*Sub:* BROADBENT

WEST HAM UNITED 2, ASTON VILLA 0
At Baltimore.
Scorers—West Ham: Peters (32 and 37).

West Ham	Aston Villa
FERGUSON	DUNN
BONDS	BRADLEY
CHARLES	WRIGHT
BOYCE	TILER
STEPHENSON	LYNCH
MOORE	HOLE
REDKNAPP	ANDERSON
PETERS	FERGUSON
BROOKING	MARTIN
HURST	BROADBENT
HOWE	GODFREY
	Sub: RUDGE

1969 LUTON

October 14th   Luton Town 0   Aston Villa 3

The 1969-70 season was both manager Tommy Docherty's and the Board of Directors' first full season together and they were looking forward to achieving their shared goal of promotion back to the big time. To improve their chances of returning to the top flight the Board had backed the manager in the transfer market by signing a number of new players including Pat McMahon, Chico Hamilton and the Rioch brothers Neil and Bruce. The latter pair were signed from Luton Town for a reported, combined record fee of around £110,000. The deal also included a clause that Aston Villa would play a friendly against Luton at Kenilworth Road later in the season.

The Rioch brothers return home

Villa's beginning to the new campaign had been less than spectacular. Following the heavy investment in both the infrastructure, as well as the playing side, everyone connected with the club had expected to be challenging for promotion. Instead they found themselves languishing at the foot of the old Second Division.

In contrast Luton Town, under the guidance of ex QPR manager Alex Stock, were technically just one position behind the Villa as they sat proudly on top of Division Three.

Going into the friendly Villa were in the midst of a goalkeeping crisis as the potential signing of John Phillips from Shrewsbury had temporarily fallen through.

(Left to right) Neil Rioch, Sir Doug Ellis, Bruce Rioch, Tommy Docherty.

This meant that Tommy Docherty's options were somewhat limited. He could either blood a fifteen year old rookie from the youth team named Gordon Knowles or call on seventeen year old Geoff Crudgington, a recent signing from Bilston who was yet to play for the club at any level. The Doc went for the latter and so Geoff much to his and the local press' surprise was selected to play his first game for the Villa. Both of the Rioch brothers were included in the starting line-up and Neil remembers the occasion fondly, "I was going back to my hometown club and playing against them. The Luton supporters were fine with both of us and I always had a good relationship with them."

As far as the actual game was concerned Aston Villa's problems were compounded after just twenty minutes when the experienced midfielder, Barrie Hole was injured and subsequently replaced by sixteen year old Jimmy Brown. The first half saw the Villa very much on the back foot however Luton's goal shy attack produced just one chance of note and that went to forward Matt Tees. The Scot found himself "one on one" with the rookie Villa 'keeper however Crudgington dived bravely at Tees' feet to send the teams in level at the break.

Neil takes up the story, "I remember in the first half we hadn't played too well and during half time Tommy Docherty gave us a roasting and told us that if we didn't improve we would return to Villa Park after the game. Once there he told us that he would have the floodlights switched on and make us train through the night on the Villa Park pitch.

We all knew he meant it – it was just the sort of thing the Doc would have done." Clearly Tommy's half-time roasting did the trick and motivated the Villa players who according to contemporary reports were much improved in the second period.

Although they gained control of midfield and were dictating play they did encounter a few scares from the eager Luton forwards, however new boy Geoff Crudginton turned up trumps and made a series of first class saves to keep Villa in the game.

With the match entering its final fifteen minutes a goalless draw looked on the cards, in spite of this Willie Anderson, not one to hide his light under a bushel, had other ideas. First of all he calmly slotted home a penalty. A few minutes later he broke down the left-wing, beat his full-back, sent in a cross that deceived everyone and sailed directly into the roof of the net. Then, with two minutes remaining, he capped off a scintillating individual display by firing in a dipping shot from over twenty yards that deceived Luton keeper Tony Read and nestled in the back of the net. Willie Anderson had completed his hat trick.

The next day the Birmingham Post enthused that, Villa were a class above Luton. Many people thought that this performance would be the spark to turn Villa's season around. How wrong they were! Just a few months later Aston Villa were relegated to the third tier of English football for the first time in their history.

1972 SANTOS

February 21st   Aston Villa 2   Santos 1

The 1970-71 season, having lost to Spurs in a hard fought League Cup Final and narrowly missed promotion, had been an "almost there" kind of experience for players and supporters alike. This meant Villa faced a second consecutive season toiling in the third tier of English football.

Villa began the 1971-72 campaign well enough and by February were comfortably placed in the league and looking forward to making a serious challenge for promotion. In addition the club's Commercial Manager Eric Woodward had arranged some exciting and very successful friendly games at Villa Park against the likes of West German giants Bayern Munich and the Polish side Gornick Zabrze. Next up on Woodward's agenda were Brazil's Santos featuring, probably the best player in the world at that time, one Edson Arantes do Nascimento or as he known in every football playing corner of the planet, Pelé.

That Woodward managed to attract such sought after opposition to Villa Park was a feat in itself but the fact that this game was played at all was a minor miracle. 1972 was the year of a national miners' strike which commenced on 9th January and lasted for seven weeks. By 5th February, factories were beginning to lay off workers because of power shortages and BBC local radio stations were warning of domestic power cuts.

This led to the Conservative government declaring a state of emergency and to save electricity, they introduced a three day working week. A direct result of this led to football matches kicking off early, including midweek games, in order to save energy. This left Villa, who according to press reports at the time had already agreed to pay Santos in the region of £13,000 for playing the game, in a very difficult situation.

Brazilian superstars display their talents at Villa Park.

They seemed to have three options. Firstly, they could bring the kick-off time forward to the Monday afternoon however this would considerably reduce the attendance. Another option was to call the game off which was seen as being completely out of the question. A third possibility was to procure a generator to run both the floodlights and the emergency lighting. This latter option would be, for obvious reasons, very difficult to pull off. After various meetings and off the record discussions it was agreed that the show must go on as originally planned and so chairman Doug Ellis embarked on the challenging mission of procuring a generator. After much searching all over Europe he eventually located one in Holland which the club bought for £5,000 however that was only part of the problem solved.

The next challenge was how to import the generator into the UK and then on to Birmingham without attracting the attention of pickets, who would have done their best to halt its progress. How this was achieved has never been properly explained but suffice to say that the said generator arrived in the Villa Park car park packed in a number of separate crates. The next task was to reassemble the machine and test it which fortunately, after a great deal of hard work, went according to plan and the game was on!

Meanwhile Pele and the Santos team had made their way to Paris and were due to fly into Birmingham the following day and then onto their hotel. So on a chilly Sunday afternoon the Brazilians were welcomed to Birmingham by an excited crowd at the Albany Hotel in the City Centre. During the subsequent press conference Pele made many friends by praising Aston Villa thus, "I know they are in the Third Division but in my country they are still great!"

Vic Crowe who was also interviewed at the event said of Pele, "I have played against him three times and this is the closest I have ever got to him"

Meanwhile Jimmy Brown, Aston Villa's exciting young midfield player, was trying desperately to get an early flight back from Iceland where he had been representing Scotland in a Youth World Cup Qualifier. The reason for his eagerness was because he wanted to be back in Birmingham in time for the Santos game. Jimmy takes up the story, "I rang Vic (Crowe) and asked him if I could play in the Santos game if I got back in time from Iceland. I told him that if I played I could mark Pele out of the game" According to Jimmy, Vic Crowe was not happy with his request and explained to him in no uncertain manner that he wanted Pele to be given some freedom to entertain the crowd. Given Vic's comments it's easy to understand why Jimmy was not selected to play, however he did manage to get back through the horrendous traffic jams in Birmingham, caused by the large crowd trying to reach Villa Park, and made it into the ground with less than ten minutes to spare.

In the meantime back at the generator there had been problems. It seemed that there was only enough power to light up three of the four floodlight pylons and the game was in danger of being called off. Thankfully following heated negotiations with the Santos officials, which included Pelé, it was agreed to play the match with the limited lighting. This meant that there would only be one floodlight pylon functioning at the Witton End of the ground.

Back in the Villa dressing room Neil Rioch, who was an unused substitute for the game, remembered the atmosphere being electric (no pun intended) and similar to a big FA Cup tie. He explained, "As a professional you want to go out and compete against top players and it couldn't get any better than playing against Santos at that time. Brazil had just won the World Cup in Mexico and players today who were around at that time all agree that the Brazil side was the greatest football team they had ever seen and here were some of that team playing against us at Villa Park."

Ray Graydon who was in his first season at Aston Villa echoed Neil's memories, "I was only a kid and was so looking forward to playing against Pelé and all these Brazilian internationals. The whole thing was like being at the 'top of the tree to me' - a massive thing"

With the floodlighting issue resolved more trouble was looming. Evidently the Santos officials were unhappy and pointed out that with a crowd of almost 55,000 inside the ground, the agreed match fee was no longer appropriate. They therefore insisted on renegotiating the deal, Jimmy Brown remembers this clearly as he was standing in the tunnel next to where the discussions took place, "Santos said they wouldn't come out unless they got another £10,000 and the Villa had to cough up" remarked Jimmy. Other reports have suggested that unless Santos' appearance fee had been increased, to reflect the large attendance, the game would still go ahead but Pele would not be selected to play. Whatever was the truth of this confrontation the game eventually went ahead, Pele played and the Villa attacked the dimly lit Witton End in the first half.

The home side lined up thus:- Cumbes; Wright, Aitken; Rioch B., Curtis, Tindall; Graydon, McMahon, Lochhead, Hamilton, Martin. Subs:- Lynch, Tiler, Hoban, Rioch N., Hughes. Straight from the kick off it was clear that the Villa were going to take the game very seriously. In doing so they marked tightly and gave Santos very little opportunity to play their exhibition football. As Charlie Aitken recalled, "The Brazilians certainly knew they were in a game."

As the game progressed Ray Graydon realised that he had the beating of the Santos left back and recalls this clearly, "I ran past the full-back more times in that game than I have in any other game in my life...I was amazed and thought well, this is great!" It was from a corner taken by Ray, following one of his many raids down the right wing that resulted in the first goal of the game. Ray's cross was helped on its way by a Charlie

Aitken header and an unmarked Pat McMahon nodded the ball out of the goalkeeper's reach and into the top of the net. The crowd went crazy and apparently the celebrations could be heard in Birmingham city centre. Aston Villa continued to press but as the first half wore on Pelé came more into the game and at last began to show his class. According to contemporary press reports some of his passes with the "inside or outside" of either foot defied logic. The Birmingham Post enthused, "As the half wore on, he ran with the ball feinting, dipping his shoulders and beating opponents with improbable ease" however for all his efforts Pelé's team went in at half time still one goal behind.

During the interval more controversy ensued with regard to the floodlights. As mentioned earlier the generator was barely able to provide enough electricity to power the emergency lighting and three of the four floodlight pylons, leaving the goal area at the Witton End in the shadows. For some reason, which has never been properly explained, someone changed the lighting around so that the Holte End became the darker end of the ground. With teams switching round at half time this would have left Santos defending the darker end of the ground for the second time in the match. Perhaps understandably Pele saw this as being unfair and consequently the Brazilans refused to appear for the second half unless the lights reverted to their original settings. Ray Graydon recalls the incident, "Pelé came out into the middle at half time and was looking up at the lights and complained to everybody that they didn't want to defend the shady end. I think it was Jack Taylor the ref who sorted it out and we attacked the Holte End, with both lights on at that end, leaving Cumbsey (Villa's goalkeeper) in the dark at the other end!"

Once the second half eventually got under way Villa didn't take long to increase their lead. Bruce Rioch embarked on one of his trademark surging runs from midfield, breaking dangerously into the opposition's penalty area where he was cynically hacked down. A young Ray Graydon stepped up in front of the packed Holte End and made no mistake from the spot. The game ebbed and flowed for the next half an hour or so until Brian Tiler who had replaced George Curtis brought Pelé down on the edge of the penalty area. The resulting free kick from Edu still ranks as one of the greatest goals ever seen at Villa Park. He curled the ball around a six man wall and watched as it nestled in the bottom corner of the goal giving Villa's keeper Jim Cumbes with absolutely no chance whatsoever. The stunned crowd reacted with a spontaneous round of applause! As Charlie Aitken said, "Edu was the star of the show, he was brilliant and that shot was amazing." There were no further incidents and so the game ended with a famous Villa win against one of the best teams in the world. Ray Graydon summed it up, "When people ask me about the highlights of my career, I always say, 'I played against Pelé and Santos and scored!'"

The generator - Villa's secret weapon!

1972 ISRAEL & CYPRUS

In May 1972 Aston Villa, newly crowned champions of Division Three, began a twelve day tour of Cyprus and Israel. Ray Graydon recalls the trip clearly as he had not been with the club very long, "I hadn't travelled much before this tour and I remember thinking what a fantastic opportunity this was going to be." Ray was so excited that he arrived at London Airport without half his luggage which he had left behind in Birmingham. Thankfully Aston Villa Vice President "Bunny" Hatfield collected the bags and drove down to the Airport with to ensure that Ray got to the middle-east with his luggage intact.

Charlie Aitken and Ray Graydon wear sarongs in Bethlehem!

Once at the airport Charlie Aitken recalls waiting in a long queue which was unusual for the period. He eventually discovered the cause of the hold up; apparently everyone booked on the flight to Israel was having their baggage searched for explosives. When the players got through security they realised that they were going to travel by Jumbo Jet which was a new experience for the majority of the party.

Happily the journey to the middle-east was trouble free and within four and a half hours they were touching down in Tel Aviv. Having passed through customs fairly swiftly the team were driven to their base for the first part of the tour; a plush hotel situated on the sea front in Herzliya close to the capital. Ray Graydon fondly remembers the hard sand on the beach, in front of the hotel, which according to Bruce Rioch was ideal for five-a-side football. Apparently, chairman Doug Ellis and former player Harry Parkes (who at that time was a director), joined in the opening game. Regrettably, Doug after just a few minutes became the first casualty of the tour suffering a strained back. George Curtis enjoyed the game and was so taken with the beach that according to Ray Graydon he got up early every morning and ran for miles on the sand and always finished off with a long swim. Ray reflected, "George was a smashing lad and a model professional. He looked after himself properly."

May 9th
Maccabi Natanya 1
Aston Villa 2

Aston Villa's first game in Israel took place on the evening of May 9th and the opposition were Maccabi Natanya who were based according to Charlie Aitken, "just down the road from the hotel" in Tel Aviv. The ground, Ray Graydon remembers, "Was a bit of a dump." Charlie Aitken has fonder memories of the place. Whilst he cannot recall the layout of the stadium, what does clearly stick in the left back's mind was his "twenty five yard right footed scorcher of a shot" that flew into the bottom corner of the net.

The Villa went on to win the game 2-1 with Andy Lochhead heading in the second. One final comment on the game came from Bruce Rioch. He recalled an Israeli international named Mordechai "Motaleh" Spiegler playing for Maccabi who clearly impressed him. The lad, an Israeli international, apparently had a short spell with West Ham at some point in his career and according to Bruce was one of the best two footed players he had ever seen. Interestingly Spiegler later played for Paris St. German and then towards the end of his career New York Cosmos where he teamed up with none other than Pele and Charlie Aitken!

May 10th
Beer Sheba 2   Aston Villa 1

After the game with Maccabi it was early to bed as the next day saw the Villa party being driven out to the edge of the Sinai desert to play Beer-Sheba. Ray Graydon's memories of this match were of the ground being very open and basic with a poor playing surface. He also recalled that Jake Findlay played in goal. What he failed to mention was that he scored Villa's only goal of the game. Bruce Rioch was quoted in the local Birmingham press as saying, "We were beaten 2-1. They got two penalties; one of them was a very strange decision."

After the game the players went back to the hotel and "had a few drinks"

The next day a trip to Jerusalem and Bethlehem had been arranged for the entire party. Ray Graydon was amazed that only about five or six players bothered to go on what he saw as a fabulous opportunity. Charlie Aitken maintained that "The rest stayed on the beach sun bathing." Ray however was more frank commenting that, "A lot of players didn't bother going because they had too much to drink the night before" Bruce Rioch must have been part of the intimate party to go on the excursion because he commented at the time that Bethlehem and Jerusalem were marvellous places and for him "this was the highlight of the tour."

Once in Bethlehem, Charlie and Ray teamed up and went to see the birthplace of Jesus however when they reached the church they were refused entry because both of them were wearing shorts. "It was made clear to us" said Ray "that we could not go into the church unless we covered our legs". The two players were very disappointed but thankfully there was help close by and an official handed them a pair of sarongs to wear. Ray continues the story, "I remember Charlie and me putting these sarong things round us like a skirt and laughing at each other!" However it did the trick and the pair were admitted and as Charlie s summed the day up thus, "It was the most fantastic day of my life!"

On their return to the hotel later that evening Ray Graydon was very surprised by the attitude of some of the more senior players especially as he was having such a good time. "It was all new for me and I was loving it. They (the senior players) complained because there weren't any night clubs and wanted to move on somewhere else." It seems that the senior pros got their own way and the stay in Israel was cut short and an extended period in Cyprus hastily arranged.

As soon as the plane carrying the Villa party landed in Cyprus at Larnaca Airport and the Villa contingent had made their way through customs they were shocked by what they saw on local television. Back in Lod airport in Israel from where the team had taken off just a few hours earlier a Belgian Airliner had been hijacked and the Villa party watched on in horror with the rest of the world. The hijackers threatened to blow up the plane, along with the passengers, unless the Israeli government released 315 convicted Palestinian terrorists who were imprisoned in Israel.

The standoff was ended when a team of sixteen Israeli commandos approached the plane disguised as technicians in white overalls. They were able to convince the terrorists that the airliner needed some repairs. The commandos then in just ten minutes stormed the aircraft and took control of the plane, killing all of the male hijackers and capturing the two women. All the passengers were rescued. Ray commented, "That could have been us!"

The Villa team was based in Famagusta at the Paradise Beach Hotel. "It had just been built, brand new and it was fabulous" commented Ray, and went on,"... that's where I learnt to water ski." Bruce Rioch however had a different memory of Ray's efforts, "Ray Graydon decided to have a go at water skiing and found it really tough. He seemed to spend most of the time being dragged along on his backside but he eventually managed to get on his feet"

Ray also recalls going to a night club in Larnaca with a number of Villa players. George Curtis apparently did the usual trick of giving the doormen some Aston Villa badges to let the group into the club without paying. When they got inside they were surprised to find that they were the only people in the club. Ray again takes up the story, "There were no women or anyone else there so we had a few drinks and ended up dancing with each other!" He then recalled Doc Taggart (The team Doctor who always accompanied the team on tours during that era) "...with his collar turned up pretending to be Billy Fury, dancing the night away on his own and thoroughly enjoying himself, of course the alcohol helped!"

May 17th

EPA Larnaca 0   Aston Villa 6

A couple of days later the Villa played their final game of the tour, the opposition this time were EPA Larnaca. The local team were no mugs and contained seven members of the Cyprus national team who had been narrowly beaten by Portugal a couple of weeks earlier. Charlie Aitken has one clear memory of the game, "This was the only time in my life when I turned up to play a football match and saw a water cart going up and down the pitch. It was so dusty they had to water the pitch!" As far as the game was concerned it took Villa a while to adjust to the unusual conditions and despite having most of the play, when the half time whistle blew there was still no score. In the second half Villa upped their game and, roared on by a large British Army contingent ran out 6-0 winners. The goals came from Ray Graydon (2), Charlie Aitken (another 25 yarder but this time with his left foot), Andy Lochhead, Bruce Rioch and Pat McMahon.

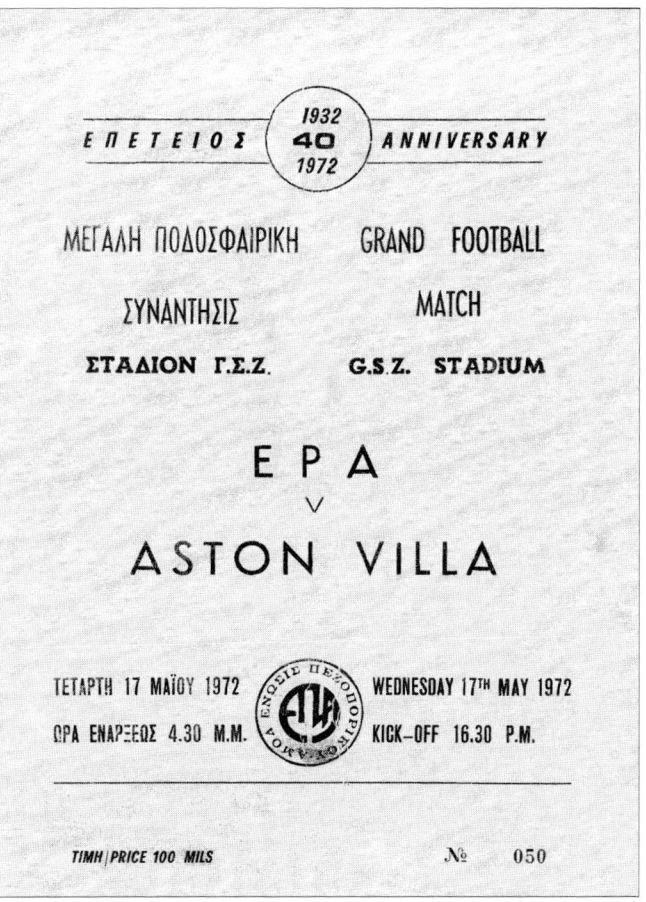

Following the game the Villa players were invited to join key army personnel and their partners at the local NAFFI for an evening meal. As usual the Villa party were sitting all together some distance away from their host's tables. The army officer in charge of the event solved this dilemma by requesting someone from each of the twelve tables to collect one Aston Villa player and take them to join their party and eat at their table. Ray Graydon enthused, "This was a great idea and all the players went along with it. I had a fabulous time and made friends with this couple who I kept in contact with for many years."

The next day it was back to airport and thankfully an uneventful flight home. Bruce Rioch in an interview with the Sports Argus said that he thought the good thing about tours like this trip was that it enabled players to mix more and get to know each other much better. "It certainly worked for us" added Bruce.

1973 TANZANIA

Aston Villa completed their 1972-73 campaign by winning the Third Division in some style and the players were rewarded with a memorable four match tour of Tanzania followed by an opportunity to go on safari in the north of the country. As Brian Little commented, "Tours in those days were a little pat on the back for having worked hard and the manager wanting to do something nice for the players."

The squad selected for the trip included Jim Cumbes, Tommy Hughes, John Robson, Charlie Aitken, Pat McMahon, Chris Nicholl, Fred Turnbull, Alun Evans, Andy Lochhead, Brian Little, Ian Ross, Geoff Vowden, Jimmy Brown, Chico Hamilton, Ray Graydon, and Neil Rioch. Unfortunately Bruce Rioch was injured and unable to make the trip and it was also uncertain whether manager Vic Crowe would be travelling with the party as speculation was rife that Villa were about to sign George Best from Manchester United. Vic after much contemplation decided to fly out with the team saying at the time, "If things start to move on the Best transfer front, I will come straight back to try and clinch the deal"

The journey started well enough with a relaxed group of players and officials boarding the coach in Birmingham destined for Heathrow Airport. From there they were scheduled to fly by East African Airways to Dar-es-Salaam via Rome, Nairobi and Mombasa. Unfortunately a number of unplanned events unfolded which resulted in the in the journey taking much longer than expected.

The first problem to beset the Villa contingent occurred just a few miles from Heathrow when the team coach broke down. The engine had overheated, there was steam bellowing from the radiator and there was no water on board to refill it. As luck would have it the players spotted a reservoir a few hundred yards from where the coach had come to a standstill.

Neil Rioch remembered the incident, "A number of us were going down to the reservoir with anything that we could carry liquid in, dipping it in the water and taking it back to the coach to fill up the radiator." This did the trick and the party were eventually on the road again and soon arrived at Heathrow, unfortunately the unplanned hold up had left them well behind schedule.

Fortuitously, on arrival at Heathrow they were greeted by staff from East African Airways who had been allocated to look after the party. This meant that their luggage was speedily loaded and the Villa contingent were moved smoothly through customs and onto a somewhat ageing VC10 aeroplane. Just as everyone had settled into their seats and the plane was preparing to take-off the engines suddenly cut out and according to Charlie Aitken, "The captain announced that there was a bomb on board the plane!" With this all the passengers filed off the airliner and were taken by coach to a hanger on the far side of the airport close to where their plane had been towed. Neil Rioch recollects the episode clearly, "There were several fire engines and other emergency vehicles with lights flashing all around the plane. The plane was emptied of all of its cargo, including the players' baggage, and every item was thoroughly searched." This evidently took almost four hours and nothing untoward was found and so it was with some relief that everyone re-boarded the plane and prepared for take-off.

Aston Villa's first ever tour in Africa

The Villa party were now well behind schedule however the first leg of the flight to Italy passed by without any major hiccoughs except that all the alcohol on the plane had been consumed during the two hour flight! This was rectified on arrival in Rome whilst the plane was refuelling in preparation for the next leg of the journey to Nairobi.

From there it was onto Mombasa and thence to their destination, Dar-es-Salaam. Unfortunately the hold-up at Heathrow had affected the travel plans and on touching down in Mombasa it became evident that the Villa party had missed their connecting flight to Dar-es-Salaam. This meant they had to take a different flight which would take them down the east African coast over a beautiful collection of tropical islands and lakes.

Neil Rioch explained that "It was so hot on the plane, there was no air conditioning and we all had our light grey Aston Villa suits on." Following take off the airliner was soon over Lake Victoria where it suddenly banked violently, almost 90 degrees and the passengers went silent. Neil really thought the plane was going to crash into the lake as the wing tip almost hit the water. He continued, "Eventually it levelled off and the pilot came on the intercom and told us that there was a ferocious storm ahead and he had to take drastic action to avoid it."

Once the plane was on an even keel a number of players decided to get up and stretch their legs whereupon they noticed that Andy Lochhead had a tell-tale damp patch in a somewhat embarrassing area of his trousers. Clearly the other players couldn't believe that a "hard as nails" player like Andy had experienced such an unfortunate accident. However everything was soon cleared up when they realised that when the plane had lurched Andy had upset a drink into his lap!

The plane finally touched down safely in Dar-es-Salaam some twenty two hours after leaving Birmingham. The players were very tired and their lovely grey suits, with the Aston Villa crest on the pockets, were by this time somewhat grubby and stained. Neil Rioch remembers, "We came down the steps from the plane and were hit by this incredible heat. There were TV crews and newspaper photographers waiting for us and I couldn't stop wondering what on earth they must be thinking of us. Here we were a group of professional footballers from England, arriving in their country dishevelled and wearing crumpled and stained suits."

Once through immigration the party were ferried fifteen miles north, in two coaches to their base for the duration of the trip, the Kunduchi Beach Hotel. Jimmy Brown takes up the story of the journey, "There were no windows that would open or air conditioning on the bus and it was so hot.

There were no proper roads either; it was just a dirt track." Evidently as the coaches passed through the small villages with mud huts and tin roofs the locals came out and waved to the players shouting, "Aston Villa, Aston Villa." Jimmy Brown had also noticed from the bus window that most of the local men seemed to be walking around with spears and machetes - which he found a little disturbing. He went on, "There was poverty all around us and we were thinking, whilst on the bus, things like 'Where have they brought us?' 'Why have they brought us to a place like this?' We thought we were supposed to be on tour!' Then we came out of the bush and were faced with this magnificent palace of a hotel with all mod cons including air conditioning, miles of white beach, a circular swimming pool and a beautiful sea."

Even with such luxury all around them and having only recently arrived, some players felt the place was boring because they suspected there would be nothing much to do, especially in the evenings. Jim Cumbes remembered, "that some of them actually wanted to go back home!" That this was taken seriously by the Villa management surprised Jim, however Vic Crowe called them all together for a team meeting.

According to Jim Cumbes, Vic he told the players that they could vote on whether they should remain in the hotel and play the four scheduled games or return home. Jim, surprised by the closeness of the vote, was relieved that the majority elected to stay and so the tour was back on!

May 13th   Young Africans   0   Aston Villa   0

The players had just one day to acclimatise before their first game against the Tanzanian champions Young Africans, so it was early to bed for a very exhausted party. The next day the players relaxed around the pool prior to boarding the coach bound for the national Stadium in Dar-es-Salaam for the five o'clock kick off. Pat McMahon said on his return, "We arrived at the Stadium at least an hour before kick- off but even so our bus had a job getting through the crowds. Once inside we drove around the track surrounding the pitch to a fabulous welcome from the 50,000 crowd who were packed in like sardines." Ray Graydon remembers a witch doctor at this and other games in during the tour, "There was a witch doctor with a live chicken on the touchline. He cut off its head and danced around the pitch with it!" It seems that this colourful addition to the team also advised the Young Africans on what tactics to employ during matches.

The game kicked off and there was plenty of good football from both teams however Aston Villa had the better goal scoring opportunities throughout the match. Brian Little recalls the game, "The pitch in Dar-es-Salaam was bone hard, it was extremely hot and the game was very rough." It didn't seem to bother Brian though because after just three minutes he had a well-placed header saved on the line by the Young Africans' goalkeeper Muhidin. Alas Brian was only to last another twenty minutes before he was badly fouled, by Young African's full back Seleman, and had to leave the field to be replaced by Chico Hamilton. Chico stepped up to the plate and revelled in the atmosphere whilst delighting the crowd with a number of jinking runs. The game was very "end to end" but at half time neither side had been able to break the deadlock.

The second half was just as lively as the first with neither side giving an inch. Ron Wylie remembered him and Vic expecting the Young Africans' to run out of steam and were astonished with their stamina as they fought tooth and nail right up to the final whistle.

Skipper Jimmy Brown remembers really wanting to win this first game and drove the Villa team on. The lads responded well, shook off the effects of the heat, matched the Young Africans' work rate and went all out for a winner. Villa's "never say die" attitude almost paid off in the very last minute of the game. Andy Lochhead headed the ball across the goal to an unmarked Pat McMahon whose point blank volley was somehow blocked on the line. Sadly there were no further opportunities to start the tour off with a victory and Villa had to settle for a well eared goalless draw.

The next day the players decided to explore the locality however they were under strict instructions that if they went into Dar-es-Salaam not to carry too much money with them and never to walk the streets after dark. Pat McMahon, Neil Rioch and Jimmy Cumbes decided against visiting the town and instead walked up to the small village located close to the Hotel to meet some of the local people. The Villa lads were surprised how friendly the locals were. Neil reflected on this saying, "It just showed us how people on the other side of the world lived. It was part of the education that football can give you as long as you are not blinkered to it all."

Chris Nichol was moved by the contrast of living conditions between those staying in the plush Kunduchi Beach Hotel and the local people who lived villages, "...sheer poverty. There were kids with no shoes living in these tiny mud and tin huts." He went on, "I can remember walking into the town and seeing young kids with part of their arms chopped off begging. We were told later that they had been severed deliberately so they would get more money. That was absolutely scary!"

Brian Little remembers going with some senior players into the town during the day where they changed money and bought souvenirs. Brian also recalled, "Money changers coming to the hotel and offering us three times the value for our English pounds."

May 16th   Zanzibar 0   Aston Villa 3

Villa's next game was against Zanzibar, a semi-autonomous region within Tanzania, which meant the opposition would be made up of the best players from the area. Once team sheets were exchanged the Villa management realised that five the opposition contained five Tanzanian full internationals.

It has to be said that this game was full of the stuff that legends are made from and consequently there are many conflicting accounts about what actually went on both prior to, during and after the match. Clearly there were a significant number of supporters from Zanzibar who had made the 40 mile or so trip to Dar-es-Salaam to see their heroes in action. Worryingly there was an even larger contingent of locals waiting to meet them! The inevitable clash took place and the police responded enthusiastically.

By this time the Villa players were safely in their dressing room however on hearing the disturbance outside they clambered onto the benches and opened the tiny windows to see what was going on. Chris Nichol was very disturbed by the whole episode, "The police were whacking the fans with batons. I saw at least five police corner one young kid and beat him viciously with their sticks. Watching something like that was very frightening." Neil Rioch added, "There was great rivalry between two areas in Tanzania and we heard this hubbub outside and I looked through the window and saw the police beating people. There was a bad atmosphere and it was all very nasty."

When the players eventually emerged onto the pitch there was still a significant amount of crowd trouble inside the stadium which was not helped by supporters trying to gain admittance to the match by scaling a 10ft high white wall which surrounded the ground. Jimmy Brown had never seen anything like it, "Inside the ground police were beating supporters with their sticks and Jimmy Cumbes was filming it all on his cine camera. The police told him to stop filming or they would confiscate it."

Meanwhile even the old heads of the squad were getting anxious. Jimmy Brown again, "Andy Lochhead says to me 'We don't want any silly tackles today Jimmy please or we could be in trouble with this crowd. Be careful please!' I agreed with him because I was just as uneasy as him about the whole situation."

The kick off was delayed for some time while the police tried to restore order in their own imitable way and even when the game eventually began the police were still trying to control the crowd. According to reports at the time the game had not been particularly riveting however after about ten minutes all hell let loose. "Not long after we kicked off rocks came flying over the wall from outside the ground" reported Ray Graydon. He went on, "I thought blow this, I'm not stopping here I'm going over onto the other wing. Then Andy Lochhead shouted at me, 'Eh! What are you doing?' I said to him, 'If you think I'm staying out there dodging rocks you're mistaken – you can go and play out there yourself!"

The game continued whilst the rocks flew over the wall and then fighting broke out inside the ground between the rival factions and people began to spill onto the pitch. The police responded with their batons and a "free for all" took place. Neil Rioch continued, "All of a sudden I heard a loud noise that sounded like gunfire. I looked across the field and almost on the half-way line there was a guy lying down on his back with a couple of people round him who I saw pull a blanket over his head!" Neil asked John Robson what had happened and he replied that the police must have shot the guy.

The word spread amongst the team and they all made for the dressing room as fast as they could. Once in the safety of the changing room Charlie Aitken pointed out to his team mates that the bangs had been caused by the police firing tear gas canisters at the supporters, who were picking up the cylinders and hurling them back onto the pitch.

With their eyes still streaming from the effects of the tear gas the players remained in the relative safety of the dressing room until order was restored. Once the game restarted Villa found little difficulty in outclassing their opponents and quickly took the lead through Alun Evans. Within fifteen minutes Villa had doubled their advantage when Charlie Aitken headed an Ian Ross free kick into the path of Chico Hamilton, who gleefully slammed the ball into the net from close range.

Leading 2-0 at the break the away team took complete control of the game in the second half and were unlucky to only add one goal to their tally. Brian Little who had been a constant thorn in the side of the Zanzibar defence, scored that third goal, just before the hour, when he forced home a Chico Hamilton cross that had been headed on by Charlie Aitken. The Villa remained in charge of the match, passing the ball around at will and running down the clock then with a minute remaining Alun Evans became involved in an altercation with one of the Zanzibar players. Sadly the Villa forward came off worse and was soon sporting a black eye. This incident once more fired up the crowd resulting in them invading the pitch and running towards the Villa players. Thankfully the baton wielding police or as they were officially known the Tanzanian Defence Force, restored order and after a short break the final minute of the match was played out without any further interruptions.

That evening the players had a party by the pool led by the "Master of Ceremonies" Jim Cumbes. For wide eyed Brian Little, an eighteen year old on his first proper tour, this party certainly opened his eyes. "It was just party after party at night time. All with a different theme and somehow Jim Cumbes came up with a different theme every time" recalled Brian. Most of the games seemed to involve forfeits which usually meant taking a drink. Chris Nichol who was not a great drinker became very drunk at one of Jim's parties and remembered that, "It was some sort of numbers game and I wasn't very good at it.

I wasn't used to the alcohol and I had to drink so much in forfeits. I think I was rooming with Geoff Vowden and I remember being sick all over our bedroom – Geoff was not best pleased!"

The next day was a rest day and the lads organised a barbecue on an uninhabited island which was not too far out to sea and visible from their rooms. The hotel staff ferried them over a few at a time in a small boat, along with the necessary cooking equipment, food and plenty of liquid refreshments. Neil Rioch described the scene, "This island was quite tiny you could walk around it in ten minutes and there were two or three beautiful beaches. In the middle of the island was a massive baobab tree. Its trunk was immense; it was the size of a house!"

With the island being uninhabited the players decided for some reason, to swim naked. They were all swimming around and having a great time when Doug Ellis and his wife Heidi came through the trees and onto the beach. Doug was in his bathing shorts and Neil remembered Jim Cumbes shouting at him, "If you want to swim here Mr Chairman then you will have to swim naked because we've designated this, 'a nude bathing beach." To which Heidi turned her back on the players and Doug said, "OK no problem" then according to Neil he dropped his shorts ran down the beach and joined them in the water.

Brian Little remembers the island too, "I can remember some of the lads getting sunburnt on this island we went out to…Neil Rioch got badly burned. It was a beautiful island and I remember swimming around and having a great time." Neil was indeed badly burned and blistered but had been selected to play against Simba a couple of days later and was desperate to play. The sunburn was hushed up and Neil played through the pain but Villa manager Vic Crowe had known about it all along. Years later he told Neil, "I was seriously in two minds about letting you (Neil) play but I wanted to test your character and see how you responded to a bit of pain!"

May 19th Simba 1 Aston Villa 1

An African welcome.

The Simba game like the previous two was held at the National Stadium in Dar-es-Salaam and kicked off once more at 5.00pm. This meant that the conditions were not too oppressive. Ian Ross, "It wasn't just the heat, we were worried about the pitch which was still bone hard!" On arrival at the ground there was another large crowd but thankfully they were all local supporters and so there was no trouble this time. Opponents Simba were very confident having just completed an impressive season in which they finished as league champions and believed that Villa were there for the taking.

The away team kicked off and were soon infuriated by the referee's interpretation of the rules which was distinctly at odds with what the players were used to back home. This was clearly illustrated after just six minutes when Chico Hamilton was sent off for persistent shouting! Chico had become quite a favourite with the locals being immediately identifiable by his flowing blonde locks and exciting surging runs, consequently the crowd were very unhappy with the referee's decision and made their feelings known. This sending off however was only the first part of a double whammy. While the Villa players were reorganising from the shock of the Hamilton dismissal Simba striker Sentara, who looked to be at least four yards offside, lobbed the ball over Jim Cumbes' head and into the back of the net to take an unexpected lead.

After the interval Villa brought on Pat McMahon and his penetrating runs immediately had the Simba defence in trouble. The away team kept up the pressure throughout the half and were eventually rewarded with just fifteen minutes left on the clock.

Andy Lochhead sent a superbly weighted pass into the path of right winger Ray Graydon who raced in and smashed the ball home for a well-deserved equaliser.

That evening at the obligatory party by the pool there was one player missing. On the team's return to the hotel Jimmy Brown was clearly not well and had taken to his bed with a stomach bug. At about 2.00 a.m. Charlie Aitken recalls Doc Taggart the club doctor receiving a call from Jimmy saying, "Come quick! I'm dying, I'm nearly dead!" According to Charlie the Doc had partaken of a few drinks with the lads and being a little refreshed he had some difficulty locating Jimmy's room. When he eventually arrived he sat on Jimmy's bed and asked him to tell him what the problem was. Jimmy replied, "Doc there's no toilet paper so I can't use the toilet." Doc stifled his laughter, checked him out and confined him to his bed.

He looked in on Jim the next morning and found him still poorly so he gave him some tablets and said that he would pop back and see him every four hours. Unfortunately Doc Taggart got somewhat side-tracked during the day and forgot about the off-colour Jimmy Brown. Neil Rioch remembers being in the Doc's room with a group of other players until well after midnight, "Suddenly there was knock on the door and we thought it was Vic Crowe come to sort us out. Doc opened the door and there was a very sick looking Jimmy Brown." Jimmy recalled that he had been left for over twelve hours all alone in his room and was in a terrible state. According to Neil Doc Taggart, "who was a fantastic guy and an extremely good doctor" sorted him out and Jimmy eventually went back to bed with some more tablets.

May 20th   Young Africans 1   Aston Villa 1

The final match of the tour was a second game against Young Africans. Villa began positively and were soon ahead thanks to a goal created by Chico Hamilton and finished off by Andy Lochhead, or "Kipara" (the bald one) as he was nicknamed by the locals. The home team were struggling and it seemed to be only a matter of time before the visitors doubled their lead. However on the twenty five minute mark Villa's plans were thrown into disarray when Andy Lochhead was given his marching orders, like Chico Hamilton the previous day, for shouting at a colleague. From then on Villa decided to play "keep ball" and they did this so effectively that, far from playing defensively, they often had the Young Africans on the back foot. It was only the exceptional goalkeeping from Muhidin that prevented the visitors from increasing their lead before half time.

The second half continued in much the same vein as the first with Villa passing the ball with consummate ease and rarely looking in trouble. That was until the 82nd minute when, under no apparent pressure, Ian Ross put through his own goal to give the Young Africans an undeserved equaliser.

The next day, with the football over, the players had to make a choice from three options as to how they wanted to spend their second week of the tour. On offer were four days on Mafia Island in the Indian Ocean with deep sea fishing laid on each day, four days on safari to Lake Manyara and Ngorogoro Crater or remain at the Kunduchi Beach Hotel with sun, swimming, water skiing, snorkelling and trips around the locality.

One young man who had no option other than to stay in bed was of course Jimmy Brown who was still unwell, "Doc Taggart came into my room, tells me he's off on safari and leaves me these pills to take and tells me I will be fine and he will see me when he gets back!" Jimmy was also told not to eat or drink anything only clean water. "

So I'm lying there and tell him that he shouldn't leave me and he says, 'Come on Jimmy you're a man for Christ's sake and that was the last I saw of him for nearly a week!" Staying behind with Jimmy were Neil Rioch, who was still getting over his sunburn, and youngster Brian Little who remembered, "Some of the lads went off on Safari others to Mafia island but I stayed at the hotel. I was not unhappy sitting around the pool sunbathing – that suited me." However when he got home Brian had other thoughts; "I've been to Africa! I should have done more than I did – that was a great eye opener for me." Neil Rioch said his decision to remain at the hotel was nothing to do with his sunburn but that both of the other options necessitated a flight in a light aircraft and after the outward journey to Africa he thought he would give it a miss and see more of the area. "We had a local guy from Dar-es-Salaam showing us around the countryside and the city – I really enjoyed that."

Ray Graydon chose to fly off to Mafia Island with Charlie Aitken, Tommy Hughes and Andy Lochhead and landed on a small airfield which consisted of a dirt runway, a weather sock and a shed. The party then travelled by bus to small village with a couple of boats, a beautiful beach lined by a few bungalows which Ray described as "paradise." They apparently went swimming, snorkelling and big-game fishing and the Villa winger remembers being fascinated by the unusual Madagascan fruit bats and thinking how wonderful the island was.

The eleven remaining members of the tour party were off on safari and had to get up at 4.30 in the morning to make the 300 mile flight from Dar-es-Salaam to Kilimanjaro. Once there they faced another 80 mile trip along dirt roads to Lake Manyara, which was once described by Ernest Hemingway as "the loveliest lake I had seen in Africa".

From the entrance gate to the lake, the road wound through jungle-like forest where baboons lazed around unperturbed alongside the track and monkeys swung between the trees.

Pre-match line-up.

In addition the party saw giraffes, gazelles, water buffalos, a rhinoceros, an elephant and a host of different tropical birds. The trip around the lake took over four hours and the only disappointment according to Jim Cumbes was that they hadn't seen any lions. However on their way back the driver suddenly stopped the truck and directly in front of them were around ten lions beginning to hunt for food.

The next day the Villa party moved on to the Ngorogoro Crater, a large dry volcanic basin. Although it was only about thirty miles from their base it took over two hours to reach because the vehicles had to drive slowly along a muddy mountain terrain with a steep drop on one side. Chris Nichol remembers the mud being so bad that at one stage the players had to get out of the Land Rovers and push one of them that had become stuck in the mud.

Once they had arrived at the lodge the group drove to the floor of the crater and across the plain in the Land Rovers. Doug Ellis recalled this episode in his book "Deadly", "Suddenly a rhinoceros, possibly disturbed by the intrusion decided to make a charge. In a flash, from all being serene one moment, a couple of tons of angry rhino was then hurtling at breakneck speed towards the (other) vehicle" Doug explained that he had never seen six heads disappear inside a Land Rover so quickly. One of those in that vehicle remembered the moment well and said that the driver knew what to do. Apparently he stopped the Land Rover then amazingly the rhino stopped as well and then it just walked away as though nothing had happened!

When the lads were together again at the Kunduchi Beach Hotel they busily exchanged stories about their various adventures and by this time even Jimmy Brown was feeling a little better. That evening was the last night of the tour a big poolside party was held which evidently went on until the early hours of the morning. Brian Little remembers it culminating in, "Andy Lochhead, who couldn't swim, throwing as many people into the pool as possible."

The players were up and around relatively early the next morning only to be greeted by dark skies and heavy rain. They made their way to the airport on the coach and boarded the plane this time without any difficulties at all. They were on their way home at last or so they thought. Charlie Aitken takes up the story, "We were all sitting in our seats on the plane and the airliner had been stationary for longer than we expected.

Apparently the airport authorities had refused permission for us to take off and had demanded a considerable amount of money before we could get airborne." So the players settled down and waited whilst Doug Ellis went to the bank and arranged a money transfer so they could take off. They eventually took to the air and fortunately had a completely trouble free journey home.

Neil Rioch summed the whole adventure thus, "It was a brilliant tour for many reasons…..it certainly created a bond between the players and if that was the purpose of the trip then it was a huge success." Jimmy Brown on the other hand who had spent most of the trip ill in bed said, "The best part of the tour was touching down in UK and thinking 'civilization again'." Let's leave the final word with Charlie Aitken who enthused, "It was a phenomenal trip, I've never laughed so much in my life!"

(Above) Half time: Ian Ross takes refreshment under the African sun.
(Below) Mixing with the locals

1975 CENTRAL AMERICA

May   Barbados International XI   0   Aston Villa   1

In the summer of 1974 Aston Villa appointed Ron Saunders as their new manager. Ron succeeded Vic Crowe into the hot seat following his dismissal at the end of the 1973-74 season. Saunders' first season in charge was "just what the doctor ordered" with Villa winning the double of the League Cup and promotion back to Division One. As a reward Chairman Doug Ellis arranged a tour of the Caribbean for the players, their wives and girlfriends. The party flew out of the UK on the 15th May to St. Lucia and from there they embarked on what was supposed to be a seven day luxury cruise around the islands on board the "Cunard Adventurer." The trip was scheduled to end in Bridgetown, Barbados in time to play a friendly against the Island's football team.

The cruise began well enough with the players eating, drinking and taking in the entertainment available. Ray Graydon remembers, "We'd had a few nights drinking and I thought, I can't be boozing every night and decided to find something else to occupy his time. The next evening Ray went off on his own to the cinema, located at the rear of the boat, to see "The Towering Inferno." Ray settled down and was enjoying the film however as it reached its climax he suddenly felt a thud, then the lights went out in the cinema and the film stopped. Ray takes up the story:

"There were maybe fifty or so people in the cinema and we all sat in silence for maybe two or three minutes and then suddenly everyone was clambering over the seats." Ray was most disgruntled by this behaviour and told them to sit down as he wanted to watch the end of the film. "I sat there for a little while and there was me and another guy left in the cinema and I said to him, 'I was enjoying that do you think we are going to see anymore?" After chatting for a while they decided that the film show must be over for the night and so they made their way out of the theatre and onto the stairs.

Here they were somewhat taken aback to see everyone rushing around in a panic many with life jackets on!

Aston Villa Cast Adrift in the Caribbean Sea!

Ray soon discovered that the thud he felt whilst in the cinema had in fact been an explosion, which resulted in one of the ship's engines catching fire. He eventually managed to get back through the confusion to the lounge where the players were still relaxing with their drinks. Here he found Jimmy Cumbes, "holding court to a group of very hot Villa players." Ray asked them if everything was alright and they replied that everything was fine except that the air conditioning had stopped working! At this point Ray realised that they had absolutely no idea that the boat was in trouble.

Ray tried in vain to explain the situation but they didn't believe him and it took him some time to persuade them to leave the bar.

Once outside they noticed everyone hurrying here and there and wearing lifejackets. This soon sobered up the Villa party and they struggled into their lifejackets before joining the majority of the passengers on deck. Once up on top they found out that the ship had lost all of its power, there was only emergency lighting available and they were drifting aimlessly. Charlie Aitken recalls, "We had no power and we spent the night on the deck" According to Doug Ellis in his book "Deadly" the boat was left drifting, "without power for twenty-six hours." Charlie who spoke to one of the ship's engineers remembered him saying how serious the situation was and how they were "lucky not to be cast adrift in the lifeboats."

After floating aimlessly in shark infested waters the crew eventually managed to get one of the engines operational and the boat crawled into the port at Caracus, over five hundred miles from Barbados, their original destination.

Doug Ellis was now faced with the problem of how to get the Villa party to their destination without a boat capable of completing the journey in time for the match. Charlie Aitken remembers the solution, "Doug managed to secure a couple of 30 seated light aircraft from somewhere to fly us to Bridgetown (Barbados). I remember they were two small propeller engine planes and ours was painted green!"

Not everyone was keen on completing the trip in planes that would probably have been more at home in an Indiana Jones movie. Doug Ellis commented in his book Deadly that, "Ron Saunders plus a leading player and a director were so nervous about flying in these planes that they wanted us to charter a jet......to fly us to Amsterdam and then return home without playing the fixture." According to Charlie, Doug Ellis was adamant that they must fulfil their commitment to play the match in Bridgetown and so he decided that everyone would have no choice but to cram into these two old planes and fly up to Barbados." The aeroplanes eventually got airborne and almost immediately some of the more anxious passengers got itchy feet and started walking around in what was a very limited space. Charlie being one of the more curious passengers decided to make his way to the flight deck and looking down below at a largish city asked the pilot the name of it. He was astounded when the pilot replied that he had no idea where it was and with that a somewhat anxious Charlie Aitken quickly returned to his seat and strapped himself in!

Meanwhile in Bridgetown the Ambassador had been waiting in hope, rather than certainty, for the Villa team to arrive in time for the match. As a precaution the government had arranged for riot police to be at the ground just in case the game had to be cancelled and the disgruntled supporters decided to cause a disturbance. Thankfully the precautions were not necessary because the planes touched down in Bridgetown with a few hours to spare. According to Doug Ellis op cit., "The Ambassador was waiting (for us) with tears in his eyes and said, 'Thank god you came. You have no idea what the radio and newspapers have been saying about the English!"

The game went ahead but the players have only a very hazy recollection of the match details. In addition neither the national nor local press appeared to have reported on the game other than giving the result. Chris Nichol recalled the pitch as being awful, "The ground was packed. We played on a cricket pitch and the square was as hard as concrete but the outfield took a stud. It was very difficult to play proper football on." Ray Graydon's memory is of the actual match is completely blank, "All I can remember is loads of frogs jumping about on the pitch!" Doug recalls the game in his book "Deadly" as the Villa winning, "by about seven or eight goals" however the Evening Mail reported the result as 2-0 to the Villa.

1976   Central America

Guadeloupe   0   Aston Villa   1

Martinique   1   Aston Villa   0

Having survived their first season amongst the elite of English football the players were relaxed with a tour to the Caribbean which included games against Martinique and Guadeloupe. Brian Little remembers a number of incidents on this tour but nothing about either of the games.

"I remember going to Martinique and staying in this absolutely fantastic hotel with a fabulous swimming pool. One of the most vivid days that I can remember was when about fifteen of us were sitting around the hotel pool bored out of our brains. At the end of the swimming pool was a beautiful girl, un-fortunately she had her boyfriend with her and he was a right poser. We all hated him, mainly because he had a beautiful girlfriend! They were obviously on holiday and we were on tour playing a bit of football but generally with nothing to do other than sit in the sun.

After a while Budgie (John Burridge) came down to the pool and said something like, 'Look at him down there – he's a right poser!' He then walked around the pool until he reached the couple then stood in front of the girl's boyfriend.

Budgie makes a point back in Central America

After standing there for a few minutes Budgie leapt into the air and stood on his hands. He then proceeded to walk around the swimming pool on his hands stopping occasionally to do a few press ups!

There was a three tier diving board at the end of the pool and Budgie's next trick was to climb to the top board, still walking on his hands, dived off and completed a full summersault before hitting the water.

He then stayed under water and swam to the other end of the pool without coming up for air! Budgie climbed out of the pool in front of the couple, stood up and then shook himself over the guy who was lying oblivious on his sun bed.

All the lads were cheering. It was ludicrously silly but so funny and it summed Budgie up a treat."

As far as the games were concerned it has not been possible to track down any reports and the players involved only have hazy recollections of them,

~ 101 ~

1976 RANGERS

October 9th   Aston Villa 2   Rangers 0
(Match abandoned after 53 mins.)

Having successfully negotiated their first season back in the top flight of English football Aston Villa were now ready to kick on by blending an exciting mix of Ron Saunders' imports with an exceptional crop of home grown players. By October they were eighth in the First Division and on course for the League Cup final having already beaten Manchester City and Norwich City.

On the Saturday 9th October a number of international games were being played therefore many English First Division matches, including Villa's against Arsenal were postponed. Facing a blank weekend Aston Villa arranged what they thought would be a prestigious home friendly against Scottish giants Rangers. However as early as three weeks before the game the Sunday Mercury's John Pearson was predicting trouble if the game went ahead, "...sadly however Aston Villa have decided to invite Rangers for a friendly match....I hope there isn't any violence or drunken behaviour – but my warning about Scots troublemakers stands." He had based his opinion on the disturbances that occurred at an earlier game between Birmingham City and Celtic.

The Rangers' fans began descending on Birmingham from the early hours of Saturday morning many already "worse for wear", and a significant number of the coaches that that had deposited the drunken hoards in the city rushed back to Scotland to collect another bus load of so called supporters. To add to the chaos there were several special trains arriving from Glasgow at New Street Station throughout the early hours and Saturday shoppers in Birmingham's Bull Ring were about to be subjected to a morning of nightmare proportions never seen in the city before! The experience of a mother and her daughter were typical of the many innocent victims caught up in the city centre mayhem.

According to a local newspaper the two women were approached by a gang of well over twenty Rangers' fans who swept through the Bull Ring shouting and singing whilst pushing shoppers and swearing at traders. The two women tried to step out of the mob's way but they turned on them swearing aggressively and threatening them with violence. Luckily the two women got off reasonably lightly compared to others; the mother had her hair pulled and was pushed to the ground whilst her terrified daughter had a full bottle of milk thrown over her.

This sadly was only the tip of the iceberg as there were numerous reports of violence, drunkenness, vandalism and general hooliganism throughout the morning. Luckily the word rapidly circulated amongst the City's publicans and the majority of pubs in the area closed their doors leaving the road to Villa Park littered with empty bottles, kicked-in doors and broken windows. Sadly many Aston Villa supporters on the way to the match were also set upon by gangs of marauding, so called, Rangers supporters. One Villa fan remembered his walk from the bus stop to Villa Park very clearly. "My friend and I were walking towards the ground and were confronted by about ten Rangers fans. We were terrified. One of them asked us in a broad Glaswegian accent if we were 'proddies' or 'papes'?" The two lads had no idea what the Rangers' supporters were talking about and said so, where upon the Scots demanded to know if they were Protestants or Catholics. When they responded by saying they were both Methodists they were told to be on their way! "God knows what would have happened if we had told them we were Roman Catholics!"

Surprisingly, given the vast numbers who had travelled from Scotland there were only around 15,000 people inside the ground by kick off.

The Battle of Birmingham.

However the atmosphere was very tense as the Rangers' supporters, many clearly drunk, had got into the ground early and were massed at the back of the Holte End which was traditionally of course occupied by the Villa fans. Luckily the police managed to contain the rivalry early on but soon minor scuffles broke out and the Villa supporters were moved to the other end of the ground. Peter Sutton, a lifelong Aston Villa fan, recalls this clearly, "When we entered the ground we were surprised to find that the rear of the Holte had been taken over by Rangers supporters. As kick-off approached Villa fans began to arrive in numbers and the front of the Holte was populated by home supporters with the Rangers hoards massed at the rear. The stadium officials recognised the potential for trouble that this represented and moved the Villa supporters from one end of the ground to the other. I don't remember the exact way in which this was carried out other than it was an orderly walk over the pitch, rather than us being chased off the Holte."

Both clubs had selected strong teams however notable absentees from the Villa line up were Andy Gray and Chris Nichol both of whom were carrying injuries. Chris' place went to rookie centre half Charlie Young who was making his home debut. The game kicked off on time and Villa enjoyed the lion's share of the possession in the first half. It was therefore no surprise when, on the half hour mark, following a series of Villa attacks the pressure finally paid off and Dennis Mortimer scored Villa's opener which the Sunday Mercury described as "sweet, swift and incisive." Alex Cropley began the move by clipping the ball out to Leighton Phillips who had made a run on the left hand side of the field. Leighton noticed a gap in the Rangers' defence and knocked the ball through it. Dennis Mortimer made a majestic run into the space, collected the ball and slotted it past the Rangers' goalkeeper Kennedy with consummate ease. Despite incessant pressure from the home team there were no further goals to report in the first half and the home side went in at the interval one goal to the good.

Whilst during the half time break the Rangers' supporters began throwing missiles once the second half began there was little indication of the chaos that was to follow. Villa began the second half in much the same vein as they ended the first playing attractive free flowing football and looked likely to increase their lead at any moment. Their persistent pressure bore fruit in the 52nd minute when a Ray Graydon corner was headed back across goal by John Deehan to Frank Carrodus, who turned and scored in one movement, with a fierce shot into the corner of the net leaving the Rangers' goalkeeper helpless.

What happened next was probably the worst case of football disorder at a Villa home game since the 19th century when a mob of Aston Villa "roughs" attacked the visiting Preston North End team with "sticks, stones and other missiles." Hundreds of Rangers' fans who were still situated at the back of the Holte End began to throw beer bottles, cans and other missiles at John Burridge's goal and then surged forward towards the front causing the crowd to spill over onto the pitch to avoid being crushed. This was the signal for the Scottish fans to invade the playing area and In no time there were hundreds of Rangers fans running onto the pitch, hurling bottles and defying all efforts by the police to hold them back. The players dashed for the safety of the changing rooms and Ray Graydon summed up their mood, "I don't remember too much about the game other than running for my life when the Rangers' fans invaded the pitch."

The invasion was unexpected and although it is still generally believed that it was a reaction to the Villa goal Brian Little pointed out, "The Rangers' fans completely flipped! Ok we were winning 2-0 but it was only a friendly and there was still over half an hour left. There must have been something else that started it off." Chris Nichol who was watching from the stands confirmed Brian's view, "I remember how surprised I was by the reaction of the Rangers supporters. I couldn't see any reason or purpose for what they did."

One possible cause of their actions, which was not widely reported at the time, may have been a response by some supporters at the Witton End of the ground when Villa scored their second goal. It seems that at this point a Celtic scarf, an Irish Tricolour flag or both were waved by some spectators located on the "Witton" in celebration, resulting in the violence that followed. Whatever the reason for the riot it has to be said that this incident was a low point for British football and the media had a field day.

The Rangers supporters' invasion quickly turned into a battle between the police and the Scottish fans and it raged all over the pitch. At this point local referee Derek Civil had no alternative but to abandon the game. Speaking afterwards to an Evening Mail reporter he said, "If I had kept the players on the pitch another thirty seconds, I would have feared for my life, and theirs...there was no way I could expose them to danger." He went on, "It was the most terrifying experience of my life! There was nothing that happened on the pitch that could have contributed to this violence."

When the players returned to their dressing rooms they passed policemen and supporters being treated for their injuries in the tunnel and they even found some Villa fans hiding in the home dressing room! Brian Little again, "I remember getting to the top of the tunnel and seeing the police dragging these Rangers fans down the tunnel and through the dressing room area and out of the ground. Their fans (Rangers) were wild and really wound up."

Brian Little

Amid this chaos John Burridge the eccentric Aston Villa goalkeeper was, according to Brian Little, extremely anxious because he had left his goalkeeping gloves in Holte End goal that Villa had been defending prior to the pitch invasion. "Budgie was walking down the tunnel and he said to me, 'Oh my gloves – I've left them behind.' Now these gloves were not the expensive ones goalkeepers use these days, they were just a cheap pair of green goalkeeper's gloves which were practically useless.

But typical of Budgie he actually went back out there, where there was a riot going on, made his way up to the Holte End goal, got his gloves and amazingly came back to the tunnel in one piece!"

Meanwhile the pandemonium on the pitch showed no sign of abating until six police-dog handlers appeared from the Witton End of the ground and immediately there was an easing of the tension as the Rangers supporters began to retreat back onto the terraces. Once people realised the game had been abandoned many well-behaved fans began drifting sadly out of the ground only to be confronted by gangs of Rangers supporters looking for trouble.

Lifelong Villa supporter Peter Sutton takes up the story again, "I had three youngsters with me as well as my elderly father and as I said we were standing on the Witton End terrace. At the end of the game we tried to exit onto Witton Lane but discovered right away that the Rangers supporters had spilled out of the Holte End and were massed at the top of the road and were obviously bent on trouble. My car was parked down by the Serpentine and we would have to pass through the Rangers supporters to reach it.

Goal!

It was clearly impossible for an elderly man and three young children to run the gauntlet of the Rangers fans to get back to the car so we agreed that they would wait at the back of the Witton End and I would go and collect the car and bring it back to pick them up."

My daughter recalls sheltering from missiles in the doorway of a house while they waited. So I left my Villa scarf with them and ran back up the road. I remember being more frightened than at any other time in my life but managed to make it to my car and get back as planned to pick up my father and the children. Most of the Rangers fans were pretty drunk and disorganised and that is probably what made it possible for me to reach my car unharmed."

That evening there was a massive police presence on the streets of Birmingham however with all the pubs and clubs either closed or appearing closed there was little trouble.

The Rangers' supporters who had been arrested, which numbered over 50, were kept in the cells until Monday when they faced the wrath of some "get tough" magistrates. According to the Evening Mail seven received custodial sentences and the magistrates, "levied fines totalling well over £1,000." The violent behaviour of the Rangers fans was controversial and widely criticised in the press but Aston Villa were exonerated. Ron Saunders was appalled by the violence commenting at the time, "I hope this is the last time that any of us will be involved in anything as distasteful as what occurred. Unfortunately the match will be remembered by the majority of people for the wrong reasons because in terms of football some good stuff was played by both sides."

Let referee Derek Civil have the final word on this sorry matter, "Villa did everything asked of them to ensure there would be no scenes and no one at the club was to blame"

1978   YUGOSLAVIA

The 1977-78 season was the first time that Villa made serious inroads into a European competition as their previous attempt in 1975 ended in humiliation at the hands of Antwerp. Aston Villa qualified for the UEFA cup this time through their efforts during the previous season and managed to reach the quarter final where they were unlucky to lose to Barcelona. In the league after many months marooned in mid table they finished the season off in style ending the campaign in a creditable eighth position.

To start the new season and help the players attain match fitness the club organised a pre-season tour of the former Yugoslavia. Most of the players were looking forward to the trip, sadly the tour got off to a bad start when the party experienced what they thought was an insignificant twenty minute hold-up at Birmingham's Elmdon airport. Unfortunately on landing in Dusseldorf, thereby completing the first leg of their journey, they noticed the Lufthansa jet that should have flown them to Yugoslavia, taking off! This brought about a hastily arranged, unscheduled overnight stay in the German city. The next morning at the crack of dawn the players and officials made their way back to the local airport and caught a flight to Yugoslavia. The journey was trouble free but regrettably when the airliner touched down in Split the players had less than twenty four hours to prepare for their first game of the tour.

Villa players sick of coaches

August 1st   Hajduk Split 4   Aston Villa 0

The next day the players and officials made their way to Hajduk Split's stadium, which Steve Stride described as being very old fashioned with, "tall, upright stands that were very close to the pitch." The Villa players on the back of a gruelling journey, soon realised that they were not properly acclimatised to the local conditions. In addition they recognised just from the warm up that the Hajduk side were three weeks further on in terms of their pre-season fitness than the Villa. The omens were not looking good.

Given their limited preparation it was no wonder that as early as the third minute the inevitable happened and the home team took the lead. As the first half progressed the visitors were given a lesson in the "passing game" and found themselves chasing shadows for much of that time. Brian Little commented, "I remember this team being the best footballing side I had ever played against. I honestly thought they were incredible! They were athletic and magically talented." With Hajduik continually pressing and the visitors making little impact it was remarkable that Villa hung on until half time with just a one goal deficit.

Following a roasting from Ron Saunders during the interval the tourists upped their game and matched the hosts until the 82nd minute when the local referee penalised a Villa defender for a heavy tackle and awarded Hajduk a penalty. The visitors protested vehemently but the official refused to change his mind and Suzac hammered home a thunderous shot from the spot to put the home side two goals to the good. Contemporary newspaper reports suggested that the Villa players' heads visibly dropped at this point and were quickly punished for it with two more well taken goals in as many minutes giving the Hajduk side a somewhat flattering 4-0 victory.

Villa's manager Ron Saunders commented after the game, "The score line presented a misleading picture of our performance which had been reasonable considering the lads were tired after a long journey and playing in hot, humid conditions." He went on, "The Hadjuk manager apologised to me after the game because of the referee's decision over the penalty and their third goal which looked offside."

The sparsely covered Kantrida Stadium of NK Rijeka.

It was a very tired group of players that made their way back to the hotel but there was no time for partying because early the next morning they faced a long coach journey to the beautiful Adriatic resort of Rijeka.

Brian Little recalled the journey clearly, "There was beautiful scenery but all we seemed to do was go round and round hairpin bends and up and down mountains. The journey took forever and there was no air conditioning on the coach it was awful." Steve Stride added, "It was so hot on that coach. I remember one of the players shouting 'Stop the coach' and ten of us piled out and were all sick by the side of the road." The party eventually arrived at their hotel in Rijeka and had a three day stay relaxing in 90 degrees Fahrenheit which must have seemed like heaven after what they had endured since leaving Birmingham.

According to Brian Little, Ron Saunders being "quite a disciplinarian" didn't allow the players do very much. It was so hot that he stopped them from lying in the sun because he believed it would tire them out therefore they were confined to their rooms for much of the daytime. Unfortunately the rooms did not have air conditioning so some of the players disobeyed Ron's instructions and went onto the cliffs and had a great time diving and swimming in the sea. If Ron knew about this, and he probably did, he chose to ignore it and the players thoroughly enjoyed their stay.

August 5th Rijeka 2 Aston Villa 0

The second game of the tour was against NK Rijeka another First Division team who had won the domestic cup for the first time, a few months earlier. Their ground, the Stadion Kantrida was very picturesque and quite unusual in that it was cut out of the side of the cliffs overlooking the Adriatic. Brian Little remembered the ground vividly, "It was in a beautiful setting. The ground was cut out of the rocks. The sea was on one side of the ground and tall cliffs on the opposite side." Leighton Phillips talking on his return observed, "As the tour drew on you could sense the lads were beginning to touch their true form and this showed itself in the game against Rijeka where although we lost 2-0 to well taken goals by Hristic after 18 minutes and Tomic ten minutes later, it was certainly not a true reflection of the game."

The next day was the final match of the tour and the Villa boys faced another two hour coach journey over the mountains to Slovenia where NK Olimpija Ljubljana were awaiting them. The bus was due to leave the hotel at three in the afternoon so the players had quite a few hours to kill. During the early afternoon they were supposed to be relaxing in their rooms but then players being players on tour soon got restless. Two of them, who must remain nameless, were rooming above a young Yugoslavian couple who were obviously on holiday or more likely, honeymoon.

The woman was very attractive and the players were watching her sunbathe on the balcony below. Getting restless and looking for some fun one of them apparently decided to pour the contents of his water bottle onto the scantily clad young lady. There was a bit of an argument and the players disappeared assuming that would be an end to it. Unbeknown to those concerned the couple called the police.

On arrival the police parked their cars across the entrance of the hotel so that the coach, which was due to take the team on the two hour journey to Ljubljana, was blocked in. By this time it was 3.00pm and kick off was scheduled for 6.00pm. Ron Saunders was becoming quite tetchy and tried to negotiate with the police officers to move their cars. They steadfastly refused unless the player who had poured the water over the young woman was identified. Of course no one would own up so eventually one of Villa party emerged with some Villa shirts which they gave to police officers and with that, in the words of Steve Stride, "The police cleared off."

August 6th   Olimpija Ljubljana   3   Aston Villa   5

This had not been the best preparation for the match especially when you consider that they faced another arduous journey aboard a hot coach going up, down and around the mountains. As it happened the players arrived at the ground with about 45 minutes to spare and were relieved to get off the bus and into the cool of NK Olimpija's stadium in Ljubijana. Once in the dressing room Ron Saunders set about announcing the team which contained a number of changes due to illness and injuries.

According to reports from the time the new-look side blended immediately and after five minutes "Dixie" Deehan headed Villa in front following an inch perfect cross from Gary Shelton. The former Walsall youngster was involved once more some five minutes later when he again crossed from the wing and this time Brian Little glanced the header into the far corner of the goal, giving the Olympia keeper no chance.

The visitors now in the ascendancy, were playing some attractive football having worked hard to gain the two goal lead. Alas, all their good work was undone in spectacular style when Olimpija striker Calasso hit a quick fire hat-trick, leaving Villa somewhat shell shocked as they went in for the half time break to face the wrath of manager Ron Saunders.

Aston Villa emerged for the second half in a very determined mood, no doubt with some choice words from Ron Saunders still ringing in their ears. Fortunately their positive attitude coupled with relentless pressure on the hosts' goal eventually paid off when Ken McNaught powered a perfectly timed header past the outstretched arms of the Olimpija Ljubljana keeper. This goal inspired Villa's makeshift team and, despite some fine saves from the opposition's goalkeeper, late goals from Brian Little and John Gregory ensured that Aston Villa finished their pre-season tour on a high note.

1981 FRANCE & SPAIN

May 11th Nantes 4 Aston Villa 0   May 18th Real Valladolid 4 Aston Villa 4

The League Champions celebrate before the tour.

Ron Saunders and the boys fresh from winning the League Champ-ionship for the first time in seventy years embarked on an end of season tour taking in games against French side Nantes and then moving on to Spain.

One story that a number of ex Villa players recall from this tour was the exploits of a somewhat "well-oiled" Gordon Cowans. The team were staying in a small hotel which they were sharing with the guests of a very up market wedding reception. According to Gordon Ron Saunders had given the players the afternoon off to investigate the local area, and probably get them out of the hotel whilst the wedding reception was taking place. The players were also told by the manager that they must be back at the hotel by 7.00pm in time for their evening meal. Sid continued, "Tony Morley, David Geddis and myself went into the town and had a few beers. David only had a couple of alcoholic drinks but Tony and me were on the beer all afternoon."

Realising that it was almost 7.00 p.m. the three of them rushed back to the hotel and just about made dinner on time. Gordon followed his two mates into the restaurant and to his horror realised that all the seats had been taken except one and that was next to "the boss" Ron Saunders and so, a somewhat inebriated Sid, had no choice but join his manager for dinner. Gordon commented, "I started to have a little chat with the boss but he soon realised that I was drunk!" Amazingly Gordon managed to finish his evening meal without any mishaps and took the sensible option of retiring to his bed. After a while some of his team mates, who had been drinking in the hotel bar, went upstairs, began banging on Gordon's door and calling him a "light weight" in an attempt to get him to join them for a drink.

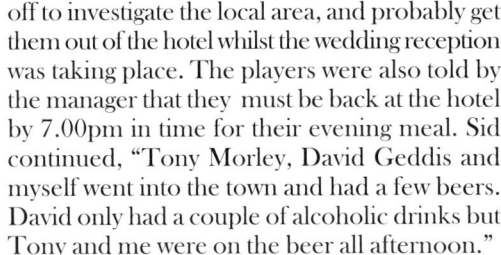
Sid Cowans "Destroys" the Wedding!

Sid told them in no uncertain terms to go away which much to his surprise, they did. Gordon recounts the story, "After a while I decided to join them as I didn't want to let them down. So I got up, got dressed and stumbled along the corridor to the top of the stairs."

Meanwhile downstairs, according to Colin Gibson, the wedding was in full swing. It was a grand military affair with all the men in uniform and the women in expensive evening dresses. At the foot of the stairs Gibbo remembers there being a large table with a wedding cake, around fifty full Champagne glasses along with an enormous bowl of punch and numerous unopened bottles.

At the top of the landing Sid began his descent of the stairs, somewhat gingerly, with both hands on one of the bannisters. He was doing okay, carefully taking one step at a time, until about halfway down when he lost his footing. At this point he tripped and tumbled to the bottom of the staircase, fell into the afore mentioned table and tipped it over. The wedding cake, bottles, glasses, punch and Champagne went everywhere and Gordon was left lying face down in the middle of a disaster area! He eventually rose to his feet apologised to the disbelieving guests who had gathered round and crawled back to bed.

According to Colin Gibson, "Gordon still tries to play the whole thing down to this day claiming that he didn't think that he upset the wedding. He is partially right he didn't upset the wedding he destroyed it!" Gordon's last words on the subject were, "I took a lot of flak from the lads for quite a while after that!"

1982 GERMANY

Having finished the 1981-82 season as Champions of Europe manager Tony Barton was eagerly anticipating the new season and in preparation Aston Villa were off to West Germany for a three match, pre-season tour. In hindsight however, having beaten the German giants Bayern Munich in the European Cup Final a couple of months earlier, this may not have been the most sensible way to prepare for the coming season. Colin Gibson, "Of all the craziest things to do was to go to Germany after beating Bayen Munich in the final. We got absolutely battered." Sid Cowans shed further light on the players view adding, "We were early in our preparation and they were at least three or four weeks ahead of us – which didn't help."

It seems from conversations with other people who were around at the time that the decision to embark on the tour in the first place was made at board level, chaired by Ronald Bendall and perhaps driven by the potential income Villa would receive from such a trip. One could easily imagine that German teams would be queuing up to take on the European Champions on their home soil and pay good money in the hope of gaining some revenge for Villa's victory over FC Bayern Munich earlier that year.

The Villa party had a trouble free flight to West Germany, made their base in a luxury hotel near Dusseldorf and travelled to and from each match by coach. The first game of the tour was against a very strong 1FC Kaiserslautern team who had reached the semi-final of the UEFA Cup the previous season. Tony Barton was quoted at the time thus, "Our credibility is at stake." He went on to point out that he wouldn't be taking any risks in the game and that he would be fielding his strongest team. He also declared that they were aiming to prove that the Villa were still the best in Europe and had a message for his players by declaring that no one's place in the team was safe. Stirring stuff then from Tony as his team boarded the coach for the two hour trip to Kaiserslautern.

August 10th
1FC Kaiserslautern 5 Aston Villa 1

As Robbie Burns once said, "The best-laid plans of mice and men go oft awry" and his quote certainly applied to this first game of the tour. The whole escapade got off to the worst possible start when the 137 mile journey to Kaiserslautern took over four hours to complete. This protracted trip, due to road works and traffic jams resulted in them arriving with just twenty five minutes to spare before the scheduled kick-off. Next, when they alighted from their air conditioned coach the party were struck by the intense 90 degrees heat that greeted them. Add to this Sid Cowan's comments about how far behind they were in terms of their fitness and the fact that the exceptionally talented West German international Hans-Peter Briegel was fit and able to play for the opposition, the omens were not looking too good.

The Villa team that began the game was the same that started the European Cup Final just a few months earlier i.e., Rimmer; Swain, Williams, Evans, McNaught; Bremner, Mortimer, Cowans, Morley; Shaw, Withe. Amongst those on the bench were Colin Gibson, Nigel Spink, Mark Walters, David Geddis and Andy Blair. Villa kicked off but were soon in trouble, quickly falling two goals behind courtesy of striker Thomas Allofs and future 1.FC Kaiserslautern manager Reiner Geye. The visitors eventually settled down and started to play some decent football however the stifling heat was making life difficult for the visitors. Colin Gibson remembers, "Our players kept running over to the touchline and dipping their heads in buckets of cold water." It was not surprising then that on the half hour the multi-talented Peter Briegel hit Kaiserslautern's third. According to contemporary reports the Villa were beginning to look more than a little jaded but just before the interval and it has to be said, against the run of play, they pulled one back through Peter Withe.

Doris Davenport takes a blow!

The squad who went on the tour.

The heat had not abated in the second half and the European Champions did well to limit the local side to just two more goals; this time from Dieter Kitzmann and another from Hans-Peter Briegel who was having a field day. So Villa opened their tour with an unconvincing performance resulting in a 5-1 defeat. At the post-match press conference Assistant Manager Roy MacLaren tried to put a positive spin on the outcome by suggesting that the Villa were in Germany for important pre-season work and that the game was just the first of their build up to the new season. He went on, "It's not the end of the world. We can use the match to our advantage, sorting out the problems we faced."

On the coach back to Dusseldorf Peter Withe decided to organise a collection which he claimed was for the coach driver. According to Gordon Cowans, "It turned out that the improvised whip-round wasn't for the driver at all.... the money was used to buy an inflatable doll!" Once purchased the fun began, christened Doris Davenport after the clubs sponsors at that time, the doll became the team's tour mascot, took up prime position at the front of the coach and travelled everywhere with them.

The fun with Doris began slowly when some of the players found a negligee and dressed Doris up in it. That evening, whilst most of the Villa party were in the bar, they made their way to the late Jim Paul's bedroom, Villa's kit man at that time, and placed the inflatable doll provocatively on his bed.

The players retired to the bar and waited for Jim to go to bed and then followed him up to his room and watched him through the crack in the door. Much to their dismay he just took "Doris" out of the bed, threw the doll on the floor, got into bed and promptly fell asleep. This was not quite what the players had hoped for so it was back to the drawing board for these unnamed players!

August 13th

SV Werder Bremen 2
AstonVilla 0

The next game was scheduled for Friday 13th August against SV Werder Bremen a newly promoted side who were destined to be runners up in the Bundesliga that season. Bremen was over 150 miles from the Villa team's base but this time they left early to make sure they arrived in good time.

The Villa again put out a strong team, played well in the first half and went in at the break with the scores level at 0-0. The second half was dominated by some bizarre refereeing decisions which culminated in Gordon Cowans being incorrectly sent off. Apparently it was a case of mistaken identity and Sid, supported by his team mates, refused to leave the field as he was at least twenty yards away from the incident when it occurred. The actual perpetrator of this very nasty flare up, substitute Gary Williams who had replaced the injured Alan Evans, was eventually identified by the linesman and given his marching orders.

Although the Villa were down to ten men their positive attacking play convinced the manager that they were very unlucky not to score on a number of occasions, "We played well. In fact it was an excellent performance. We created four very good chances but we didn't put them away. Even when we were down to ten men I was sure we would win but our legs tired towards the end and we gave away two soft goals."

August 16th
FC Shalke 04 4   Aston Villa 2

The lads spent the next few days chilling by the pool or shopping in Dusseldorf until their final game of the tour came round on the Monday evening. This game entailed a short trip to Gelsenkirchen where FC Shalke 04 and a 4-2 defeat awaited them. Villa were angry at three of Shalke's goals not being ruled out for offside. "It sounds like sour grapes but they were dubious goals that took away the shine from a much improved performance" said manager Tony Barton. Still Villa did at least get on the score sheet through a Mark Walters' volley and powerful headed goal from Peter Withe.

On their return to base Doris Davenport made her second appearance away from the bus. This time according to Gordon Cowans, who was rooming with Colin Gibson, two players who must remain nameless decided to take the joke a little further. This time they dressed the inflatable doll in a Villa shirt with the number 12 on the back and a black wig. They then wrote Colin Gibson's wife's name on Doris' forehead with a thick black felt tip marker. In addition they had raided Gibbo's jewellery and put some of his gold chains around Doris' neck and other parts of her anatomy.

Eventually, in the early hours of the morning, Colin and Sid made their way to bed. When Colin went into their room he was confronted by the inflatable Doris Davenport hanging from the ceiling in all her glory and according to Gordon, Colin was very angry and said, "What the (expletive deleted) is going on here then?" Sid continued, "He looked at the doll closer, saw his wife's name on it but what really got him angry was the substitute's number twelve on the back of the shirt. This upset him most because he had been sub in the European Cup Final and never got on!" Sid continued the story, "Anyway Gibbo got hold of a pair of scissors and stabbed Doris all over! I was killing myself with laughter I thought it was so ridiculous but he kept slashing away and swearing...." Colin takes up the story "....I took the doll into the foyer and threw it out of the window unfortunately it stuck in a pine tree for everyone to see and that's where it still is as far as I know..." Sid added, "....by this time all the lads had gathered around and were in bits with laughter! And Colin even saw the funny side of it eventually."

The trip back to the UK was without incident and the tour as a whole is still remembered fondly by former players. Tony Barton summed it up at the time by concentrating on the positives, "We came out here to get our sharpness and our fitness back and that's exactly what we have been able to do."

1983 SPAIN

Aston Villa began the 1982-83 season as the newly crowned Champions of Europe and whilst they were unable to retain their hold on the trophy, they made a sterling effort finally bowing out to a multi-talented Juventus side in the quarter finals. Unfortunately Villa fell at the first hurdle in their League Cup campaign however they had better luck in the FA Cup progressing to the 6th Round where they were beaten by Arsenal at Highbury. They also lost in the World Club Championship to Penerol in Japan but did much better against a strong Barcelona team over two legs to secure the European Super Cup for the first time in their history. Predictably, with all the cup distractions, Villa's league form was somewhat erratic however they still managed to finished a creditable sixth in the First Division.

In August 1983 following a couple of pre-season friendlies Villa took part in a prestigious Spanish football tournament organised by the Real Zaragoza club. This annual competition or to give it its correct title, "The Trofeo Ciudad de Zaragoza" began back in 1971. In addition to Real Zaragoza and Aston Villa, the 1983 tournament also included Club America from Mexico and the Rumanian outfit Politehnica Timi°oara. The tournament was organised on a knock out basis and all the games were played at the Estadio La Romareda, home of the host team. This meant that two semi-finals were planned for the Thursday and Friday with the play off for third place and the final reserved for the following day.

August 18th   Club America 2   Aston Villa 2
(Club America won 4-3 on penalties)

The first match was between Real Zaragoza and Politehnica Timi°oara and saw the home team cruise to a 4-1 victory. The next day Aston Villa took on the Mexican giants Club America who were about to enter their golden era. Hoping to get off to a positive start in the tournament Villa fielded a sound team which consisted of Spink; Williams, Gibson, Evans, McNaught; McMahon, Curbishly, Cowans; Withe, Walters, Shaw.

According to the Birmingham Mail, Aston Villa played some excellent football and seemed to be hitting top form just at the right time with the new season round the corner. It took however over half an hour for their dominance to be converted into a goal when Steve McMahon fired home. Unfortunately the boys in claret and blue were unable to take advantage of their superiority and just before the break Echaniz, the Argentinian defender, slotted home an equaliser very much against the run of play. The second half was more even but once Aston Villa took the lead through Allan Evans in the 51st minute it looked like there was only going to be one winner.

F.C. America however had different ideas and on the hour the Mexican league side broke away and their top scorer, Argentinian Norberto Outes, equalised against the run of play.

Both teams decided to go flat out for the winner and a great tussle ensued, however what happened next has been described by those who witnessed it as one of the most sickening tackles they had ever seen. Colin Gibson takes up the story, the game was going from end to end when "Gordon Cowans went in for a 50/50 ball with this guy (Andreus Manso) who went in hard over the top of the ball. He just went straight through Sid. When I saw Gordon fall you could see his leg was flopping and we knew he'd broken it." Sid Cowan's recalls the incident thus, "Gary Shaw laid the ball off to me and it was a bit short and I was sprinting towards the ball when their centre half came over the top of the ball with his studs up and hit me full on. As soon as he hit me I knew my leg was broken because the bottom of it was facing the wrong way!"

Sid Cowans breaks his leg and Paul Rideout breaks a record.

He continued, "So I was lying there in agony and there was a bit 'going on' between the players, when suddenly the guy who had 'done me' came up and smashed the ball against me whilst I was lying on the floor. All our lads were round me and there was a lot of pushing, shoving and swearing then the lad that 'done me' just walked away! I don't think he was even booked!" Sid continued somewhat ruefully, "I'd never pulled out of a tackle in my life but I wish I had avoided that one!" Eventually Sid was stretchered off, put into an ambulance and taken to the local hospital but more of that later.

Back to the game which, according to Colin Gibson, became a bit tetchy to say the least, "I remember Steve McMahon had just joined us and was looking forward to teaming up with Gordon. He made this tackle on the half way line. He went in so hard but it was a fair tackle he slid in, hit the ball against this guy's knee, the ball bounced off him and actually ended up in their goalkeeper's hands without bouncing!" Thankfully there were no further incidents and when the final whistle blew the scores were still level so the game went to a penalty shoot-out.

As one might imagine it was hardly surprising that the Villa players were not at their best mentally to concentrate on taking effective spot kicks. Gary Shaw started well enough by firing his shot home and he was followed by successful efforts from Allan Evans and Steve McMahon. The score then went to 4-3 in the Mexicans' favour when Alan Curbishley stepped up and unluckily hit the post with the goal keeper beaten. Nigel Spink made a great save next and gave Villa a real chance of getting back into the competition.

Unfortunately substitute Paul Rideout saw his decisive effort well saved at the foot of the post and Villa had lost the game.

At the end of the penalty shoot-out feelings were still running high amongst the Villa players and they tried to get into the opposition's dressing room. Thankfully some quick thinking from the Villa management team along with some of the senior players averted what could have turned into a very nasty situation.

Meanwhile back with Sid Cowans who was all alone at the local hospital because Villa's "physio" couldn't be with him as he was required to be at the game in case there were any more injuries. Interestingly it is worth pointing out that Steve Stride remembers accompanying Sid to the hospital however Gordon maintains that he had been lying on a hospital bed with no one else around, waiting for a doctor to see him, for over forty minutes. In Sid's own words, "A doctor eventually came running through the doors with a cigarette in his mouth and was trying to put his white coat on at the same time. He ran up to my bed finished putting his coat on but carried on smoking his cigarette. This was in a hospital!" The doctor began chatting to Sid who was clearly suffering and asked him in broken English, "Are you in pain – it was a terrible tackle" Sid replied, "I beg your pardon – were you at the game?" The doctor replied in the affirmative which meant that he had stayed at the match until the end knowing that Gordon was at the hospital with a broken leg, waiting for him!

Sid Cowans

According to Sid, the doctor began manipulating his leg in an attempt to slot the bones together but unfortunately this was not possible because Gordon's leg was shattered. He went on, "I was in absolute agony! I hadn't had any painkillers. He was pulling my leg all over the place and still had a cigarette in his mouth!" Gordon was eventually put into plaster, given some pain killing injections and told that he would be kept in the hospital overnight. That evening Tony Barton and the Villa physio visited him and Sid made it very clear to the pair that he wanted to go back to the hotel so that he could be with people he knew. After some persuasion by the Villa pair the hospital agreed that he could return to the hotel the next day and so Gordon had to spend just one night in hospital. When he made it back to his hotel room the next day he was once again alone because his team mates were back in the La Romareda stadium preparing for the 3rd/4th playoff game against FC Polytechnica Timisoara.

August 19th   Politechnica Timisoara   1   Aston Villa   1
(Aston Villa won 4-2 on penalties)

The Villa players were in a determined frame of mind for this game following the appalling injury to their pal Sid Cowans. The Villa team for the game saw a few changes from the previous day, one of which was the inclusion of Paul Rideout making his first full senior appearance in place of Peter Withe. Manager Tony Barton explained the reason for the change, "I wanted to have a good look at Paul in a full match." Alas, Tony wasn't given much time to assess Rideout's abilities because with the game just thirty two seconds old the new signing was sent off for deliberately kicking the Polytechnica goalkeeper! Surely this must have been one the shortest Villa full debuts on record.

Aston Villa played out a goalless first half which they spent predominantly on the back foot. The second half held no respite and in the 68th minute the inevitable transpired and Villa went one behind. Tony Barton immediately replaced a very tired Gary Shaw, who had been foraging alone upfront since Rideout's early dismissal, with Peter Withe and Villa immediately looked a different team.

Pushing forward constantly, their intense pressure was eventually rewarded when Withe scored an equaliser. Although Villa pressed hard for the winner they drew a blank and so once again Villa faced the dreaded penalty shoot-out. Thankfully Alan Evans, Steve McMahon, Brendan Ormsby and Dennis Mortimer were on target to win the match on penalties and take third place in the competition.

Meanwhile back at the hotel a very sober Gordon Cowans was eager to hear all about the game however it was a bunch of "well refreshed players" who piled into his room to give him chapter and verse. Sid recalled the situation clearly, "They had obviously had a few drinks and I was in bed. They brought a lot of beers with them and the more they drunk the more boisterous they got." Gordon continued, "They were jumping up and down all over the bed. Seriously, there was me with a broken leg and they were all bouncing around on and off the bed." Sid loved the fact they were all there with him but he summed it up thus, "I could have done without them using the bed as a trampoline - I was in agony!"

1985   THE BRADFORD DISASTER

On Saturday May 11th 1985 a crowd numbering just above the 11,000 mark gathered at Valley Parade, home of Bradford City, to see the local side's captain Peter Jackson presented with Third Division Championship trophy, prior to kick off in a league game against Lincoln City.

The match was good natured and without incident until about five minutes before the interval when a small fire was noticed in the old wooden main stand. The blaze spread rapidly and very soon the whole stand was going up in flames. As it increased in intensity the police had to struggle past supporters, who under-standably were rushing for the exits, to save those too stunned or weak to escape. One survivor spoke to the local newspaper at the time commenting on the horror that he witnessed. "It spread like a flash," said 46-year-old Bradford City fan Geoffrey Mitchell. "I've never seen anything like it. The smoke was choking. You could hardly breathe." He continued, "There was panic as fans stampeded to an exit which was padlocked. Two or three burly men put their weight against it and smashed the gate open. Otherwise I would not have been able to get out."

Fifty six fans lost their lives in the tragedy and of those fifty-four were Bradford supporters whilst the other two were Lincoln City fans. Hundreds more were injured in the disaster and had it not been for the courage of the police and some very brave supporters, the death toll may well have been much higher.

It was subsequently revealed that the probable cause of the blaze was due to a spectator disposing of his cigarette, or possibly a match, into a polystyrene cup. The receptacle then accidentally fell through a gap in the stand's wooden floor and ignited a pile of rubbish that had been accumulating underneath the old stand for many years.

In the aftermath of the tragedy many football clubs arranged charity games in aid of the Bradford Disaster Appeal and Villa "stepped up to the plate" a week after the Valley Parade fire with a the hastily arranged charity game against West Bromwich Albion on Friday 17 May 1985.

May 17th

Aston Villa   3   West Bromwich Albion   3

In terms of the football, this game is probably remembered by most of those in attendance for the exploits of one George Best. George had returned from a premature retirement, his last game for Manchester United had been eighteen months earlier, to guest for Aston Villa and hopefully boost the attendance figure. Best, as one might expect, stole the show. The Birmingham Mail's Mike Ward enthused, ".....the former Manchester United idol was almost untouchable." With George enjoying himself so much, Aston Villa were soon in front with a well worked goal that was finished off by clinically by Steve McMahon. The home side added another before the break when Allan Evans powered home an effort which was created by none other than the mercurial Best.

In the second half George continued to delight the crowd and gave the Albion defenders the run around for another twenty minutes attracting enthusiastic cheers every time he had the ball at his feet. The Albion players must have been glad to see the back of him when in the 65th minute he made way for the Frenchman Didier Six. George was applauded by the entire stadium all the way to the dugout.

This was the signal for the visitors to begin their fight back and following a series of attacks they were soon level. The first came from a firmly despatched penalty by Steve Mackenzie and was followed up with an equaliser from Tony Grealish. The excitement didn't end there and the Albion fans were in ecstasy when future Villan Gary Thompson gave them the lead with a firm header.

It was now the home side that needed to regroup and try to get something from the game. The clock was ticking down but with just four minutes remaining Villa's tiny left winger Didier Six rounded off an excellent move with an outstanding goal. As the Evening Mail reporter concluded, "It was a fitting climax to a match in which Villa, Albion and Best combined to help soothe the horrible memory of Bradford." It was estimated that the game raised in excess of £10,000 for the Disaster Fund.

The Bradford Disaster Appeal Match featuring George Best in a Villa shirt.

Allan Evans and George Best.

1986 SHREWSBURY

February 15th   Shrewsbury Town 0   Aston Villa 3

Appointed in the summer of 1984 the former Shrewsbury Town manager Graham Turner was half way through his second season in charge of the former European Champions and things were not going too well. Despite reaching the semi-final of the League Cup, Villa's position in the First Division was causing some concern and a relegation battle was looming on the horizon.

Due to the postponement of their league game against Newcastle United, Aston Villa found themselves with a free February Saturday afternoon. Graham Turner decided that the first team needed an outing prior to their Milk Cup Semi-Final first leg scheduled for the following Wednesday at Villa Park. Conveniently, not only were Villa's third string scheduled to play a Midland Intermediate League game on the afore mentioned date against his old club Shrewsbury Town, but also the Shrews' first team game at Hull had also become a victim of the weather. A swift call to his counterpart Chic Bates at Gay Meadow resulted in both managers using the fixture to give their first team players some Saturday action.

A meagre crowd of around 350 turned out on a cold winter's afternoon to watch the spectacle which essentially featured Villa's first choice eleven with the exception of Andy Gray and Paul Elliot who were rested. The first half was uneventful in terms of scoring opportunities however Simon Stainrod remembered getting a "a bang on the chest" and "coughing blood," following a clash with Shrewsbury's Steve Cross which resulted in the Villa man watching the rest of the game from the stands.

The second period saw Alan Evans emerge from the break with a heavily strapped right thigh resulting from a hard tackle in the first half. Unfortunately the strapping failed to help the injury and he was pulled out of the action after just three minutes.

> *How a third team league game become a first team friendly.*

Following Alan's withdrawal a goal was scored that settled a game that the Sports Argus described as being "pretty dour" and played on "bone hard heavily sanded ground". Mark Walters, who had been the star of the show lost his marker on the edge of the penalty area and sent in a quality cross which Paul Kerr headed clinically past Malcolm in the Shrewsbury Town goal.

Villa took control from that point and seemed to be cruising towards a 1-0 victory against their less illustrious Shropshire neighbours when, two minutes before the final whistle, Kevin Poole in the Villa goal pulled off the save of the game. The ball was whipped into the box from the left with pace and Steve Cross timed his header perfectly and seemed certain to end up in the back of the Villa net but Poole in the visitors' goal saved instinctively from point blank range. The Villa managed to see out the remaining few minutes of the game and duly collected two points for the Midland Intermediate League side in what, to all intents and purpose, was a friendly!

```
       SHREWSBURY   TOWN   FOOTBALL   CLUB
          MIDLAND   INTERMEDIATE   LEAGUE
       SHREWSBURY TOWN   v.   ASTON VILLA
    Saturday, 15th February, 1986.  K.O. 10.45 a.m.
    ---------------------------------------------
    SHREWSBURY TOWN                ASTON VILLA
    Gold and Blue                  Claret and White

    PAUL MALCOLM         1.        KEVIN POOLE
    WAYNE WILLIAMS       2.        DAVID NORTON
    PAUL JOHNSON         3.        ANTHONY DORIGO
    BERNARD McNALLY      4.        ALAN EVANS
    RICHARD GREEN        5.        BRENDAN ORMSBY
    COLIN GRIFFIN        6.        DEAN GLOVER
    TIM STEELE           7.        PAUL BIRCH
    MARK KELLY           8.        PAUL KERR
    GARY STEVENS         9.        SIMON STAINROD
    STEVE CROSS         10.        STEVEN HODGE
    GERRY DALY          11.        MARK WALTERS
    JONATHAN NARBETT    12.        DARREN BRADLEY

                        REFEREE
              MR. M. A. LOVERIDGE, Shrewsbury
                        LINESMEN
             Red Flag - MR. N. W. PRYCE
             Yellow Flag - MR. K. G. SHINGLER

              NEXT MATCHES AT THE GAY MEADOW
    Saturday, 22nd February. Midland Intermediate Leag
                      CHESTERFIELD. Kick off 10.45 a.m.
    Saturday, 1st March. Div.II. CARLISLE UNITED
                      Kick off 3 p.m.

    Price: 2p
```

1989 TRINIDAD AND TOBAGO

The 1988-89 season was Villa's first back in the top flight of English football having gained promotion at the first time of asking under future England team manager Graham Taylor. The season thus far had been a little disappointing and having made no headway in the cup competitions they were finding the going back in Division One pretty tough as well. In fact by the end of February, following a disastrous slump in form, they were just three points clear of the relegation zone. With a free Saturday scheduled for 4th March, due their early FA Cup exit at the hands of Wimbledon, Aston Villa took advantage of an offer to play in the Caribbean against Trinidad and Tobago. The West Indian side were in the middle of their qualification games for the Italia '90 World Cup and needed some class opposition to help with their preparation.

According to Graham Taylor the Villa party flew out to Trinidad on the 4th March and he apparently used the tour to explain in no uncertain terms to the players about the mess they were in back home. According to the Birmingham Mail he read the riot act to them and made sure that they didn't view the break as a holiday by pushing them extremely hard in the 100 degree heat. Gordon Cowans explained, "There was no way you could go along for the ride under this manager. You had to pull your weight or you would soon be moving on."

March 5th   Trinidad & Tobago 0   Aston Villa 1

Villa's first game was against the islands' World Cup team in the national stadium. According to Dwight Yorke's official biography by Hunter Davies, the match "was a huge event" for the local population. Interestingly the Birmingham Mail reported that the ground, which had a capacity of over 30,000, was only a third full. Whatever the attendance, the Villa team braved the heat and did not fail to please an enthusiastic crowd with a polished performance, eventually running out 1-0 winners.

Following the game Villa's Steve Stride had the task of collecting the match fees for both games. "We were a bit uncertain as to whether we were going to get paid. Usually you received at least half of or the complete fee in full before you set off on tour but as this trip had been hastily arranged we agreed to collect it all after the game in Trinidad." He continued, "Anyway we played the game and the money still hadn't materialised!" The next morning everyone was due to fly to Tobago for the second game of the tour. Everyone that was, except Steve who had offered to stay behind in Tobago and try to locate the money.

He was eventually met by an official from the Trinidad and Tobago FA who took him to the bank where they settled up, much to Steve's surprise, in cash!

Steve's next task was to make his way to the local airport, with a bag full of money, where he hoped to make the short flight to join the Villa party in Tobago. When he eventually reached the airport he was not feeling very well, "When I saw the plane I certainly felt a bit queasy!" Apparently it was a four-seater light aircraft. Once he was on board he realised that there was only one other passenger who turned out to be none other than the infamous FIFA Executive Committee member and soon to be CONCACAF President, Jack Warner.

The plane took off and the flight was apparently a "bit bumpy" according to Steve however this didn't seem to worry Jack. "He sat there with a brown paper bag on his lap and when he opened it up and started to consume the contents, I realised that he was eating curried rabbit. I looked at it, started heaving and then I threw up in the plane!"

March 6th   Tobago XI 0   Aston Villa 5

Steve eventually made it to the packed Shaw Stadium where a crowd of over 4,000 supporters were becoming restless because the kick off had been delayed, at Villa's request, due of the heat. Dwight Yorke op cit, "It was a massive game for Tobago. We just didn't see these sorts of players in Tobago. In fact I don't think it had happened before - having a professional team playing in Tobago."

How Aston Villa discovered Dwight Yorke still appears to be a matter of conjecture. Contrary to popular belief Steve Stride maintains that on arrival at the Shaw Stadium the Villa management were already aware of Dwight Yorke. The locals had been telling some members of the Villa party that they had, "....this fantastic lad, a fantastic player – boy wonder" and it was just a matter of Graham checking him out. There are however other versions of how Dwight was spotted. Doug Ellis' version, which Steve claims to have heard him recount many times, was that Doug was apparently sitting next to Graham Taylor in the first half of the game and said, "I turned to Graham on the bench and said to him, 'Have you spotted their number eight? He looks a good player'..." and according to Steve, Doug claimed that Graham replied thus, "Oh thanks chairman. Yes you're quite right he is a good player."

Graham Taylor has a different recollection of the game. "I remember it was an open ground with no stands, it was a lovely sunny day and Doug had got a comfy chair – like a deck chair. He sat in this chair roundabout the halfway line where we were standing watching the game. Doug fell asleep, I would guess for most of the game."

An unknown West Indian youngster impresses the Villa management!

Graham Taylor inspects the pitch!

Graham went on, "In the first half this boy (Dwight Yorke) turned up and I thought goodness me! He lead our centre halves Steve Sims and I think it was Martin Keown, a merry dance" Graham continued, "At half time I decided to go into the Tobago dressing room and said to Doug, who had been asleep, 'I'm going to try and get that lad to play on our side in the second half and Doug asked why?" Graham remembers explaining to him that he wanted to see how he handled playing with professional players. Unfortunately the Tobago officials refused Graham's request pointing out that if Dwight scored for the Villa in the second half and still remained in Tobago after the game, life would be very difficult for him. Graham understood what they were talking about and said, "Okay that's fine."

Steve Stride recalls the events a little differently. "I can remember going to the game. It was a very small ground with just one stand and that was behind the goal. I sat next to Doug in that stand behind the goal and there were punters everywhere – it wasn't very VIP that's for sure. Anyway we watched the game and Dwight was great. I think Graham asked him if he could play for us in the second half."

When reading contemporary reports of the game, Aston Villa seemed to be a class above their opposition passing the ball sweetly whilst hammering in five goals without reply. Unfortunately there does not appear to be a record of the goal scorers. Meanwhile Graham Taylor's main concern was how to sign Dwight Yorke before anyone else spotted him and somehow the club managed it. The rest, as they say, is history!

1989 LINCOLNSHIRE

December 20th   Nettleham 1   Aston Villa 5
(Match abandoned after 65 minutes)

On a dark and dank Wednesday night in December, the day before the club's Christmas party, manager Graham Taylor took his first team to a village in rural Lincolnshire to play a friendly against a Standard League side. Their exact destination was Nettleham and the occasion was to celebrate the opening of their new flood-lights. Accord-ing to Graham Taylor the reason Villa agreed to the game so close to Christmas was "...nothing more than looking after a local club that I knew. It may be wrong and it was 'an old pal's act' but that does happen now and again."

A capacity crowd of around 1,000 welcomed the two teams onto the field and history was made when Aston Villa played their first ever game in the Lincolnshire village.

The quality of the Villa team was such that by half time they were perhaps somewhat predictably 4-0 in front. The home side reduced the deficit early in the second period but the visitors hit back on the hour. Following Villa's fifth goal the packed crowd was enjoying some exhibition football from the visitors when in 65th minute the entire ground was suddenly plunged into complete dark-ness. The players hung around on the pitch in the hope that the problem could be rect-ified but after twenty minutes of trying it was discovered that the fault was with the local Elect-ricity Board and so the game was abandoned!

Graham's final word on the affair was, "I did my best for my friends but they let me down!"

Lighting-up Time in Nettleham

1991 MALAYSIA

Following the appointment of Graham Taylor to the England manager's job, Aston Villa's chairman Doug Ellis raised a few eyebrows with the appointment of Josef Vengloš. Dr Jo, as he soon became known, had previously managed Czech side Slovan Bratislava where he had been relatively successful having won their domestic league on two occasions. Following this he had spells in charge of the Czechoslovakian national team and in 1990 took them to the quarter finals of the World Cup. His achievements in this tournament alerted the Villa chairman and Dr. Jo was subsequently installed as Graham's replacement, making him the first foreign manager to take charge of Aston Villa. Sadly "Doctor Jo" found life in the top flight of English football somewhat challenging and in this his first and only season in charge he contrived to turn the previous season's runners up into relegation candidates.

Farewell Dr. Joseph Venglos!

Prior to his successful period with the Czech national team, Jo had a period of time coaching in Malaysia where in 1991 he was still highly regarded and it was his connections in that part of the world which led to Villa undertaking an end of season tour to south-east Asia. According to former chief executive Steve Stride, Dr. Jo took responsibility for the organisation of the travel arrangements and utilised his connections with Czech Airlines to save the club money. This resulted in the Villa party taking a protracted route via Denmark, when there were plenty of direct flights to their far-east destination from the UK.

The flight to Copenhagen went without a hitch however once they had arrived it became apparent that they would have an eight hour wait for their connecting flight. The players had not expected this but undaunted Kent Nielsen took the bull by the horns and decided to show some of the players the delights of his home city. Gordon Cowan's takes up the story, "Kent, Paul McGrath, myself and a few others went along with Kent's suggestion and visited the famous Tivoli Gardens."

He continued, "We hadn't been there long before we got bored and asked Kent where the nearest pub was."

The group ended up in a city centre bar where they spent over six hours drinking and only realised in the nick of time that they needed to be back at the airport for their flight to the Far East. Taxis were ordered but when they arrived Paul McGrath steadfastly refused to leave the bar. Sid again, "I tried so hard to get him to come with me in a taxi to the airport but he was having none of it!" Paul wanted the two of them to stay for "one more drink" and Sid agreed as he thought this was the only way to get him to the airport in time. Unfortunately one drink lead to two and then another. Gordon continued, "Well I eventually got him out of the bar and we made it to the airport with only a few minutes to spare but to be honest neither of us were in the best of states when we arrived!" Waiting for them at the airport were Joseph Vengloš and Doug Ellis who were not amused. According to Sid, Jo said, "Come on boys! To be in this state is not professional. You are professional athletes and shouldn't be doing this." Gordon replied to the exasperated Dr. Jo, "Boss this is the way its always been!"

Thankfully for all concerned the Czech Airlines direct flight to Kuala Lumpur took off on time and the eleven hour journey passed without incident until they were due to land. The plane circled the airport for a while and then the cabin crew reported that there was a problem with the runway and they would have to divert to Singapore. When they eventually touched down an exhausted Villa party faced more difficulties. Steve Stride again, "Once we had landed we had to stay on the plane for what seemed like an age before they eventually ferried us off to a hotel for the night."

The next morning the players and officials realised that they had the luxury of a whole day in Singapore before flying back to Kuala Lumpur.

Steve remembered telling some of the players that he was going to see as much of the city as he could and asked if any of them wanted to go with him. He had no takers so he spent a fascinating day sight-seeing whilst the players remained in the hotel bar!

Sid Cowans takes up the story, "The flight from Singapore to Kuala Lumpur was scheduled to leave at seven o'clock the next morning but after sitting around and having a few drinks in our hotel some of us decided to have a night out in a city centre bar." Remarkably, given their previous exploits in Denmark, all the players made the early morning flight on time but most of them, in Gordon's words, "were a bit worse for wear and we had a game scheduled for the next day."

Venglos Farewell.

On touching down in Kuala Lumpur the exhausted players were ferried directly to their hotel where they behaved like model professionals and had an early night.

May 14th   Kuala Lumpur   1   Aston Villa   2

The following day the players and officials were taken by coach to the stadium where Dr. Josef Venglos gathered his boys together in the changing room to talk tactics and announce the team. Having gone through these formalities Stuart Gray observed that the manager had named twelve players in the starting line-up. With this Doctor Jo went through the names again and realised his mistake. Whilst he was deliberating as to who he should leave out Ian Ormonroyd rose to his feet and said, "Sod it gaffer – just leave me out!"

There does not seem to be a great deal of information available regarding the game itself and the only recollection Gordon Cowans has of it was the enormous moths that were everywhere, "I'm not joking they were the size of sparrows!"

What surprised him more was the fitness of the opposition and how good they were. David Platt opened the scoring but the home side were level at the interval. Sid again, "We weren't really up for the game. They were in better shape than us especially after our long flight and the drinking!" Villa played a good deal better in the second half and Gary Penrice nicked a winner just before the end.

The next day the team flew to Sarawak and experienced the luxury of a day's break before they played the local team. Housed in a first class hotel, close to the beach in a fabulous holiday resort the players relaxed by swimming and taking in the odd round of golf. Gordon Cowans enjoyed the stay commenting, "It was a really nice place and we were very well looked after."

May 16th

Sarawak 0   Aston Villa 4

The following day saw the tourists up against Sarawak, unfortunately accessible reports of the game are difficult to locate. Suffice to say that a hat-trick from David Platt along with a rare goal from full-back Gary Williams gave the visitors a 4-0 victory. The next day "Platty" flew back to the UK alone as he had been picked by Graham Taylor to play for his country against Russia at Wembley.

May 20th

Malaysian Select XI 0   Aston Villa 4

David Platt

For the remaining match Villa had to return to Kuala Lumpur where a strong Malaysian XI awaited them. Both Tony Cascarino and Paul McGrath seemed likely to miss out on the game due to them both having international commitments with the Republic of Ireland however Doctor Jo had a different view. His idea was for them both to play the first half of the game and then go by taxi to the airport at half time. Tony and Macca were against this suggestion but it made no difference and Jo got his way. However according to Steve Stride, Venglos didn't enjoy the game at all because "he spent the entire first half worrying about where the taxi was!"

Fortunately for the Irish lads the taxi did arrive on time and they reached the airport with time to spare. As far as the game was concerned Villa went on to win 4-0 with contributions from Gary Penrice and Tony Cascarino in the first half with Neil Cox and Gareth Williams doubling the lead in the second period.

On his return to the UK Doctor Jo had a brief conversation with Doug Ellis in which according to Doug's book "Deadly" Jo said, "I love it here and you have always been very good to me but if you feel, for the sake of the club, that you ought to appoint someone else, it will not be a problem." Farewell Doctor Joseph Venglos!

1994 SOUTH AFRICA

Given how close they had come to securing the league title the previous season, the 1994-95 campaign was somewhat disappointing as they only managed to finish in tenth position. Alongside their erratic league campaign Aston Villa's progress in the League Cup continued unabated. This culminated in a famous 3-1 Wembley victory over Manchester United to win the Coca Cola Cup under the guidance of their mercurial manager, Ron Atkinson.

With the season at a close the Aston Villa players and officials embarked on a short tour of South Africa. The party flew out from London's Heathrow Airport during the evening of Thursday 19th May with South African Airways bound for Johannesburg. Arriving at 7.30 a.m. the next day the players and officials were met by a reception party which included a large contingent of the South African branch of the Aston Villa supporters club. After exchanging niceties the Villa group moved on to their hotel, The Holiday Inn in Sanderton, where they held a well-attended press conference.

On Saturday 21st May the players made their way to the Ellis Park Stadium in Johannesburg for a training session prior to the showpiece game against Liverpool scheduled for the following day.

This was followed by a visit to the previously mentioned Aston Villa South African Supporters club where the Villa players and management received an enthusiastic welcome from an audience of over 200 "Villa mad" South Africans.

The fans forum consisted of just about everyone in the excited audience wanting to ask questions, shake the players' hands and obtain autographs. According to then club secretary Steve Stride, "These people were Villa fanatics....eighteen of them had made their way to England to watch the League Cup Final and quite a few more went to a number of other Villa games during the season."

Villa meet with Nelson Mandella

After the meeting Doug Ellis and director Dr. David Taggart decided to take in the game between Kaiser Chiefs and their bitter rivals Orlando Pirates. Steve takes up the story, "This was a big mistake! Half way through the second half the match was abandoned after a penalty decision lead to a crowd riot." In fact The Doc and Doug had a very frightening experience when they left the game in their car. Surrounded by mobs of hostile and angry supporters of both teams, they had to inch their vehicle though the ensuing confusion and scuffles for over half an hour before they could begin their journey back to the hotel. Thankfully they managed it and lived to tell the tale.

May 22nd   Aston Villa   1   Liverpool   2

The next day was a Sunday and also the day that Villa took on Liverpool in the impressive Ellis Park Stadium. There was a healthy crowd of around 30,000 inside the ground which included a surprising number of Liverpool and Aston Villa supporters who had made the long trip from the UK to support their teams. Villa had done the double over Liverpool the previous season and so it was a buoyant bunch of players that manager Ron Atkinson sent out to face the "Reds." The Villa team comprised of:- Bosnich, Barrett, Froggatt, Teale, Ehiogu, Cox, Fenton, Beinlich, Whittingham, Breitkreutz, Yorke.

Liverpool, who had been in South Africa a little longer than the Villa boys, settled the quicker and were extremely unlucky not to be ahead as early as the eighth minute, when Don Hutchison's lob hit the post with Mark Bosnich well beaten. Liverpool continued to pile on the pressure and so it was against the run of play when Aston Villa took the lead following a mistake by Liverpool goalkeeper and future Villan David James. The goal was set up by winger Stephen Froggatt who sent in a regulation cross which James missed completely and Neil Cox, who was lurking unmarked at the far post, confidently lobbed the ball into the net.

Liverpool responded positively, looked dangerous and only some sterling defensive work kept them at bay. The incessant pressure however eventually paid off for the reds and within ten minutes the scores were level. The versatile Scot, Dominic Matteo, collected the ball in midfield, evaded two tackles and then turned quickly to slip a pass through to the mercurial Robbie Fowler who carried the ball a few yards before coolly slotting it past the outstretched arms of the Villa keeper Mark Bosnich.

Following the goal the game ebbed and flowed with chances falling to both teams but there were no further goals before the interval.

The second half followed a similar pattern to the first with Liverpool very much on top and in the 57th minute their pressure paid off when injury plagued Michael Thomas raced through, latched onto a perfectly weighted ball and drove a fierce shot past Mark Bosnich and into the bottom right-hand corner of the net. Villa tried hard to fight back and inspired by Earl Barrett's surging runs had some decent late chances to level the scores. Unfortunately all this pressure came to nothing and Liverpool ran out winners by the odd goal in three.

Ron Atkinson, in the post-match interview, claimed that the altitude had left many of his players breathless during the match. Villa captain Sean Teale agreed commenting that most of the Villa team were, "….suffering from sore throats and lack of breath as the game wore on."

The tourists' next game necessitated an early morning flight to Durban before facing the now defunct local team Manning Rangers. Once in Durban the Villa party were transported by coach a few miles from the airport to a luxury hotel located in the lavish holiday village of Umhlanga Rocks.

Once the players and officials had checked into their rooms they attended a high profile press conference. Steve Stride explained, "There was a big media interest in the tour and this was shown by the large numbers of journalists, radio and TV people who came along."

May 24th   Manning Rangers 0   Aston Villa 1

On the day of the game the weather was extremely wet and although the match was not scheduled to kick off until 8.10pm there had been no respite in the rain and sadly the appalling conditions affected the attendance. Nevertheless Villa fielded a sturdy team for the game and lined up thus: - Bosnich, Barrett, Small, Teale, Ehiogu, Richardson, Cox, Yorke, Whittingham, Breitkreutz, Froggatt.

Probably as a result of the conditions the first half was a very scrappy affair as the away team took time to come to terms with the tight, on-the-ball control of the Manning Rangers' players. This skill was demonstrated time and time again by their clever midfield player Solo Ndimande whose contribution was an integral component of the home team's domination. Aston Villa were clearly on the back foot and defending doggedly, however it was they who had the better chances to take the lead. For example as early as the seventh minute Neil Cox was on the end of a Dwight Yorke cross but his shot was well smothered by the Rangers' goalkeeper Neil Blankenberg. Following this initial period of Villa domination the game panned out into an exciting end to end affair but amazingly there were no more clear-cut chances before the interval.

The Aston Villa players came out very positive in the second half, no doubt following a few choice words from manager Ron Atkinson and were soon in front through Guy Whittingham. The striker latched on to a weak back pass by a South African defender and swept the ball confidently past the stranded Manning Rangers goalkeeper. Following the goal both sides had good opportunities to score and Villa really should have increased their lead when efforts from Earl Barrett, Kevin Richardson, Guy Whittingham and Substitute David Farrell were all denied by the agile Blankenberg in the Manning Rangers' goal. For all their pressure it was the Villa players that breathed a collective sigh of relief when, a few minutes from time Zambian International Evans Sakala was denied an almost certain equaliser by Mark Bosnich who pulled off a quite remarkable save that ensured a Villa victory.

Ron Atkinson summed up the game at the time, "We would have liked to have scored more goals but you have to give them credit for stopping us. Their goalkeeper had a great game". The players had a lie in the following morning but once up they were off to help with a football development clinic arranged specially for local players. Apparently this went really well with over 100 youngsters taking part in the session. As Steve Stride said at the time, "This event was one of the big successes of the tour."

The next day the party were off once again on the early flight this time to Johannesburg, followed by a gruelling three hour coach journey to their luxurious base in Sun City. Once settled in many of the players and officials went on safari. Steve Stride was one of these and remembered that they were split into two groups and riding in jeeps they saw ".....zebras, giraffes and a rather daunting elephant among the various types of wildlife in the game park." Once back at the hotel the players relaxed with a barbecue which Steve reckoned was used more for warmth than eating purposes.

The day prior to the final match of the tour was used both as a training session and a promotional appearance by the players, on behalf of the sponsors of the trip. The next day however, Sunday 29th May still remains the highlight for those lucky enough to be there. This was the day when the players and officials met Nelson Mandela who was, at that time, the new president of South Africa. Steve Stride once again takes up the story. "I was so thrilled to meet him (Nelson Mandela). He shook my hand and said, 'It's an honour to meet you sir" Steve was gobsmacked and embarrassed by the humility of the great man.

May 29th   Moroka Swallows   0   Aston Villa   0

Officials arrive for the last match.

Over 60,000 spectators packed into the Ellis Park Stadium to watch the double header with Villa and Liverpool playing local opposition. The first match saw Aston Villa pitted against Soweto based Moroka Swallows. Ron Atkinson described the Aston Villa team for the last game of the tour as, "... a mix of experience and youth." And lined up thus:- Bosnich, Barrett, Small, Teale, Ehiogu, Richardson, Cox, Yorke, Whittingham, Froggatt, Beinlich.

Aston Villa seized control of the game from the outset and it was one way traffic for most of the first half. Dwight Yorke had a fantastic first twenty minutes where he ran the Swallows defence ragged and was only denied a number of goals by some great saves from the Swallows' keeper. Towards the end of the first half Neil Cox should have done better with a superb cross from Stephen Froggatt, unfortunately he failed to control the ball, had he done so he would have had just the goalkeeper to beat.

The second half carried on in much the same vein as the first with Froggatt running riot on the wing getting to the goal line and sending in numerous inviting crosses, all of which were squandered by the Villa strikers.

Perhaps frustrated by the lack of finishing Froggatt tried a different option. First he cut inside, then played a clever one-two with Guy Whittingham and scampered towards the South African's goal. Regrettably he made a complete hash of his shot which went well wide for a goal kick. It seemed as though it was not going to be Villa's day and then with just ten minutes left on the clock the visitors looked to have won the game with the goal they so richly deserved.

Substitute David Farrell sent in a perfect cross which Riccardo Scimeca failed to properly connect with, however the miscued header went back across goal and was met by Guy Whittingham who made no mistake this time and hammered the ball home. His celebrations were cut short sadly when he looked across and saw the linesman's flag raised for offside.

So Villa rounded off their South African tour with a goalless draw and even the second match of the day which the Aston Villa players and officials stayed on to watch between Kaiser Chiefs and Liverpool couldn't muster a goal between them to reward a packed Ellis Park Stadium. Once this game was over the Villa players and officials were transported by coach directly to the airport and an overnight flight home.

1999 NEW YORK

The Villa's 1998-99 campaign began with the sad but inevitable departure of Dwight Yorke to Manchester United and the addition of a couple of experienced imports in Paul Merson and Dion Dublin. These signings rejuvenated the side and Christmas saw Aston Villa sitting proudly at the top of the Premier League. Unfortunately due to a mixed second half to the season their challenge faded but Villa still ended the season in a creditable sixth position.

Villa's preparations for the 1999-2000 campaign saw them visit Stevenage Borough in a friendly before flying off to New York to take part in the four club Gotham Cup knock-out tournament. The competition, organised to raise the profile of "soccer" in the USA, included the Greek club Panathinaikos in addition to Villa, Fiorentina and Ajax. Initially it had been hoped that the Portuguese side Benfica would take part in the tournament as this would have increased interest in the competition amongst New York's large Hispanic community. Sadly for the organisers the Portuguese side pulled out in the March and were replaced by Aston Villa.

Even though this prestigious competition had been heavily advertised and had the backing of a local Major League Soccer team the MetroStars (now known as New York Red Bulls) the crowds were disappointing. Doug Ellis, Aston Villa's chairman at the time commented, "They suffer a bit because they try to 'Americanise' football. They won't just let a game come to an end without a decisive result. If it's a draw, they have to have a shoot-out. The MetroStars people told us that puts a lot of the minority audiences off, such as Italians and Brazilians because they obviously know what football's about; they don't need the Americans to repackage it."

Villa in the big apple!

July 23rd

Aston Villa 2   Ajax 2
(Villa won 3-2 on penalties)

The tournament got under way with the first semi-final which was played between Panathinaikos and Fiorentina and saw the Italians ease through to the final. Next up was the mouth-watering prospect of a game between Aston Villa and Ajax and the two clubs did not fail to please. The Villa team comprised of:- James; Delaney, Southgate, Ehiogu, Wright; Thompson, Taylor, Boateng, Barry; Joachim, Dublin.

According to contemporary reports Villa appeared nervous in the early stages of the game as the talented Ajax side plied their brand of "total football." Thankfully the Villans worked hard, came to terms with their opposition's style of play and began to show some excellent free flowing football themselves. It was therefore no surprise when, after thirteen minutes, Julian Joachim opened the scoring for the Villa with a classy effort. This was followed a quarter of hour later with the Birmingham team's second this time from the head of Dion Dublin.

Rather than settling the Villa team down this second goal seemed to spur the Dutch into action and just before half time they were back in the game following a well worked goal by Greek international Nikos Machlas. Former Chelsea striker Brian Laudrup, was sent clear with an accurate from Richard Witsshge but Laudrup's shot was superbly blocked by Villa keeper David James, only for the ball to fall at the feet of Machlas who tapped it in from close range.

The second half was a very exciting end to end affair that saw Ajax pushing for an equaliser and Villa responding with lightening breaks thanks to the blistering pace of Julian Joachim. According to the Evening Mail, George Boating was magnificent in the centre of midfield during this period, "displaying all the qualities that made him a £4.5million must buy for Gregory, matching grit with hard tackling and smart passing." Just as Villa were turning their thoughts to a final against Italian side Fiorentina, their defence unexpectedly cracked.

Ian Taylor who had run his heart out throughout the game was at last beaten by the tricky and illusive Brazilian, Wamberto de Jesus Sousa Campos (Wampie to the fans) who curled the ball from distance, around the hard working Taylor and into the top left hand corner of the net, giving David James no chance. Following the goal both teams appeared to settle for the draw and as expected the game went to a penalty shoot-out. First up for the "sudden death" was none other than Gareth Southgate who suffered another dose of Euro 96 misery when his shot was easily saved by Ajax goalkeeper Fred Grim. John Gregory's team however battled back in the tense contest which finished 3-2 to in their favour, thanks to Alan Wright's final effort wrong footing the otherwise excellent Ajax goalkeeper.

The next day saw the Villa boys enjoying a day off to take in the delights of New York City before they played Fiorentina in final of the competition that was scheduled for Sunday 25th July. At the press conference prior to the match skipper Gareth Southgate was unexpectedly asked about an ex-colleague who was about to join local New York team Metro Stars.

That player was none other than Sasa Curcicand and Gareth showed great maturity in his answer diplomatically pointing out that, "Curcicand is a very skilful player and I think he'll be a player who will excite the spectators. He's quite an off-the-wall character. I guess in time you will get to know some of his intricacies."

July 25th

Aston Villa 0   Fiorentina 4

Following a day's rest the Villa players were well prepared for their Gotham Cup final against the Italians. Included in the Fiorentina line-up was an Argentinian striker named Gabriel Batistuta who by the end of his career had scored over 50 goals for his country in just 78 games. John Gregory's boys were confident of a victory and the Villa side lined up thus:- James; Wright, Ehiogu, Southgate, Barry, Watson; Thompson, Taylor, Boateng; Dublin, Joachim, in a 5-3-2 formation designed to stifle the Italians' creativity.

Villa kicked off in 90 degree heat and found the going difficult. A number of their players struggled to get their breath in the stifling humidity and this undoubtedly affected their game. It was therefore clear to the majority of spectators in the ground that it would only be a matter of time before the English Premier League team fell a goal behind. Sure enough the inevitable happened when on twenty minutes the Italians took the lead through Pedrag Mijatovic. The excellent Rui Costa provided the assist and Mijativic clinically side-footed the ball into the bottom corner of the goal. John Gregory commented, "I felt sorry for David James because he was left exposed and that was all down to individual errors. Fiorentina hadn't had a shot on goal until Mijatovic put them ahead."

A sparse crowd watch as Fiorentina make it 2-0, from the penalty spot.

The Aston Villa team, prepared for a Gotham Cup match.

The Villa were not overwrought by the setback and soon had an opportunity to get back on equal terms. A foul in the area resulted in a penalty, unfortunately Dion Dublin's weak effort from the spot was easily saved by Francesco Toldo in the Fiorentina goal. A very curt Gregory commented later, "Dion's not our penalty taker anymore! I don't expect players to miss penalties and that was a bad miss!" The miss was to prove costly as the Gabriel Batistuta produced a Gotham Cup winning double strike either side of half time.

The first on 36 minutes came from the penalty spot after he was fouled by Gareth Southgate just inside the area. Batistuta made it a brace just three minutes into the second half with a goal described by the Evening Mail as a "superb finish" which was laid on by the former Villa transfer target Pedrag Mijatovic.

The rout was complete three minutes from time when Gregory's team once again showed their weakness against teams that broke quickly. Villa were in control on the edge of their opponents' penalty area and looking the more likely to score, when a loose pass from a Villa forward allowed Abel Balbo to regain control. In the blink of an eye he had slipped the ball to Rui Costa who in no time at all was bearing down on David James. The Villa goalkeeper spread his massive frame but Costa's shot was superbly placed and Aston Villa's miserable night in New York was over!

Vince Ellis of the Evening Mail summed up the competition very succinctly, "The standard of football was very good. If you were a neutral at the final to see Batistuta on fire would have been superb and Villa in their first game also played really well. So there was a lot to see."

Fixtures lists and results from the early days......

......*At this time in the pre-Football League days, of course, most matches were Friendlies, with just the occasional cup game or testimonial.*

FOOTBALL SUMMARY, 1877-8.

ASTON VILLA FOOTBALL CLUB.

FIRST TEAM.

Matches played, 17; won, 12; ties, 2; lost, 3; goals obtained, 71; goals lost, 17.

1877.
Oct. 6—Brownhills, Perry Barr; won by 8 goals.
 " 13—Wolverhampton (Stafford Road), Wolverhampton; lost by 2 goals.
 " 20—Coventry, Coventry; won, by 3 goals.
 " 27—Wednesbury Old Athletic, Perry Barr; tie, 3 goals each.
Nov. 3—St. George's (cup tie), Fentham Road; won, by 2 goals.
 " 10—Saltley College, Saltley; lost by 4 goals.
 " 17—West Bromwich, Perry Barr; tie, 1 goal each.
Dec. 1—Coventry, Perry Barr; won, by 8 goals.
 " 22—Saltley College (cup tie), Perry Barr; lost, 4 goals to 1.
 " 29—Burton (Allsopp's), Perry Barr; won, by 6 goals.
1878.
Jan. 19—West Bromwich, West Bromwich; won, 4 goals to none.
 " 26—Burton Robin Hood, Perry Barr; won, by 8 goals.
Feb. 16—Calthorpe, Perry Barr; won, 4 goals to 2.
 " 23—Burton (Allsopp's), Burton; won, 4 goals to 1.
Mar. 2—St. George's, Perry Barr; won, by 6 goals.
Apr. 22—Sheffield (Heeley), Perry Barr; won, by 4 goals.
 " 23—St. George's, Perry Barr; won, by 9 goals.

SECOND TEAM.

Matches played, 19; won, 12; tie, 1; drawn, 4; lost, 2; goals obtained, 29; goals lost, 8.

1877.
Oct. 13—Rushall Rovers, Perry Barr; won by 2 goals.
 " 20—Wolverhampton (Stafford Road), Perry Barr; tie, 1 goal each
 " 27—Wednesbury Old Athletic, Wednesbury; drawn.
Nov. 10—Harborne (first team), Harborne; won by 2 goals.
 " 17—West Bromwich, West Bromwich; drawn.
 " 24—Calthorpe, Perry Barr; won by 5 goals.
Dec. 1—Heathfield (first team), Handsworth; won by 3 goals.
 " 15—Ocker Hill (first team), Tipton; won by 1 goal.
 " 25—Westminster (first team), Perry Barr; won, 5 goals to 1.
 " 29—Harborne (first team), Harborne; won by 1 goal.
1878.
Jan. 12—West Bromwich, Perry Barr; drawn.
 " 19—West Bromwich, Perry Barr; lost 2 goals.
Mar. 2—St. George's, Fentham Road; won by 1 goal.
 " 9—Ocker Hill (first team), Perry Barr; won by 2 goals.
 " 23—Wolverhampton (Stafford Road), Wolverhampton; drawn.
 " 23—Oscott (first team), Perry Barr; won by 1 goal.
 " 30—Excelsior (first team), Perry Barr; won by 3 goals.
Apr. 6—Oscott (first team), Oscott ; lost by 4 goals.
May 4—Oscott Unity (first team), Perry Barr; won by 2 goals to 1.

Aston Villa 1887-8.

Date	Name of Club	Where Played			Name of Club	Where Played		lost
Sep. 3	London Caledonians	Lower Grounds			Stoke, B.C. repayed	Stoke	0	0
" 5	W. O. Athletic	Wednesbury	4	1	" 28 Mitchell's St. George's	Cape Hill	4	2
" 7	Burton Wanderers	Burton	7	1	" 30 Blackburn Olympic	Perry Barr	5	1
" 10	Long Eaton Rangers	Perry Barr	5	0	Feb. 4 Association Matches	"	7	0
" 17	Sheffield Wednesday	"	6	1	" 6 Notts Rangers	"	–	–
" 24	Welsh Druids	"	4	2	" 11 Derby County	"	7	1
" 26	Walsall Town	Walsall	4	3	" 13 Oxford University	Oxford	5	0
Oct. 1	London Caledonians	London	4	0	" 18 Glasgow Rangers	Perry Barr	3	0
" 8	Warwick County B.C.	County Ground	11	0	" 20 Long Eaton Rangers	Long Eaton	5	1
" 15	Old'y Town C'wells E.C.	Oldbury	4	0	" 25 Westbromwich Albion	Westbromwich	5	5
" 17	Small Heath Alliance	Perry Barr	3	0	" 25 W Bromwich Albion BC	Lower Grounds	1	4
" 22	Notts County	Nottingham	2	8	Mar. 3 Cambridge University	Cambridge	3	2
" 24	Halliwell	Perry Barr	2	0	" 7 Westbromwich Albion	Perry Barr	3	2
" 29	Lockwood Brothers	"	12	1	" 10 Blackburn Rovers	Blackburn	2	4
Nov. 5	S. Heath Alliance EC	Small Heath	4	0	" 17 Burnley	Burnley		
" 12	Aston Unity	Perry Barr	9	0	" 19 Everton	Everton	2	2
" 14	Blackburn Olympic	Blackburn	2	1	" 24 Corinthians	Perry Barr	2	1
" 19	W. O. Athletic B.C.	Perry Barr	5	0	" 31 Queen's Park	Perry Barr	5	2
" 21	Horncastle	Perry Barr	13	0	Apr. 2 Dumbarton Athletic	"	1	2
" 26	Oxford University	Perry Barr	7	0	" 7 Notts County	"	2	1
" 28	Stoke	Stoke	4	2	" 9 Walsall Town Swifts	"	3	3
Dec. 3	Derby County	Derby	3	0	" 14 Mitchells Charity Cup	Lower Grounds	0	0
" 5	Blackpool South Shore	Perry Barr	9	0	" 21 Blackburn Rovers	Perry Barr	6	2
" 10	Notts Rangers B.C.	"	4	1	" 23 Bl'kpool South Shore	Blackpool	2	0
" 17	Shankhouse E.C.	Newcastle-on-T.	9	0	" 28 Crewe Alexandria	Perry Barr	5	2
" 19	Cambridge University	Perry Barr	12	0	May 5 Glasgow Rangers	Glasgow	4	2
" 24	Battlefield	"	3	0	" 7 Ayr	Ayr	1	3
" 26	Mitchell's St. George's	"	7	2	" 12 Bolton Wanderers	Bolton		3
" 27	London Casuals	"	1	0	" 14 S. H. Alliance	Small Heath	3	4
1888					" 19 Preston North End	Perry Barr	4	1
*Jan. 7	Preston North End EC	"	1	3	" 21 Newton Heath	Manchester	4	1
			169	26	" 26 W. B. Albion	Perry Barr	–	1

* Declared "No Cup Tie" (A. V. disqualified).

In February 1898, Villa visited Tufnell Park, home of the famous amateur Casuals team from London, in this last match between the two.

Aston Villa versus Bohemian (in Dublin) - April 1905.

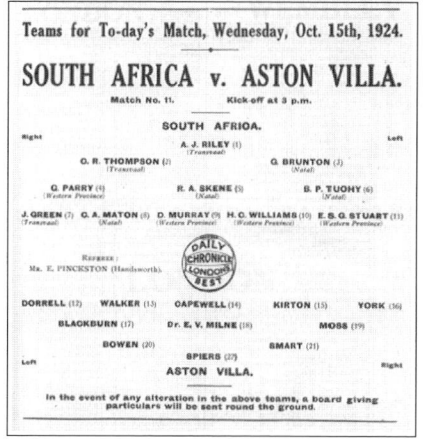

(Left) The first official team from South Africa came to Villa Park in 1924.

(Right) Presented to Harry Cooch during the Scandanavian tour of 1926.

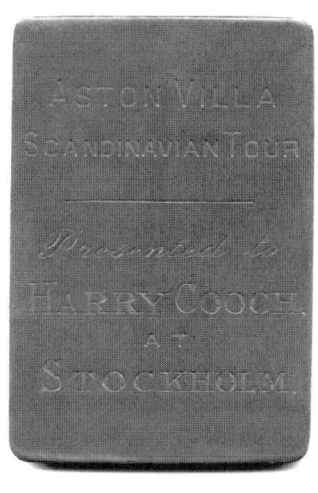

Action from a match in Norway, 1926.

*Kerr, Cobley and Maund take it easy on a river boat trip,
during the 1938 Germany tour.*

*(Above) Villa beat Ipswich Town (their debut sea-
the Football League in Third
Division South) 3-2.*

(Above, right) These amateurs from the west country were beaten 5-0.

(Below) The Aston Villa party await before boarding the ship for the Norway tour of 1946.

This match (an 8-0 victory) was the last at the end of the 1948/49 season tour.

This Friendly produced 11 goals, seven from from Villa.

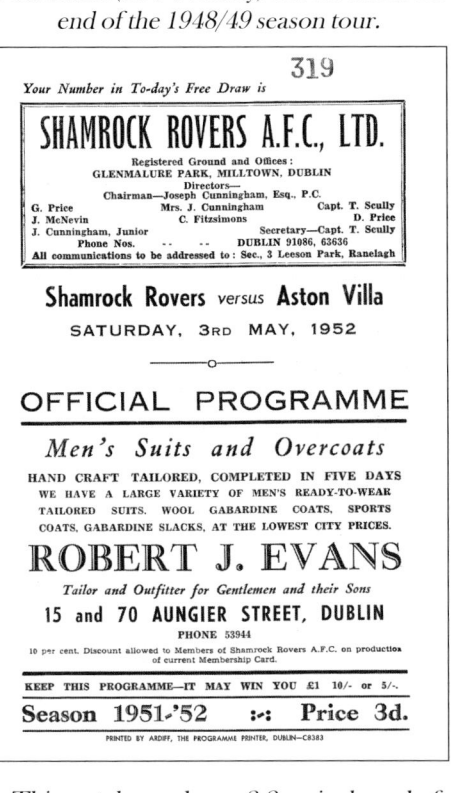

This match was drawn 2-2, a single end of 1951/52 season match in Ireland.

Players from the mid-1950s.

(Left) A close fought friendly that finished 4-3 in Villa's favour.
(Above) This pre-season match in Germany ended as a 1-0 defeat to Villa.

Relaxing whilst on tour in Milan in 1962:

(Left to right)

Burrows,

Sidebottom,

MacEwan,

Dougan,

Mercer (Manager)

Eric Woodward (Public Relations Officer) welcomes Pele to Villa Park for the 1972 Friendly match.

The July 1999 competition played in the USA.

Date		Opposition	Venue	Match Type	Result	Note
1874-1875						
Jan	9	Aston Park Unity	H	Friendly	?	*1*
Jan	?	Aston Park Unity	H	Friendly	0 - 9	
Mar	13	Aston Brook St Mary's	H	Friendly	1 - 0	*2*
1875-1876						
Dec	21	St. Georges	H	Friendly	1 - 0	
Jan	8	Wednesbury Old Athletic	H	Friendly	0 - 2	
?	?	Wednesbury Old Athletic	H	Friendly	3 - 3	
?	?	Grasshoppers	H	Friendly	5 - 1	
?	?	Tipton	N	Benefit - Wednesbury Town FC	0 - 1	
?	?	Hearts of Oak	H	Friendly	5 - 1	
?	?	Walsall Albion	H	Friendly	6 - 0	
?	?	Hockley Belmont	H	Friendly	4 - 0	
?	?	Stafford Road	A	Friendly	0 - 7	
?	?	Stafford Road	H	Friendly	0 - 1	
?	?	Stafford Road	H	Friendly	9 - 0	
?	?	Wednesbury Old Athletic	H	Friendly	0 - 3	
1876-1877						
Sep	30	Wednesbury Town	H	Friendly	1 - 0	
Oct	14	Stafford Road	A	Friendly	1 - 1	
Oct	21	Wednesbury Old Athletic	H	Friendly	0 - 1	
Nov	4	Saltley College	A	Friendly	0 - 5	
Nov	25	Burton (Allsop's)	H	Friendly	0 - 1	
Dec	2	Wednesbury Old Park	H	Friendly	2 - 0	*3*
Dec	9	Royal	N	Friendly	1 - 1	
Dec	16	West Bromwich	A	Friendly	0 - 1	
Dec	23	Calthorpe	H	Friendly	0 - 0	
Dec	26	Aston Park Unity	H	Friendly	0 - 0	
Dec	30	West Bromwich	H	Friendly	2 - 0	
Jan	6	Wednesbury Old Athletic	A	Friendly	1 - 1	
Jan	13	Coventry Royal	H	Friendly	4 - 0	
Jan	20	Wednesbury Old Park	A	Friendly	1 - 1	
Feb	3	Aston Park Unity	A	Friendly	2 - 2	
Feb	10	Stafford Road	H	Friendly	0 - 2	
Feb	17	Saltley College	H	Friendly	2 - 0	
Feb	24	Victoria Swifts (Walsall)	A	Friendly	1 - 0	
Mar	10	Tipton	A	Friendly	2 - 0	
Mar	17	St George's Athletic	H	Friendly	3 - 0	
Apr	2	Aston Park Unity	H	Friendly	2 - 0	
1877-1878						
Oct	6	Brownhills	H	Friendly	8 - 0	
Oct	13	Wolverhampton Stafford Road	A	Friendly	0 - 2	
Oct	20	Coventry Royal	A	Friendly	3 - 0	
Oct	27	Wednesbury Old Athletic	H	Friendly	3 - 3	
Nov	10	Saltley College	A	Friendly	0 - 4	
Nov	17	West Bromwich	H	Friendly	1 - 1	
Dec	1	Coventry Royal	H	Friendly	8 - 0	
Dec	29	Burton Allsopp's	H	Friendly	6 - 0	
Jan	19	West Bromwich	A	Friendly	4 - 0	
Jan	26	Burton Robin Hood	H	Friendly	8 - 0	
Feb	16	Calthorpe	H	Friendly	4 - 2	
Feb	23	Burton Allsopp's	A	Friendly	4 - 1	
Mar	2	St George's	H	Friendly	6 - 0	
Apr	22	Heeley FC	H	Friendly	4 - 0	
Apr	23	St George's Athletic	H	Friendly	9 - 0	
1878-1879						
Oct	12	Burton Robin Hood	A	Friendly	1 - 1	
Oct	19	Rushall Rovers	H	Friendly	4 - 0	
Oct	26	Shrewsbury Engineers	H	Friendly	6 - 2	
Nov	16	West Bromwich	H	Friendly	2 - 1	
Nov	23	The Birmingham Club	A	Friendly	2 - 1	*4*
Nov	30	Wednesbury Old Athletic	A	Friendly	2 - 3	
Dec	7	Nottingham Sneirton Wanderers	H	Friendly	3 - 0	
Jan	11	West Bromwich	A	Friendly	2 - 0	
Jan	20	Queens Park (2nd Team)	H	Friendly	1 - 2	
Jan	25	The Birmingham Club	H	Friendly	2 - 0	
Feb	1	St George's	A	Friendly	0 - 0	
Feb	8	Nottingham Sneirton Wanderers	A	Friendly	4 - 2	

Notes:

1 The game was played under Sheffield Association Association Football rules, with each team fielding fourteen players. A match report states a victory for Unity but gives no score.

2 The first half of this game was played under Rugby Football rules with fifteen players on each team. The second half was contested under Association rules with eleven players on each team.

3 This game was played at Calthorpe's ground

4 This match was played at Aston Lower Grounds

FRIENDLIES

TOURS

TESTIMONIALS

The Complete List

1878-1879 (Contd.)

Feb	15	Aston Unity	H	Friendly	2 - 0	
Feb	22	Arcadians	H	Friendly	8 - 0	
Mar	22	Stafford Road	A	Friendly	1 - 0	
Apr	5	Wednesbury Old Athletic	H	Friendly	3 - 0	
May	3	Stoke	A	Friendly	1 - 2	

1879-1880

Sep	27	Small Heath Alliance	A	Friendly	0 - 1	**5**
Oct	4	The Birmingham Club	H	Friendly	4 - 1	
Oct	11	Stoke	H	Friendly	4 - 1	
Oct	25	Nottingham Wanderers	H	Friendly	3 - 2	
Nov	1	Stafford Road	A	Friendly	4 - 1	
Nov	8	Stoke	A	Friendly	1 - 1	
Nov	15	Park Grove (Glasgow)	H	Friendly	4 - 2	
Dec	20	Walsall Town	A	Friendly	2 - 1	
Dec	26	St George's	H	Friendly	2 - 0	
Dec	27	Stoke	H	Friendly	2 - 2	
Jan	3	Aston Unity	H	Friendly	4 - 3	
Jan	10	Calthorpe	A	Friendly	3 - 1	
Apr	17	Sheffield Zulus	H	Friendly	3 - 1	
Apr	24	Elwells	A	Friendly	1 - 1	
May	29	Walsall Swifts	A	Benefit - Birchills Ironworks Explosion	1 - 2	

1880-1881

Aug	16	U/K (Definite Game)	U/K	Benefit - J.Wright Memorial Fund	?	
Sep	25	Small Heath Alliance	H	Benefit	?	
Oct	2	Nottingham Forest	H	Friendly	2 - 0	
Oct	9	Derby Town	H	Friendly	4 - 0	
Oct	16	Walsall Swifts	H	Friendly	4 - 0	
Oct	23	Stafford Road	A	Friendly	2 - 1	
Oct	30	St George's	H	Friendly	0 - 0	**6**
Nov	13	Nottingham Forest	A	Friendly	2 - 0	
Nov	27	Stafford Road	H	Friendly	4 - 1	
Dec	11	Wednesbury Strollers	H	Friendly	2 - 1	
Jan	1	Heart of Midlothian	H	Friendly	4 - 2	
Jan	8	Darwen	H	Friendly	4 - 0	
Jan	15	Stafford Road	H	Friendly	?	**7**
Jan	29	Blackburn Rovers	H	Friendly	4 - 3	
Mar	12	Nottingham Wanderers	A	Friendly	0 - 4	**8**
Apr	18	Blackburn Rovers	A	Friendly	0 - 3	

1881-1882

Aug	15	Small Heath Alliance	A	Benefit - Nechells Amateur Floral Society	?	
Sep	10	Heart of Midlothian	H	Friendly	5 - 0	
Sep	17	Oldbury	H	Friendly	1 - 1	
Sep	24	Wednesbury Old Athletic	H	Friendly	3 - 0	
Sep	29	Wednesbury Strollers	A	Friendly	2 - 3	**9**
Oct	1	Pollockshields	H	Friendly	6 - 1	
Oct	8	Walsall Swifts	H	Friendly	2 - 1	
Oct	15	Wednesbury Old Athletic	H	Friendly	3 - 3	
Oct	20	Queens Park	H	Friendly	0 - 4	
Oct	29	Saltley College	H	Friendly	2 - 1	
Nov	19	Darwin	A	Friendly	4 - 4	**10**
Nov	21	Blackburn Rovers	A	Friendly	2 - 7	
Nov	26	Wednesbury Old Athletic	A	Friendly	1 - 2	
Dec	3	Notts County	H	Friendly	2 - 2	
Jan	28	Wednesbury Strollers	H	Friendly	3 - 1	
Feb	4	Sheffield Town	H	Friendly	3 - 0	
Feb	11	Derby Town	A	Friendly	3 - 0	
Feb	18	Saltley College	H	Friendly	2 - 0	
Mar	4	Darwen	H	Friendly	2 - 2	
Mar	11	Blackburn Rovers	H	Friendly	1 - 4	
Mar	22	Deby Midland	A	Friendly	3 - 0	
Mar	25	Rangers	H	Friendly	3 - 2	
Apr	8	Heart of Midlothian	A	End of Season Tour (Scotland)	6 - 2	
Apr	10	Rangers	A	End of Season Tour (Scotland)	1 - 7	
May	13	The Grove	H	Friendly	2 - 2	
May	20	Stourbridge	H	Friendly	3 - 7	

5   Some sources suggest this game ended 1-0 in Villa's favour.

6   Aston Villa played Wednesbury Strollers in a cup tie on this day and so the Villa side that faced St Georges was probably somewhat weak-ened.

7   The Villa were also playing Fenton in the Senior Cup on this day and so the team that played against Stafford Road was probably somewhat weakened.

8   Aston Villa fielded a weakened team.

9   This game was abandoned with half an hour remaining due to poor weather conditions.

10   The result of this game is disputed. Darwin insisted that they had won the game 5-4.

1882-1883						
Aug	26	Sheffield Wednesday	H	Friendly	0 - 1	**11**
Sep	2	Walsall Swifts	A	Friendly	1 - 4	
Sep	14	Stafford Road	A	Benefit- Birchfield Harriers	8 - 0	
Sep	23	Darwen	H	Friendly	2 - 1	
Sep	30	Blackburn Rovers	H	Friendly	1 - 0	
Oct	7	Notts County	H	Friendly	1 - 2	
Oct	14	Sheffield Wednesday	H	Friendly	6 - 1	
Oct	26	Queens Park	H	Friendly	0 - 3	
Oct	28	Derby Midland	A	Friendly	2 - 3	
Nov	11	Darwin	H	Friendly	1 - 2	**12**
Nov	27	Blackburn Rovers	H	Friendly	2 - 3	**13**
Dec	16	Stoke	H	Friendly	5 - 1	
Dec	21	Cambridge University	H	Friendly	2 - 1	
Jan	1	Pollockshields Athletic	H	Friendly	4 - 2	
Jan	8	Notts County	A	Friendly	2 - 2	
Jan	20	Derby Midland	H	Friendly	4 - 0	
Feb	3	Blackburn Rovers	A	Friendly	4 - 3	
Feb	5	Darwin	A	Friendly	2 - 1	**14**
Feb	19	Oxford University	A	Friendly	0 - 1	
Mar	5	Oxford University	H	Friendly	1 - 1	
Mar	10	Wrexham	H	Friendly	6 - 0	
Mar	24	Rangers	A	Mid Season Tour (Scotland)	1 - 4	
Mar	26	Ayr United	A	Mid Season Tour (Scotland)	5 - 1	
Mar	31	Rangers	H	Friendly	2 - 1	
Apr	14	Stoke	A	Friendly	9 - 1	
Apr	23	Edinburgh University	H	Friendly	1 - 1	
Apr	28	Blackburn Olympic	H	Friendly	5 - 1	
May	14	Llangollen	A	Friendly	0 - 4	
May	21	Leek	H	Friendly	4 - 2	
1883-1884						
Sep	1	Walsall Swifts	H	Friendly - Benefit S. Law	4 - 0	
Sep	22	Blackburn Olympic	A	Friendly	0 - 2	
Oct	6	Sheffield Town	H	Friendly	14 -0	
Oct	13	Blackburn Olympic	H	Friendly	3 - 2	
Oct	20	Walsall Town	H	Friendly	4 - 0	
Oct	25	Queens Park	H	Friendly	0 - 1	
Oct	27	Wednesbury Old Athletic	H	Friendly	3 - 0	
Nov	3	Derby Midland	A	Friendly	1 - 4	
Nov	5	Notts County	H	Friendly	2 - 1	
Nov	17	Darwen	A	Mid Season Tour (Lancashire)	3 - 2	
Nov	19	Blackburn Rovers	A	Mid Season Tour (Lancashire)	1 - 0	
Nov	26	Oxford University	A	Friendly	1 - 2	
Dec	8	Small Heath Alliance	H	Friendly	4 - 0	
Dec	13	Dunbarton	A	Friendly	7 - 0	
Dec	15	Cambridge University	H	Benefit - Perry Barr Institute	3 - 3	
Dec	22	Walsall Swifts	H	Friendly	1 - 2	
Dec	31	Dunbarton	H	Friendly	1 - 0	
Jan	1	Spital	H	Friendly	3 - 1	
Feb	2	Oxford University	H	Friendly	2 - 1	
Feb	11	Edinburgh University	H	Friendly	7 - 0	
Feb	16	Derby Midland	H	Friendly	2 - 2	
Feb	23	Notts County	A	Friendly	0 - 2	
Feb	26	Sheffield	A	Friendly	3 - 0	
Mar	3	Blackburn Rovers	H	Friendly	1 - 2	
Mar	15	Darwen	H	Friendly	6 - 1	
Mar	24	Wednesbury Town	H	Friendly	1 - 4	
Mar	29	Nottingham Forest	A	Friendly	2 - 0	
Apr	7	Bolton Wanderers	H	Friendly	0 - 1	
Apr	12	Dunbarton	A	Friendly	1 - 5	
Apr	14	Bangor	A	End of Season Tour (Wales)	0 - 3	
Apr	15	Caernarvon	A	End of Season Tour (Wales)	1 - 4	
Apr	19	Walsall Town	H	Friendly	5 - 1	
May	3	Bolton Wanderers	A	Friendly	1 - 2	

11 Other accounts appear to suggest Villa won this match 6-1.

12 Villa fielded a weakened team because they also played a cup match on the same day.

13 This game was abandoned during the second half. Some sources suggest that the scores were 2-2 when heavy rain ended the game early.

14 There is some evidence to suggest that this game was won 5-2 by the Villa.

1884-1885

Aug	23	Walsall Swifts	A	Testimonial - W. Brandrick	0 - 1	
Aug	25	West Bromwich Albion	H	Benfit-Andy Hunter	3 - 2	
Sep	13	Stafford Road	A	Benefit - Archie Hunter	4 - 0	
Sep	20	Sheffield Wednesday	H	Friendly	2 - 3	
Sep	27	Castle Blues (Shrewsbury)	A	Friendly	1 - 1	**15**
Sep	27	Aston Unity	H	Friendly	3 - 4	
Oct	4	Bolton Wanderers	H	Friendly	1 - 2	
Oct	11	Northwich Victoria	H	Friendly	3 - 3	
Oct	18	Blackburn Olympic	H	Friendly	4 - 0	
Oct	25	Derby Midland	H	Friendly	1 - 1	
Nov	1	Blackburn Rovers	H	Friendly	2 - 1	
Nov	8	Queens Park	H	Friendly	2 - 1	
Nov	22	Bolton Wanderers	A	Friendly	1 - 4	
Nov	24	Blackburn Rovers	A	Friendly	4 - 5	
Nov	29	West Bromwich Albion	A	Friendly	4 - 2	
Dec	1	Oxford University	A	Friendly	1 - 1	
Dec	13	Cambridge University	H	Friendly	3 - 1	
Dec	26	Nottingham Forest	H	Friendly	2 - 0	
Dec	27	Blackburn Olympic	A	Friendly	1 - 5	
Dec	29	Northwich Victoria	A	Friendly	5 - 3	
Jan	1	Queens Park	A	Friendly	3 - 4	
Jan	5	Dunbarton	H	Friendly	1 - 1	
Jan	17	Derby Midland	A	Friendly	2 - 1	
Jan	27	Notts County	H	Friendly	3 - 1	
Jan	31	Small Heath Alliance	A	Friendly	4 - 3	
Feb	7	Stoke	A	Friendly	3 - 1	
Feb	9	Edinburgh University	H	Friendly	4 - 2	
Feb	14	Great Lever (Bolton)	H	Friendly	3 - 1	
Feb	16	Cambridge University	A	Friendly	1 - 1	
Feb	21	Accrington	A	Friendly	3 - 4	
Feb	28	Oxford University	H	Friendly	3 - 1	
Mar	7	Nottingham Forest	A	Friendly	1 - 1	
Mar	14	West Bromwich Albion	H	Friendly	1 - 2	
Mar	30	Sheffield Wednesday	A	Friendly	2 - 1	
Apr	3	Great Lever (Bolton)	A	Friendly	1 - 3	
Apr	4	Battlefield (Glasgow)	H	Friendly	2 - 0	
Apr	6	Accrington	H	Friendly	2 - 2	
Apr	?	Old Carthusians	H	Friendly	4 - 0	
Apr	11	Corinthians	H	Friendly	1 - 0	
Apr	24	Aston Unity	H	Friendly	2 - 0	
Apr	25	Preston North End	A	Friendly	2 - 7	**16**
May	9	Preston North End	H	Friendly	1 - 5	
May	16	Wolverhampton Wanderers	A	Friendly	0 - 2	
May	18	Walsall Swifts	H	Friendly	2 - 1	
May	27	Walsall Swifts	H	Friendly	1 - 1	

* 15 Villa fielded a weakened team in this game because they also played Aston Unity on the same day. The match was abandoned after two balls had burst and there were no others available.

* 16 Press reports imply that Aston Villa could only raise a scratch side for this game.

1885-1886

Aug	15	Blackburn Rovers	H	Benefit - Arthur Brown	2 - 0
Aug	29	Bolton Wanderers	A	Friendly	2 - 7
Sep	5	Blackburn Olympic	H	Friendly	1 - 2
Sep	12	West Bromwich Albion	A	Friendly	0 - 5
Sep	12	Burslem Port Vale	A	Friendly	2 - 2
Sep	19	Walsall Town	H	Friendly	0 - 0
Sep	26	Blackburn Rovers	A	Friendly	1 - 2
Oct	3	Halliwell	H	Friendly	6 - 0
Oct	10	Derby County	H	Friendly	4 - 2
Oct	24	Nottingam Forest	A	Friendly	0 - 0
Nov	2	Oxford University	H	Friendly	1 - 3
Nov	7	Gloucester County	H	Friendly	11 - 1
Nov	21	Mitchells St George's	H	Friendly	3 - 2
Nov	23	Oxford University	U/K	Friendly	4 - 2
Nov	28	West Bromwich Albion	H	Friendly	4 - 5
Dec	5	Burnley	H	Friendly	1 - 1
Dec	12	Bolton Wanderers (Reserves)	H	Friendly	4 - 3
Dec	14	Cambridge University	H	Friendly	3 - 1

1885-1886 (Contd.)

Dec	19	Blackburn Rovers	H	Friendly	1 - 3	**17**
Dec	21	Corinthians	H	Friendly	4 - 1	
Dec	26	Acton	H	Friendly	13 - 0	
Dec	28	London Caledonians	H	Friendly	7 - 0	**18**
Dec	30	Casuals	A	Friendly	3 - 4	
Jan	1	Queens Park 2nd team	H	Friendly	2 - 2	**19**
Jan	2	Aston Unity	H	Friendly	5 - 0	
Jan	4	Great Lever (Bolton)	H	Friendly	2 - 3	
Jan	16	Accrington	H	Friendly	2 - 0	
Jan	23	Wolverhampton Wanderers	A	Friendly	3 - 1	
Jan	30	Birmingham Excelsior	H	Friendly	3 - 0	
Feb	6	West Bromwich Albion	A	Friendly	2 - 3	
Feb	13	Notts County	A	Friendly	5 - 3	
Feb	15	Cambridge University	A	Friendly	1 - 5	
Feb	20	Oxford University	H	Friendly	3 - 0	
Feb	22	Derby County	H	Benefit - E Davis	2 - 1	
Feb	27	Burnley	A	Friendly	1 - 2	**20**
Feb	27	Birmingham Excelsior	H	Friendly	0 - 3	**20**
Mar	8	Stoke	A	Friendly	0 - 2	
Mar	9	Notts County	H	Friendly	3 - 2	
Mar	13	Wolverhampton Wanderers	A	Friendly	1 - 1	**21**
Mar	13	Stafford Rangers	A	Friendly	4 - 4	**21**
Mar	20	Derby County	A	Friendly	3 - 3	
Mar	22	Bolton Wanderers	H	Friendly	3 - 1	
Mar	27	Small Heath	A	Friendly	8 - 1	**22**
Apr	8	Third Lanark	H	Friendly	3 - 4	
Apr	10	Corinthians	H	Friendly	1 - 3	
Apr	17	Accrington	A	Friendly	1 - 2	
Apr	19	West Bromwich Albion	H	Benefit - West Bromwich Albion's Ex Players	3 - 1	
Apr	24	Scottish Crusaders	H	Friendly	1 - 2	
Apr	26	Hibernian	H	Friendly	2 - 1	
Apr	27	Vale of Leven	H	Friendly	3 - 0	
May	?	Small Heath Alliance	H	Friendly	7 - 0	
May	10	Blackburn Rovers	H	Friendly	2 - 1	
May	29	West Bromwich Albion	H	Friendly	1 - 3	
May	31	West Bromwich & District League	H	Benefit - Joe Simmonds	3 - 1	
Jun	16	Small Heath Alliance	A	Friendly	3 - 4	

1886-1887

Jul	19	West Bromwich Albion	A	Friendly	1 - 5	
Jul	24	West Bromwich & District League	H	Benefit-S.Richardson	6 - 3	
Aug	?	Renton (Glasgow)	A	Pre Season Tour (Scotland)	2 - 6	
Aug	21	Greenock Morton	A	Pre Season Tour (Scotland)	0 - 1	
Aug	23	Airdrieonians	A	Pre Season Tour (Scotland)	0 - 1	
Aug	25	Falkirk	A	Pre Season Tour (Scotland)	3 - 2	
Aug	27	East Stirlingshire	A	Pre Season Tour (Scotland)	5 - 2	
Aug	28	Dundee Harp	A	Pre Season Tour (Scotland)	2 - 3	
Aug	29	St.Johnstone	A	Pre Season Tour (Scotland)	11 - 1	
Aug	30	Arbroath	A	Pre Season Tour (Scotland)	5 - 4	
Sep	4	London Caledonians	H	Friendly	11 - 0	
Sep	6	Exelsior	H	Friendly	3 - 2	
Sep	11	Lincoln City	H	Friendly	4 - 1	
Sep	18	Welsh Druids	H	Friendly	5 - 0	
Sep	25	Cowlairs (Scots)	H	Friendly	3 - 2	
Oct	2	Sheffield Wednesday	H	Friendly	7 - 0	
Oct	7	Queens Park	H	Friendly	3 - 1	
Oct	11	Halliwell	H	Friendly	3 - 0	
Oct	16	Nottingham Rangers	H	Friendly	7 - 0	
Oct	18	Burslem Port Vale	A	Friendly	1 - 0	
Oct	23	Church (Accrington)	H	Friendly	4 - 1	
Oct	25	Small Heath Alliance	A	Friendly	1 - 1	
Nov	6	Wolverhampton Wanderers	H	Friendly	5 - 1	
Nov	8	Oxford University	H	Friendly	5 - 2	
Nov	13	Middlesbrough	H	Friendly	8 - 0	
Nov	15	Derby County	H	Friendly	3 - 0	

17   This game was abandoned due to heavy rain.

18   This match was abandoned, with fifteen minutes remaining, due to heavy rain.

19   Both clubs fielded only amateur players for this match.

20   There were two games played on this day but there is no evidence to imply that one Villa team was any weaker than the other.

21   There were two games played on this day but there is no evidence to suggest that one side was weaker than the other.

22   There are other reports that allude to this game being won 5-1 by Aston Villa.

		1886-1887 (Contd.)				
Nov	22	Stoke	A	Friendly	1 - 2	
Nov	27	Stafford Rangers	H	Friendly	3 - 1	
Dec	4	Derby County	A	Friendly	3 - 0	
Dec	13	Cambridge University	H	Friendly	6 - 1	
Dec	18	West Bromwich Albion	H	Friendly	1 - 1	
Dec	20	Corinthians	H	Friendly	4 - 1	
Dec	25	Battlefield	H	Friendly	5 - 1	
Dec	27	Greenock Morton	H	Friendly	7 - 3	
Dec	28	Casuals	H	Friendly	2 - 1	
Jan	1	Hibernian	A	Friendly	8 - 3	
Jan	3	Queens Park	A	Friendly	5 - 1	**23**
Jan	24	Accrington	H	Friendly	2 - 2	
Jan	31	Small Heath Alliance	H	Friendly	3 - 2	
Feb	14	Walsall Town	H	Friendly	4 - 2	
Feb	17	Oxford University	A	Friendly	4 - 3	
Feb	19	Lockwood Bros. (Sheffield)	H	Friendly	4 - 0	
Feb	22	Shiffnal & District	A	Friendly	3 - 1	
Feb	26	Notts. County	A	Friendly	3 - 1	
Feb	28	Rangers	H	Friendly	1 - 0	
Mar	7	Burslem Port Vale	H	Friendly	3 - 0	
Mar	12	Blackburn Rovers	A	Friendly	3 - 3	
Mar	19	Church (Accrington)	H	Friendly	4 - 1	
Mar	23	Small Heath Alliance	A	Friendly	7 - 0	
Mar	26	Blackburn Olympic	A	Friendly	3 - 0	
Apr	9	Hibernian	H	Friendly	3 - 0	**24**
Apr	?	Old Carthusians	H	Friendly	3 - 1	
Apr	11	Notts County	H	Friendly	10 - 1	
Apr	?	Vale of Levan	H	Friendly	?	
Apr	12	Dunbarton	H	Friendly	4 - 1	
Apr	16	Everton	A	Friendly	2 - 2	
Apr	23	Birmingham & District Association	N	Benefit - B'ham Charity Festival	2 - 1	
Apr	30	Blackburn Rovers	H	Benift - Aston Villa Festival	2 - 0	
Apr	?	Sheffield Wednesday	U/K	Friendly	7 - 0	
May	7	Preston North End	A	Friendly	1 - 11	
May	9	Wolverhampton Wanderers	H	Friendly	1 - 0	
May	14	West Bromwich Albion	A	Friendly	1 - 3	
May	21	Preston North End	H	1st Benefit - H. Vaughton & Archie Hunter	2 - 1	
May	28	Scottish Crusaders	A	Friendly	0 - 1	
May	28	Blackburn Rovers	H	Friendly	2 - 0	
Jun	4	Midland Select XI	H	2nd Benefit - H.Vaughton & Archie Hunter	3 - 0	
		1887-1888				
Jul	2	Blackpool South Shore	A	Friendly	3 - 4	
Aug	23	Small Heath Alliance	A	Friendly	3 - 0	
Sep	3	The Caledonians (London)	N	Benefit - Birmingham Charity Sports	8 - 0	
Sep	5	Wednesbury Old Athletic	A	Friendly	4 - 1	
Sep	7	Burton Wanderers	A	Friendly	7 - 1	
Sep	10	Long Eaton Rangers	H	Friendly	5 - 0	
Sep	17	Sheffield Wednesday	H	Friendly	6 - 1	
Sep	24	Wesh Druids	H	Friendly	4 - 2	
Sep	26	Walsall Town	A	Friendly	4 - 3	
Oct	1	London Caledonians	A	Friendly	4 - 0	
Oct	17	Small Heath Alliance	H	Friendly	3 - 0	
Oct	22	Notts County	A	Friendly	2 - 8	
Oct	24	Halliwell	H	Friendly	2 - 0	
Oct	29	Lockwood Bros. (Sheffield)	H	Friendly	12 - 1	
Nov	12	Aston Unity	H	Friendly	9 - 0	
Nov	14	Blackburn Olympic	H	Friendly	2 - 1	
Nov	21	Horncastle	H	Friendly	13 - 0	
Nov	26	Oxford University	H	Friendly	7 - 0	
Nov	28	Stoke	A	Friendly	4 - 2	
Dec	3	Derby County	A	Friendly	3 - 0	
Dec	5	Blackpool South Shore	H	Friendly	9 - 0	
Dec	19	Cambridge University	H	Friendly	12 - 0	
Dec	24	Battlefield	H	Friendly	3 - 0	

23 This game was abandoned at half time when the Queens Park players refused to play in the second half due the weather.

24 This game was played between The English Cup Winners and the Scottish Cup Winners.

1887-1888 (Contd.)

Dec	26	Mitchell St George	H	Friendly	7 - 2	
Dec	27	Casuals	H	Friendly	1 - 0	
Dec	31	Ayr	A	Friendly	4 - 2	
Jan	2	Rangers	A	Friendly	1 - 1	
Jan	10	Scoottish Crusaders	H	Friendly	7 - 4	
Jan	24	Accrington	H	Friendly	2 - 0	
Jan	28	Mitchell St George	A	Friendly	5 - 1	
Jan	30	Blackburn Olympic	H	Friendly	7 - 0	
Feb	4	Wolverhampton Wanderers	H	Friendly	3 - 1	
Feb	6	Nottingham Rangers	H	Friendly	7 - 1	
Feb	11	Derby County	H	Friendly	5 - 0	
Feb	13	Oxford University	A	Friendly	3 - 0	
Feb	18	Rangers	H	Friendly	5 - 1	
Feb	20	Long Eaton Rangers	A	Friendly	5 - 5	
Feb	25	West Bromwich Albion	A	Friendly	1 - 4	
Feb	29	Cambridge University	A	Friendly	2 - 2	
Mar	5	Derby Midland	H	Friendly	3 - 2	
Mar	7	Cambridge University	A	Friendly	3 - 2	
Mar	10	West Bromwich Albion	H	Friendly	0 - 4	
Mar	17	Blackburn Rovers	H	Friendly	6 - 4	
Mar	19	Burnley	A	Friendly	2 - 2	
Mar	24	Everton	A	Friendly	2 - 1	
Mar	31	Corinthians	H	Friendly	5 - 2	
Apr	2	Queens Park	H	Friendly	1 - 2	
Apr	3	Dunbarton	H	Friendly	2 - 1	
Apr	5	Sheffield Wednesday	A	Friendly	1 - 2	
Apr	7	Notts County	H	Friendly	3 - 3	
Apr	9	Walsall Town Swifts	H	Friendly	0 - 0	25
Apr	21	Blackburn Rovers	H	Friendly	2 - 0	
Apr	23	Blackpool South Shore	A	Friendly	5 - 2	
Apr	28	Crewe Alexandra	H	Benefit - Dawson	4 - 2	
May	5	Rangers	A	Friendly	1 - 3	
May	7	Scottish Crusaders	H	Friendly	7 - 4	
May	7	Ayr	A	Friendly	2 - 3	
May	12	Bolton Wanderers	H	Friendly	3 - 4	
May	14	Small Heath Alliance	A	Friendly	4 - 1	
May	19	Preston North End	H	Friendly	4 - 1	
May	21	Newton Heath	A	Friendly	0 - 1	
May	26	West Bromwich Albion	H	Friendly	1 - 1	

1888-1889

Aug	18	Birmingham & District FA XI	N	Benefit-Birmingham Charity Sports Day	1 - 0	
Sep	1	Ayr United	H	Friendly	10 - 0	
Oct	4	Nottingham Forest	A	Friendly	4 - 1	
Oct	22	Canadians	H	Friendly	4 - 2	*
Nov	12	Oxford University	H	Friendly	4 - 2	
Dec	26	St. George's	H	Friendly	0 - 3	
Dec	27	Casuals	H	Friendly	6 - 3	
Feb	18	Oxford University	A	Friendly	1 - 5	
Feb	23	Mitchell St Georges	A	Friendly	1 - 4	
Mar	5	Sheffield Wednesday	A	Friendly	1 - 2	
Mar	30	St George's	A	Benefit - St. George's players	2 - 3	
Apr	20	Renton	H	Benefit - A. Brown	1 - 3	
Apr	22	Queens Park	H	Friendly	2 - 6	
Apr	23	London Caledonians	H	Friendly	5 - 1	

1889-1890

Sep	2	Wolverhampton Wanderers	A	Opening Of Wolverhampton's New Ground	0 - 1	
Sep	16	St George's	A	Friendly	7 - 2	
Oct	7	Druids of Wales	H	Friendly	11 - 2	
Oct	14	London Caledonians	A	Friendly	4 - 3	
Nov	18	(Mitchell) St George's	H	Friendly	2 - 2	26
Feb	15	West Bromwich Albion	H	Friendly	0 - 1	
Feb	22	Derby County	H	Friendly	2 - 0	
Feb	24	Casuals	H	Friendly	4 - 0	
Mar	1	Bootle	A	Friendly	3 - 1	

25 Some sources imply that this was a Birmingham Charity Cup game that ended in a 2-2 draw.

26 This game was abandoned with fifteen minutes remaining.

			1889-1890 (Contd.)			
Mar	9	Middlesbrough Ironopolis	A	Friendly	0 - 1	
Mar	15	St George's	H	Friendly	2 - 1	
Mar	29	West Bromwich Albion	A	Friendly	2 - 2	
Apr	4	Newcastle West End	A	End of Season Tour (The North)	0 - 1	
Apr	5	Sunderland	A	End of Season Tour (The North)	2 - 7	
Apr	7	Notts County	H	Friendly	3 - 1	
Apr	12	Kilbirnie	H	2nd Benefit - Archie Hunter	7 - 3	
Apr	26	Oldbury Town	H	Friendly	5 - 0	
May	5	Small Heath	A	Benefit- C.Charsley	2 - 2	
May	10	Shropshire Association XI	A	Benefit - Shropshire Charities	7 - 1	
May	24	West Bromwich Albion	H	Benefit - J.Burton & A Allen	1 - 0	
			1890-1891			
Sep	1	Small Heath	H	Friendly	0 - 4	
Sep	8	Kidderminster Harriers	H	Friendly	6 - 0	
Sep	15	Kidderminster Harriers	A	Friendly	1 - 3	
Sep	29	Stoke	A	Friendly	4 - 4	
Oct	6	Walsall Swifts	H	Friendly	2 - 1	
Oct	23	Nottingam Forest	A	Friendly	0 - 3	
Nov	3	Oxford University	H	Friendly	7 - 1	
Nov	17	Warwick County	A	Friendly	4 - 0	
Dec	1	Small Heath	A	Friendly	2 - 2	
Dec	8	West Bromwich Albion	H	Friendly	4 - 2	
Dec	15	Cambridge University	H	Friendly	3 - 1	
Dec	22	Accrington	A	Friendly	0 - 6	**27**
Dec	25	St George's	H	Friendly	5 - 2	
Dec	27	London Casuals	H	Friendly	7 - 2	
Jan	3	Preston North End	H	Friendly	2 - 1	**28**
Jan	19	West Bromwich Albion	A	Friendly	2 - 4	
Feb	14	Small Heath	A	Friendly	3 - 0	
Feb	21	Stoke	H	Friendly	2 - 1	
Mar	7	Derby County	A	Friendly	11 - 0	
Mar	16	Nottingham Forest	A	Friendly	3 - 2	
Mar	28	Partick Thistle	A	Friendly	10 - 0	
Apr	2	Corinthians	H	Friendly	8 - 3	
Apr	4	Small Heath	A	Friendly	5 - 4	
Apr	13	Notts County	H	Benefit - New Hospital Fund	2 - 0	
			1891-1892			
Sep	1	Small Heath	H	Friendly	5 - 1	*
Sep	7	Wolverhampton Wanderers	A	Friendly	0 - 0	
Sep	14	St George's	A	Friendly	4 - 1	
Sep	26	Canadians	H	Friendly	3 - 1	
Nov	30	West Bromwich Albion	H	Friendly	8 - 2	
Dec	25	Small Heath	A	Friendly	3 - 0	
Jan	11	West Bromwich Albion	A	Friendly	1 - 2	
Jan	23	Nottingham Forest	H	Friendly	3 - 2	
Feb	1	Sheffield United	A	Friendly	4 - 2	
Apr	4	Wednesbury OA/St. Georges Combined	H	Benefit - Wednesbury OA & St. Georges	8 - 0	
			1892-1893			
Sep	3	West Bromwich Albion	A	Friendly	1 - 0	**29**
Sep	26	West Bromwich Albion	H	Friendly	3 - 2	
Oct	24	Wolverhampton Wanderers	H	Friendly	6 - 1	
Nov	14	Liverpool	H	Friendly	2 - 3	
Dec	5	West Bromwich Albion	A	Friendly	1 - 1	**30**
Dec	26	Small Heath	H	Friendly	3 - 2	
Jan	2	Battlefields	H	Friendly	6 - 2	
Jan	23	Wolverhampton Wanderers	A	Friendly	3 - 2	
Jan	28	Middlesbrough	H	Friendly	3 - 5	
Jan	30	Preston North End	H	Benefit - D.Hodgetts	1 - 3	
Feb	4	West Bromwich Albion	H	Friendly	4 - 4	
Feb	18	Stoke	H	Friendly	3 - 1	
Feb	20	Notts County	H	Benefit - Warwickshire CCC	6 - 2	
Mar	4	West Bromwich Albion	A	Friendly	0 - 2	
Mar	9	Liverpool	A	Friendly	3 - 1	
Mar	11	Corinthians	A	Friendly	7 - 2	
Mar	13	(Woolwich) Arsenal	A	Friendly	1 - 0	
Mar	15	Burton Wanderers	A	Bass Charity Vase	1 - 2	
Apr	8	Corinthians	H	Friendly	8 - 3	**31**
Apr	1	Corinthians	A	Friendly	5 - 2	

27 The Villa team arrived late and so the league game was postponed. The two teams then played a friendly match.

28 This match was scheduled to be a league game but due to fog and frost the two sides agreed to play a friendly instead.

29 This match was originally played as a league game. Unfor-tunately Villa fielded an illegal player and so the game was downgraded to a friendly.

30 This game was abandoned due to bad weather.

31 Some sources suggest that Villa won this game 8-0.

1893-1894

Sep	25	Wolverhampton Wanderers	A	Friendly	0 - 4	
Sep	28	Queens Park	H	Friendly	3 - 3	
Oct	23	Sunderland	H	Benefit - McGregor	4 - 2	
Nov	13	Blackburn Rovers	H	Benefit - G. Cox	2 - 2	
Nov	20	Wolverhampton Wanderers	H	Friendly	1 - 3	
Nov	27	Walsall	H	Friendly	4 - 1	
Dec	7	Notts County	A	Benefit - Notts. County Club	2 - 0	
Dec	11	Stoke City	A	Benefit - Proctor's Wife & Family	1 - 4	
Dec	15	Corinthians	A	Friendly	?	*32*
Jan	1	Small Heath	H	Friendly	4 - 3	
Jan	8	Sheffield United	H	Benefit - H. Devey	4 - 0	
Jan	13	Corinthians	A	Friendly	6 - 4	
Jan	15	Royal Arsenal	A	Friendly	3 - 1	
Jan	20	Corinthians	H	Friendly	2 - 3	
Jan	30	Preston North End	H	Friendly	1 - 3	
Feb	17	Sunderland	H	Friendly	2 - 0	
Feb	27	Rangers	H	Friendly	3 - 1	
Mar	9	Celtic	H	Friendly	3 - 2	
Mar	21	Celtic	A	Friendly	1 - 2	
Mar	30	Small Heath	A	Benefit - Small Heath FC	3 - 3	

1894-1895

Sep	3	West Bromwich Albion	A	Benfet - West Bromwich Albion	4 - 5	
Sep	24	Football League XI	H	Benefit-William McGregor	1 - 3	
Oct	1	Wolverhampton Wanderers	A	Benefit - Baugh	2 - 4	
Oct	15	Bristol & District	A	Friendly	8 - 0	
Oct	29	Birmingham & District Association	H	Benefit - W.H.Mason's Widow & Children	1 - 1	
Nov	19	Wolverhamton Wanderers	H	Benefit - James Cowan	2 - 2	
Nov	26	Cambridge University	A	Friendly	3 - 1	
Dec	15	Corinthians	A	Friendly	5 - 3	*33*
Jan	19	Cambridge University	H	Friendly	11 - 0	
Feb	9	London Caledonians	A	Friendly	5 - 0	*34*
Feb	18	Wolverhamton Wanderers	A	Benefit - Wolverhampton Club	2 - 1	
Apr	13	Rangers	H	Friendly	2 - 3	
May	7	Wolverhampton Wanderers	H	Friendly	2 - 2	
May	14	Wolverhampton Wanderers	A	Benefit - Wolverhampton Club	0 - 3	

1895-1896

Sep	16	Burnley	H	Friendly	2 - 1
Sep	23	West Bromwich Albion	A	Benefit - Widow of Archie Hunter	2 - 1
Oct	14	Small Heath	A	Testimonial - W.Devey	3 - 1
Nov	18	West Bromwich Albion	A	Testimonial - R.McLeod	1 - 1
Nov	25	Wolverhampton Wanderers	A	Benefit - Family of David Wilkes	1 - 4
Nov	30	Crystal Palace	A	Friendly	7 - 3
Feb	15	Small Heath	H	Friendly	1 - 2
Feb	17	Small Heath	A	Friendly	0 - 1
Feb	29	Preston North End	H	Friendly	1 - 1
Apr	4	Hibernian	H	Friendly	1 - 2
Apr	7	Bristol and District League XI	A	Friendly	0 - 2
Apr	11	Tottenham Hotspur	H	Friendly	3 - 1
Apr	18	Hibernian	A	End of Season Tour (Scotland & The North)	2 - 5
Apr	20	Celtic	A	End of Season Tour (Scotland & The North)	2 - 3
Apr	21	Ayr United	A	End of Season Tour (Scotland & The North)	3 - 1
Apr	27	Newcastle United	A	End of Season Tour (Scotland & The North)	1 - 1

1896-1897

Sep	1	Small Heath	H	Benefit Match - Part Of Weldon Transfer	3 - 1	
Sep	10	Grimsby Town	A	Friendly	3 - 3	
Sep	21	Leicester Fosse	A	Friendly	3 - 2	
Oct	5	Derby County	H	Benefit - John "Jack" Devey	2 - 1	*
Nov	30	Stoke City	A	Benefit - William "Billy" Dickson	0 - 3	
Dec	5	Corinthians	A	Challenge Match - Friendly	4 - 4	
Dec	7	Woolwich Arsenal	A	Benefit - Joe Powell	3 - 1	
Dec	29	Small Heath	H	Benfeit - James Elliot	1 - 1	
Jan	11	Small Heath	A	Benefit - W.Walton	1 - 2	
Jan	23	Tottenham Hotspur	H	Friendly	2 - 2	
Apr	3	Bristol and District League XI	A	Opening of Eastville - Friendly	5 - 0	
Apr	28	West Bromwich Albion	H	Benefit - Aston Villa players	3 - 1	
Apr	29	Notts County	A	Benefit - W. Bramley	2 - 1	

32 This game was played at Queen's Club in West Kensington.

33 This game was played at Kennington Oval.

34 This game was played in Kentish Town.

1897-1898

Aug	25	Walsall	A	Friendly	1 - 0		
Sep	13	Derby County	H	Testimonial - C. Athersmith	6 - 2		
Sep	15	Derby County	A	Benefit - J. Methven	1 - 2		
Oct	18	West Bromwich Albion	A	Testimonial - J.Reader	0 - 2		
Dec	6	Halliwell Rovers	H	Friendly	9 - 1		
Dec	13	Loughborough	H	Friendly	5 - 1		
Jan	20	Small Heath	H	Friendly	4 - 0	**35**	35 This match was abandoned, with twenty minutes remaining.
Feb	12	Sunderland	A	Friendly	1 - 4		
Feb	19	Wolverhampton Wanderers	H	Friendly	5 - 0		
Feb	23	Casuals	A	Friendly	6 - 1	**36** *	36 This game was played at Tufnell Park.
Feb	26	Suffolk County	A	Friendly	4 - 1		
Mar	14	Rushden	A	Friendly	4 - 2		
Mar	19	Small Heath	A	Friendly	3 - 0		
Apr	4	South Wales League	A	Friendly	3 - 2		
Apr	9	Millwall Athletic	H	Friendly	3 - 1		
Apr	12	Norfolk County	A	Friendly	8 - 0		
Apr	14	Kings Lynn	A	Friendly	2 - 3		
Apr	18	Burslem Port Vale	H	Testimonial - R. Chatt	2 - 3		
Apr	23	Leicester Fosse	A	Friendly	1 - 2		
Apr	25	Tottenham Hotspur	A	Friendly	3 - 2		

1898-1899

Sep	1	Walsall	A	Benefit	1 - 0		
Sep	5	West Bromwich Albion	H	Testimonial - F. Burton	6 - 1		
Oct	3	Wolverhampton Wanderers	A	Benefit	2 - 1		
Oct	31	West Bromwich Albion	A	Testimonial - T.Perry	0 - 4		
Feb	11	Corinthians	A	Friendly	1 - 1		
Feb	14	Newton Heath	A	Benefit	1 - 1		
Feb	25	Rangers	A	Friendly	1 - 3		
Mar	13	Sheffield Wednesday	H	Benefit H.Davies	5 - 2	**37**	37 Prior to this match kicking off Aston Villa and Sheffield Wednesday played the ten minutes remaining from an earlier game in the season, which had been abandoned.
Apr	4	Burnley	A	Benefit - Walter Place	0 - 8		
Apr	8	Bristol Rovers	A	Friendly	4 - 4		
Apr	10	Rangers	H	Friendly	8 - 4		

1899-1900

Sep	11	Wolverhampton Wanderers	H	Benefit - Steve Smith	2 - 2		
Oct	2	Woolwich Arsenal	A	Friendly	0 - 1		
Nov	20	The Kaffirs	H	Friendly	7 - 4		*
Dec	26	Small Heath	H	Friendly	5 - 2		
Jan	3	Southampton	H	Friendly	4 - 2		
Apr	17	Norfolk County	A	End of Season Tour (East Anglia)	11 - 0		
Apr	18	Suffolk County	A	End of Season Tour (East Anglia)	0 - 1		
Apr	19	Yarmouth	A	End of Season Tour (East Anglia)	6 - 0		
Apr	21	Tottenham Hotspur	H	Friendly	4 - 3		
Apr	28	Portsmouth	A	Friendly	1 - 2		
Apr	30	Rangers	A	Friendly	0 - 0		
?	?	Sunderland	A	Friendly	2 - 7		

1900-1901

Oct	1	Woolwich Arsenal	A	Friendly	0 - 3		
Dec	21	Celtic	H	Benefit - A J Evans	3 - 1		
Dec	27	Sheffield United	H	Benfit - H. Spencer	5 - 1		
Jan	7	Berlin Select XI	H	Friendly	6 - 2		*
Jan	14	Sheffield United	A	Benefit	5 - 1		
Mar	4	Sussex County	A	Benefit	4 - 0		
Apr	9	Bury	H	Benefit - Crabtree	1 - 3		

1901-1902

Sep	2	Celtic	H	Friendly	2 - 1
Sep	18	Milwall	A	Opening of Milwall's New Ground	0 - 2
Dec	21	Celtic	H	Benefit - A. Evans	3 - 1
Mar	1	Portsmouth	H	Friendly	6 - 0
Apr	14	South Wales	A	End of Season Tour	5 - 0
Apr	16	Bristol City	A	End of Season Tour	1 - 0
Apr	17	Dorset	A	End of Season Tour	4 - 2
Apr	19	Plymouth Argyle	A	End of Season Tour	7 - 0
Apr	22	Southampton	A	End of Season Tour	4 - 2
Apr	23	West Ham United	A	End of Season Tour	0 - 2
Apr	30	Small Heath	H	Benefit - Ibrox Disaster Fund	1 - 1

			1902-1903				
Sep	1	Small Heath	H	Friendly	4 - 2		
Sep	8	Kettering Town	A	Friendly	3 - 1		
Oct	20	West Bromwich Albion	A	Testimonial - H.Hadley	5 - 1		
Dec	29	West Bromwich Albion	H	Testimonial - W.George	2 - 1		
Jan	5	Corinthians	H	Benefit	4 - 0		
Jan	19	Corinthians	H	Benefit	3 - 1		
Mar	18	G. Robey's Team	H	Friendly	3 - 4		
Apr	20	Wolverhampton Wanderers	N	Benefit for Dudley Town	2 - 3		
			1903-1904				
Sep	7	Wolverhampton Wanderers	H	Benefit - W. Garraty	4 - 0		
Oct	26	West Bromwich Albion	A	Testimonial - C. Simmonds	3 - 3		
Nov	9	Southampton	A	Testimonial - H. Wood	1 - 1		
Dec	29	West Bromwich Albion	H	Testimonial - G.Johnson	3 - 0		
Jan	4	Corinthians	H	Friendly	2 - 1		
Mar	5	Everton	A	Friendly	2 - 2		
Apr	4	Third Lanark	H	Friendly	2 - 0		
Apr	11	Wolverhampton Wanderers	A	Benefit	1 - 1		
Apr	25	Southampton	H	Benefit - A. Wilkes	2 - 3		
			1904-1905				
Oct	3	Burton United	A	Benefit	4 - 0		
Nov	5	Corinthians	A	Friendly	5 - 0		
Dec	27	Corinthians	H	Friendly	1 - 1		
Apr	24	Belfast Distillery	A	Mid - Season Tour (Ireland)	1 - 1	**38**	38 This game was played at Grosvenor Park.
Apr	25	Bohemians	A	Mid - Season Tour (Ireland)	3 - 1		
			1905-1906				
Apr	7	Corinthians	A	Friendly	1 - 7		
Apr	28	Linfield	A	End of Season Tour (Ireland)	2 - 0		*
Apr	30	Bohemians	A	End of Season Tour (Ireland)	4 - 1		*
			1906-1907				
Oct	30	Cambridge University	A	Friendly	2 - 0		
Nov	26	Cambridge University	H	Friendly	6 - 0		
Feb	11	George Robey's International XI	H	Benefit - Local Charities	4 - 3		
			1907-1908				
Apr	28	Manchester City	A	Benefit - Rawdon Colliery Disaster Fund	2 - 2		
			1908-1909				
Mar	2	Birmingham	H	Charity Festival	2 - 1	**39**	39 This match was abandoned.
			1909-1910				
Jan	25	West Bromwich Albion	H	Benefit - Birmingham Theatrical Sports	0 - 1		
Feb	22	George Robey's XI	H	Benefit - Local Charities	3 - 1		
Apr	20	Bristol Rovers	A	Friendly	1 - 2		
Apr	25	Northwich Victoria XI	A	Benefit- Working Men's Hospital Sat. Fund	4 - 1		
			1910-1911				
No matches							
			1911-1912				
Apr	15	Stourbridge	H	Friendly	1 - 4		
Apr	25	Third Lanark	A	End of Season Tour (Scotland)	1 - 0		
Apr	27	Celtic	A	End of Season Tour (Scotland)	1 - 1		
			1912-1913				
Apr	30	Stoke City	A	Testimonial - T.Wilkes	2 - 1		
			1912-1913				
Apr	29	Combined Bristol XI	A	Benefit Match - Locke	3 - 0		
			1913-1914 & 1914-15				
No macthes							
			1915-1916				
Apr	22	West Bromwich Albion	H	Benefit - War Fund	1 - 1		
Apr	24	West Bromwich Albion	A	Benefit - War Fund	1 - 3		
			1916-1917				
Dec	26	West Bromwich Albion	A	Benefit - War Fund	1 - 5		
Apr	7	West Bromwich Albion	H	Benefit - War Fund	1 - 2		
			1917-1918				
Dec	24	West Bromwich Albion	A	Victory Benefit Match - Charity Fund	2 - 1		
Dec	26	West Bromwich Albion	H	Victory Benefit Match - Charity Fund	0 - 2		
			1918-1919				
Aug	5	West Bromwich Albion	A	Benefit - National Footballers War Fund	4 - 3		
May	3	Birmingham	H	Benefit - War Charity Fund	1 - 2		

			1919-1920			
Apr	28	Bristol Rovers	A	Testimonial - A.G. Homer	2 - 2	
			1920-1921			
Jan	17	Birmingham	H	Benefit - Lord Mayor's Unemployment Fund	1 - 1	
			1921-1922			
Nov	9	Oxford University	H	Friendly	11 - 2	
Dec	14	Army FA	H	Friendly	3 - 1	
			1922-1923			
Oct	11	Army FA	H	Friendly	4 - 3	
			1923-1924			
Oct	17	Army	A	Friendly	7 - 2	
			1924-1925			
Oct	15	South Africans	H	Friendly	0 - 3	*
Oct	29	Army	A	Friendly	1 - 0	
May	4	West Bromwich Albion	H	Benefit - Rowley Regis Ambulance Fund	5 - 5	
			1925-1926			
Oct	28	Army	A	Friendly	1 - 5	
Apr	28	Birmingham	H	Benefit - Widow of E.W.Strange	6 - 3	
May	26	Orgryte Idrott Sallskap	A	End of Season Tour (Scandinavia)	2 - 5	*
May	29	Kombineral Gotesburgslag	A	End of Season Tour (Scandinavia)	1 - 2	*
May	30	Lyn OG Frig	A	End of Season Tour (Scandinavia)	11 - 2	*
Jun	2	Stockholm (Combined team)	A	End of Season Tour (Scandinavia)	5 - 4	*
Jun	5	Copenhagen (Combined team)	A	End of Season Tour (Scandinavia)	4 - 1	*
Jun	6	Copenhagen (Combined team)	A	End of Season Tour (Scandinavia)	5 - 2	*
			1926-1927			
Nov	10	Army	A	Friendly	4 - 5	
Apr	30	Corinthians	H	Friendly	4 - 2	
			1927-1928			
Nov	23	Army	A	Friendly	7 - 2	
Mar	3	Airdrieonians	H	Friendly	7 - 2	
			1928-1929			
Nov	21	Army	A	Friendly	7 - 3	
			1929-1930			
Oct	31	Oxford University	A	Friendly	3 - 0	
Nov	13	Army	A	Friendly	5 - 0	
Apr	28	Walsall	A	Friendly	8 - 2	
			1930-1931			
Oct	23	Cambridge University	A	Friendly	8 - 0	
Nov	19	Army	H	Friendly	7 - 1	
Nov	27	Oxford University	A	Friendly	10 - 0	
Feb	14	Corinthian FC	H	Friendly	8 - 2	
			1931-1932			
Dec	6	Army	A	Friendly	6 - 0	
Feb	13	Cowdenbeath	H	Friendly	4 - 2	
			1932-1933			
Nov	9	Army	A	Friendly	4 - 4	
			1933-1934 to 1937-1938			
No Matches						
			1937-1938			
Nov	4	Cardiff City	N	Benefit - Yeovil Charities	0 - 3	**40**
May	15	German Select XI	A	End of Season Tour (Germany)	3 - 2	*
May	18	Die Deutsche Auswahlelf	A	End of Season Tour (Germany)	0 - 1	*
May	22	Greater German XI	A	End of Season Tour (Germany)	2 - 1	*
			1938-1939			
Aug	20	West Bromwich Albion	A	Benefit - Football League Jubilee Fund	1 - 1	
May	8	Ipswich Town	A	Ipswich Hospital Cup	3 - 2	
May	13	Coventry City	H	Friendly	1 - 0	
			1939-1940			
Aug	19	West Bromwich Albion	H	Benefit - Football League Jubilee Fund	1 - 1	
Sep	16	Leicester City	A	Friendly	0 - 3	
Apr	13	Birmingham	A	Testimonial - H. Hibbs	1 - 2	
Apr	20	Chelmsford City	A	Friendly	1 - 2	
?	?	ICI Metals	N	Benefit - Charity	5 - 1	**41**

40   This game was played at Yeovil.

41   This game was played at Perry Barr.

				1940-1941			
Sep	28	Birmingham	A	Friendly	3 - 0		
Dec	7	Revo Electric	A	Worcestershire Cup	1 - 2		
May	10	Worcester City	A	Worcester Infirmary Cup	1 - 2		
May	17	Walsall	A	Friendly	3 - 4		
				1941-1942			
Sep	28	Birmingham	A	Friendly	0 - 3		
Nov	15	Birmingham	H	Friendly	7 - 0		
Nov	29	Birmingham	A	Friendly	1 - 0		
Dec	13	Revo Electric	H	Worcester Charity Cup	1 - 2		
Dec	27	Birmingham	H	Friendly	4 - 1		
Mar	14	Birmingham	H	Friendly	4 - 0		
Mar	28	West Bromwich Albion	A	Challenge Match - Friendly	2 - 1		
Apr	6	Birmingham	A	Friendly	1 - 2		
May	2	Worcester City	A	Infirmary Cup	3 - 0		
May	25	West Bromwich Albion	A	Challenge Match - Friendly	4 - 3		
May	30	RAF XI	H	Benefit - Wartime Charity	1 - 2		
				1942-1943			
May	8	Portsmouth	H	Benefit - Wartime Charity	1 - 1		
				1943-1944			
May	13	Portsmouth	H	Benefit - Red Cross & Sailors Fund	3 - 3		
				1944-1945			
Aug	5	Edinburgh Select XI	A	Benefit - Red Cross Fund	4 - 3	*42*	* 42 This game was played at Tynecastle.
May	9	Portsmouth	A	Benefit - Victory Match (VE Day) for Charity	4 - 3		
				1945-1946			
Aug	15	Woverhampton Wanderers	H	VJ DAY	2 - 3		
Aug	18	Wolverhampton Wanderers	A	VJ Celebrations	3 - 1		
May	6	Wolverhampton Wanderers	H	Benefit - National Association Of Boys Clubs	3 - 2		
May	9	Boston United	A	Boston Hospital Cup - Charity Fund Raiser	3 - 4		
May	28	South Norway/Oslo	A	End of Season Tour (Scandinavia)	2 - 2		*
May	30	Oestfold District	A	End of Season Tour (Scandinavia)	4 - 2		*
Jun	5	Combined West Norway XI	A	End of Season Tour (Scandinavia)	9 - 1		*
Jun	8	Edinburgh Selected XI	A	Charity Game @ Easter Road	3 - 3	*43*	* 43 This game was played at Easter Road.
				1946-1947			
Mar	1	Celtic	H	Friendly	1 - 2		
May	3	Cornwall County XI	A	Friendly	5 - 0		
				1947-1948			
Nov	10	Army	A	Friendly	1 - 1		
Jan	17	Northampton Town	H	Friendly	4 - 2		
Jan	24	Birmingham City	H	Friendly	2 - 1		
Feb	7	Newcastle United	H	Friendly	1 - 2		
Mar	13	Brentford	A	Friendly	2 - 2		
				1948-1949			
Feb	5	Celtic	A	Friendly	2 - 0		
May	4	Reading	A	Testimonial M. McPhee	1 - 1		
May	20	Shamrock Rovers	A	End of Season Tour (Ireland)	2 - 2		
May	25	Limerick	A	End of Season Tour (Ireland)	8 - 1		
May	29	Munster XI @ Mardyke, Cork	A	End of Season Tour (Ireland)	8 - 0		
				1949-1950			
Oct	26	Army	A	Friendly	7 - 3		
Nov	2	Shamrock Rovers	H	Friendly	2 - 1		
Jan	28	Birmingham City	H	Friendly	3 - 1		
Feb	11	Hibernian	H	Friendly	5 - 2		
Feb	22	Army	H	Friendly	3 - 0		
May	1	Merthyr Tydfil	A	Friendly	4 - 7		
May	14	Shamrock Rovers	A	Friendly	3 - 4		
				1950-1951			
Sep	20	Shamrock Rovers	H	Friendly	4 - 1		
Oct	25	Army	A	Friendly	3 - 1		
Feb	10	Luton Town	A	Friendly	2 - 1		
May	19	Frem	H	Festival of Britain - Friendly	1 - 1		
May	25	Shamrock Rovers	A	Friendly	5 - 1		

			1951-1952			
Sep	26	Shamrock Rovers	H	Friendly	1 - 1	
Oct	1	Army	A	Friendly	2 - 1	
Feb	23	Birmingham City	H	Friendly	3 - 2	
May	3	Shamrock Rovers	A	Friendly	2 - 2	
May	13	JYDSK Pokalturnering	A	End of Season Tour (Scandinavia)	2 - 1	
May	15	International Combination	A	End of Season Tour (Scandinavia)	3 - 0	
May	18	Goteborg Alliansen	A	End of Season Tour (Scandinavia)	1 - 3	
May	20	International Combination	A	End of Season Tour (Scandinavia)	2 - 6	
			1952-1953			
Oct	15	Army	A	Friendly	1 - 3	
Apr	13	Kettering Town	A	Benefit - Jummerly & Mead	2 - 1	
May	9	Birmingham City	H	Coronation Festivities 1953	1 - 1	
May	17	Waterford Select XI	A	Friendly	8 - 1	
May	24	Shamrock Rovers	A	Friendly	1 - 1	
			1953-1954			
Oct	14	Army	A	Friendly	3 - 2	
Jan	30	Nottingham Forest	A	Friendly	2 - 0	
May	9	FC Nurenberg	A	End of Season Tour (Germany)	1 - 3	
May	12	FC St. Pauli	A	End of Season Tour (Germany)	3 - 2	
May	16	Preussen	A	End of Season Tour (Germany)	1 - 0	
			1954-1955			
Oct	13	Army	A	Friendly	1 - 0	
			1955 -1956			
Nov	16	Army	A	Friendly	1 - 0	
			1956 -1957			
Oct	10	Army	A	Friendly	7 - 1	
May	18	HSV Hamburg	A	End of Season Tour (Germany)	3 - 1	
May	21	FSV Frankfurt	A	End of Season Tour (Germany)	3 - 1	
May	29	Toulouse	N	FA Cup Winners v French Cup Winners	1 - 2	*44*
			1957-1958			
Oct	16	Army	H	Friendly	4 - 3	
May	11	TSV 1860 Munich	A	End of Season Tour (Germany)	1 - 2	
May	14	Aachen	A	End of Season Tour (Germany)	0 - 0	
May	17	Duisburger & Meidericher Combined	A	End of Season Tour (Germany)	0 - 0	
			1958-1959			
Oct	29	G.A.I.S.	H	Friendly	3 - 0	
Nov	19	Heart of Midlothian	H	Friendly	3 - 3	
May	1	Bedford Town	A	Friendly	4 - 2	
			1959-1960			
Oct	19	Rapid Vienna	H	Friendly	2 - 1	
Oct	28	Raith Rovers	H	Friendly	5 - 1	
Nov	4	Army	H	Friendly	4 - 2	
Apr	25	Heart of Midlothian	A	Friendly	2 - 2	
May	5	Swindon Town	A	Testimonial - Hudson & Cousins	4 - 3	
May	6	Bedford Town	A	Friendly	4 - 3	
May	10	Gotenburgs Alliansen	A	End of Season Tour (Scandinavia)	1 - 2	
May	12	Helsingborg	A	End of Season Tour (Scandinavia)	3 - 2	
May	17	Raufoss Idrettslag	A	End of Season Tour (Scandinavia)	13 - 1	
May	19	Bollnas	A	End of Season Tour (Scandinavia)	6 - 0	
May	24	Trondheim	A	End of Season Tour (Scandinavia)	6 - 0	
May	26	IFK Ostersund	A	End of Season Tour (Scandinavia)	7 - 1	
			1960-1961			
Sep	27	Raith Rovers	A	Friendly - Opening of floodlights	1 - 2	
May	11	Dynamo Moscow	A	End of Season Tour (Russia)	0 - 2	
May	14	Dynamo Tbilisi	A	End of Season Tour (Russia)	0 - 2	
May	17	Moscow Combined XI	A	End of Season Tour (Russia)	1 - 0	
			1961-1962			
Nov	13	Dynamo Kiev	H	Friendly	2 - 1	
May	3	Swindon Town	A	Testimonial - Darcy & Chamberlain	2 - 1	
May	15	FC Internazionale Milano	A	End of Season Tour (Italy)	2 - 1	*45*
			1962-1963			
Feb	20	West Bromwich Albion	N	Friendly	2 - 3	*46*
Feb	23	Swansea Town	A	Friendly	4 - 3	*47*
Apr	23	Coventry City	A	Festival of Sport	2 - 2	

* 44   This game was played in Paris.

45   The game in Italy was agreed as part of the transfer fee that took Gerry Hitchens to Inter-Milan.

46   The winter of 1962-63 was known as the big freeze and the majority of league and cup games were postponed. During this this period many clubs played friendlies when they were able to locate a fit ground. Villa and West Brom played a friendly at Stourbridge which surprisingly was passed fit.

47   See 46. Swansea's ground was playable.

				1963-1964		
Aug	14	Shrewsbury Town	H	Public Practice Match	2 - 2	
Aug	17	Northampton Town	H	Public Practice Match	8 - 0	
Nov	20	Hereford United	A	Roly Morris Testimonial	3 - 1	
Mar	14	Portsmouth	A	Friendly	1 - 2	
				1964-1965		
Aug	15	Southampton	A	Pre Season Friendly	2 - 3	
Apr	30	Bournemouth	A	Friendly	1 - 1	
				1965-1966		
Aug	10	D.O.S. Utrecht	A	Pre Season Tour (Holland)	3 - 3	
Aug	12	FC Twente (Enschede)	A	Pre Season Tour (Holland)	2 - 2	
Aug	16	Port Vale	A	Pre Season Friendly	2 - 3	
Mar	7	Peterborough United	A	Friendly	1 - 2	
Mar	21	FC Twente (Enschede)	H	Friendly	2 - 1	
				1966-1967		
Jul	31	Schalke 04	A	Pre Season Tour (Holland & Germany)	3 - 2	*
Aug	3	AFC Ajax	A	Pre Season Tour (Holland & Germany)	0 - 2	*
Aug	6	1 FC Nuremburg	A	Pre Season Tour (Holland & Germany)	2 - 1	*
Aug	13	Swindon Town	A	Pre Season Friendly	1 - 2	
Jun	5	Aalborg Boldklub	A	End of Season Tour (Scandinavia)	1 - 4	
Jun	7	Malmo FF	A	End of Season Tour (Scandinavia)	2 - 1	
Jun	8	STDJSK Fodbold AKK	A	End of Season Tour (Scandinavia)	4 - 2	
				1967-1968		
Aug	7	Oxford United	A	Pre Season Friendly	3 - 2	
Aug	9	Burnley	A	Pre Season Friendly	0 - 0	
Aug	12	Blackburn Rovers	H	Pre Season Friendly	2 - 1	
May	13	Wellington Town	A	Testimonial - J. Bently	3 - 2	
May	15	Yeovil Town	A	Testimonial - Muir & Herrity	3 - 1	
May	9	Kidderminster	A	Testimonial - D.Gilbert	1 - 3	
				1968-1969		
Jul	27	Bedford Town	A	Pre Season Friendly	0 - 2	*
Jul	29	Shrewsbury Town	A	Pre Season Friendly	3 - 2	
Aug	1	Walsall	A	Pre Season Friendly	1 - 0	
Aug	5	Wellington Town	A	Friendly	2 - 2	
Feb	4	Walsall	A	Friendly	0 - 3	
Apr	21	Bedford Town	A	Testimonial-Joe Campbell's dependants	2 - 2	
May	3	Kilmarnock	A	USA Tournament (Atlanta)	2 - 1	*
May	9	Dundee United	A	USA Tournament (Atlanta)	2 - 2	*
May	10	Dundee United	A	USA Tournament(Dallas)	2 - 0	*
May	14	Wolverhampton Wanderers	A	USA Tournament (Atlanta)	1 - 2	*
May	17	Tottenham Hotspur	A	Exhibition Match (Atlanta)	2 - 2	*
May	19	West Ham United	A	USA Tournament (Atlanta)	2 - 2	*
May	24	Woverhampton Wanderers	A	USA Tournament (Kansas	0 - 5	*
May	25	Kilmarnock	A	USA Tournament (St.Louis)	1 - 2	*
May	27	West Ham United	A	USA Tournament(Baltimore)	0 - 2	*
May	30	Atlanta Chiefs	A	Exhibition Match (Atlanta)	2 - 0	*
				1969-1970		
Jul	26	Italy U21	H	Pre Season Friendly	1 - 0	
Jul	29	SSV Jahn Regensburg	A	Pre Season Tour (Germany)	0 - 1	
Aug	2	Dunfirmline Athletic	H	Pre Season Friendly	3 - 2	
Aug	3	Clydebank	A	Pre Season Friendly	1 - 0	
Oct	14	Luton Town	A	Friendly	3 - 0	*
Oct	20	Hibernian	A	Friendly	4 - 1	
Apr	20	Coventry City	H	Testimonial - Charlie Aitken	3 - 3	
Apr	21	Southend	A	Testimonial - Dave Robinson	2 - 3	
May	5	SSC Napoli	H	Friendly	1 - 1	
				1970-1971		
Jul	27	Coleraine	A	Pre Season Tour (Ireland & Scotland)	4 - 0	
Jul	29	Glentoran	A	Pre Season Tour (Ireland & Scotland)	0 - 0	
Aug	1	Motherwell	A	Pre Season Tour (Ireland & Scotland)	1 - 3	
Aug	3	Clydebank	A	Pre Season Tour (Ireland & Scotland)	1 - 3	
Aug	8	West Bromwich Albion	H	Pre Season Friendly	1 - 1	

1971-1972

Jul	29	Alemannia Aachen	A	Pre Season Tour (Germany)	0 - 1
Jul	31	Kickers Wurzburg	A	Pre Season Tour (Germany)	4 - 2
Aug	2	Bayreuth	A	Pre Season Tour (Germany)	3 - 2
Aug	3	Goppingen	A	Pre Season Tour (Germany)	2 - 2
Aug	7	Birmingham City	H	Friendly	2 - 1
Dec	1	Gornik Zabrze	H	Friendly	1 - 1
Feb	21	Santos	H	Friendly	2 - 1 *
May	9	Maccabi Natanya (Tel Aviv)	A	End of Season Tour (Israel & Cyprus)	2 - 1 *
May	10	Beer Sheba	A	End of Season Tour (Israel & Cyprus)	1 - 2 *
May	17	EPA Larnac (Cyprus)	A	End of Season Tour (Israel & Cyprus)	6 - 0 *

1972-1973

Jul	26	Groningen	A	Pre Season Tour (Holland)	2 - 1
Jul	29	Nijmegen	A	Pre Season Tour (Holland)	3 - 0
Aug	2	Tottenham Hotspur	H	Pre Season Friendly	0 - 0
Aug	7	Shrewsbury Town	A	Pre Season Friendly	2 - 2
Oct	24	Exeter City	A	Testimonial for Bryan Sharples	2 - 2
Nov	21	St Martin's (Gurnsey)	A	Friendly	5 - 0
Jan	23	Bayern Munich	H	Friendly	1 - 1
Mar	19	Hereford	A	Len Weston Challenge Cup	2 - 2
May	1	Coventry City	A	Machin Testimonial	1 - 1
May	4	Wimbledon	A	Friendly	2 - 0
May	13	Young Africans SC	A	End Of Season Tour (Tanzania)	0 - 0 *
May	16	Zanzibar XI	A	End Of Season Tour (Tanzania)	3 - 0 *
May	19	Simba SC	A	End Of Season Tour (Tanzania)	1 - 1 *
May	20	Young Africans SC	A	End Of Season Tour (Tanzania)	1 - 1 *

1973-1974

Aug	15	Oldenburg	A	Pre Season Tour (Germany)	3 - 2
Aug	18	Leicester City	H	Friendly	0 - 1
Mar	9	Southampton	A	Friendly	3 - 1
Apr	30	Feyenoord	H	Friendly	7 - 1

1974-1975

Jul	27	VFL Osnabruck	A	Pre Season Tour (Germany)	1 - 1
Jul	29	Borusia Dortmund	A	Pre Season Tour (Germany)	1 - 0
Aug	7	Leeds United	H	Centenary Game	1 - 2
Aug	10	Bury	A	Friendly	1 - 0
May	5	Stoke City	H	Testimonial - Michael Wright	3 - 1
May	8	West Bromwich Albion	A	Ray Wilson Testimonial	2 - 2
May	15-29	Barbados International XI	A	End of Season Tour (West Indies)	1 - 0

1975-1976

Aug	2	Port Vale	A	Pre Season Friendly	3 - 2
Aug	5	Bristol Rovers	A	Pre Season Friendly	0 - 2
Aug	9	Walsall	H	Friendly	2 - 1
Nov	4	SK Brann	H	Friendly	11 - 0
Apr	26	West Bromwich Albion	H	Testimonial - Fred Turnbull	0 - 1
Apr	27	SK Brann	A	Friendly	1 - 0
May	?	Guadeloupe	A	End of Season Tour (Central America)	1 - 0 *
May	?	Martininque	A	End of Season Tour (Central America)	0 - 1 *

1976-1977

Jul	30	St. Etienne	A	Pre Season Tour (France & Portugal)	2 - 1	
Aug	1	Rheims	A	Pre Season Tour (France & Portugal)	0 - 0	
Aug	4	Oporto	A	Pre Season Tour (France & Portugal)	1 - 1	
Aug	11	Royal Antwerp	H	Pre Season Friendly	3 - 1	
Oct	9	Rangers	H	Friendly	2 - 0	**48**
Nov	22	Eintracht Frankfurt	H	Dunlop Sponsored Friendly	3 - 1	
May	26	Midland Select XI	H	2nd Testimonial - Charlie Aitken	1 - 6	

48 Match abandoned due to crowd invasion.

1977-1978

Aug	8	Athletico Bilbao	A	Pre Season International Tournament	0 - 2	
Aug	10	RSC Anderlecht	A	Pre Season International Tournament	3 - 4	
May	5	Walsall	A	Testimonial - Bob Davies	3 - 0	
May	17	Sweden World Cup XI	A	End of Season Tour - Friendly	0 - 1	**49**

49 This match was played in Gothenburg

1978-1979

Aug	1	HNK Hajduk Split	A	Pre Season Tour (Yugoslavia)	0 - 4 *
Aug	5	NK Rijeka	A	Pre Season Tour (Yugoslavia)	0 - 2 *
Aug	6	NK Olimpija Ljubljana	A	Pre Season Tour (Yugoslavia)	5 - 3 *

1978-1979 (Contd.)

Aug	12	NEC Nijmegen	A	Pre Season Friendly	1 - 1		
Sep	25	Aston Villa 74/75	A	Testimonial - Keith Leonard	1 - 2		
Oct	30	John Robson's International XI	A	Testimonial - John Robson	6 - 6		

1979-1980

Aug	2	Heart of Midlothian	A	Pre Season Tour (Scotland)	3 - 1		
Aug	4	Dundee United	A	Pre Season Tour (Scotland)	0 - 3		
Aug	10	FC Twente	H	Pre Season Friendly	2 - 0		
May	7	Birmingham City	H	Testimonial - Ron Saunders	2 - 3		

1980-1981

Jul	30	FC Bochult	A	Pre Season Tour (Germany)	1 - 0		
Aug	2	Nurnberg	A	Pre Season Tour (Germany)	2 - 1		
Aug	5	VFL Bochum	A	Pre Season Tour (Germany)	1 - 1		
Aug	9	VFL Bochum	H	Pre Season - Friendly	2 - 1		
Jan	26	Rapid Vienna	H	Friendly	4 - 0		
May	5	Birmingham City	A	Testimonial - Joe Gallagher	6 - 3		
May	?16	Nantes	A	End of Season Tour (France & Spain)	0 - 4		*
May	?18	Real Vallodolid	A	End of Season Tour (France & Spain)	4 - 4		*

1981-1982

Aug	4	Servette	A	Pre Season Tour (Switzerland & Greece)	1 - 2		
Aug	7	Frauenfeld (Zurich)	A	Pre Season Tour (Switzerland & Greece)	4 - 0		
Aug	10	AEK Athens	A	Pre Season Tour (Switzerland & Greece)	2 - 2		
Aug	12	Olympiakos	A	Pre Season Tour (Switzerland & Greece)	1 - 1		
Aug	17	German Democratic Republic XI	H	Pre Season Friendly	4 - 2		
May	18	England XI	H	Testimonial - Brian Little	3 - 2		
May	23	Moroccon League Select XI	A	Friendly - Morocco National Sports Week	2 - 3		

1982-1983

Aug	8	Shrewsbury Town	A	Pre Season Practice Match	3 - 1		
Aug	10	1 FC Kaiserslautern	A	Pre Season Tour (Germany)	1 - 5		*
Aug	13	Werder Bremen	A	Pre Season Tour (Germany)	0 - 2		*
Aug	16	Shalke 04	A	Pre Season Tour (Germany)	2 - 4		*
Aug	21	Dukla Prague	H	Friendly	1 - 2		
Aug	23	Portsmouth	A	Testimonial - Alex Cropley	4 - 3		
Oct	11	Hereford United	A	Testimonial - Tommy Hughes	2 - 1		
Nov	15	Rotherham	A	Testimonial - Richard Finney	3 - 1		
May	4	Mansfied	A	Testimonial - Kevin Bird	3 - 1		

1983-1984

Aug	8	Torquay United	A	Testimonial - Ian Twitchin	1 - 2		
Aug	10	Plymouth Argyle	A	Testimonial - Brian Johnson	3 - 0		
Aug	18	FC America	A	Pre Season Tournament in Spain - Zaragosa	2 - 2	50	* 50 Aston Villa lost on penalties
Aug	19	Polytechnica	A	Pre Season Tournament in Spain - Zaragosa	1 - 1	51	51 Aston Villa lost on penalties
Aug	22	Derby County	A	Pre SeasonFriendly	3 - 1		
Nov	14	Chelmsford City	A	Opening of Floodlights	1 - 0		
Jan	23	Bideford	A	Friendly	2 - 1		
Apr	10	Poole Town	A	Friendly	1 - 0		
Apr	30	West Bromwich Albion	A	Testimonial - Brendon Batson	2 - 1		
May	14	Worcester City	A	Testimonial - Malcolm Phelps	6 - 4		
May	16	Portsmouth	A	Friendly	1 - 0		

1984-1985

Aug	4	Millwall	A	Pre Season Friendly	4 - 2		
Aug	11	Rotherham	A	Pre Season Friendly	1 - 2		
Aug	14	Shrewsbury Town	A	Pre Season Friendly	2 - 0		
Aug	15	Wolverhampton Wanderers	A	Pre Season Friendly	1 - 0		
Aug	21	Bayern Munich	N	Pre season Tournament in Spain	1 - 2		
Aug	22	Boca Juniors	N	Pre season Tournament in Spain	0 - 2		
Sep	11	Bristol Rovers	A	Benefit - Mike Barrett Memorial	1 - 2		
Nov	25	Australia	H	Friendly	2 - 0		
Nov	27	Aldershot	A	Testimonial - Joe Jopling	1 - 4		
Dec	3	Cardiff City XI	A	Testimonial - Jeff Hemmerman	0 - 3		
Jan	15	Leeds United	A	Charity Match - Ethiopia Appeal	3 - 1		
Jan	23	Hotels International	A	Mid Season Tour (Bermuda)	6 - 0		
Jan	25	Somerset	A	Mid Season Tour (Bermuda)	12 - 0		
Feb	13	Central Wales League	A	Friendly	6 - 1	52	52 This game was played at Latham Park in Newtown
Feb	16	Exeter City	A	Friendly	3 - 0		
May	14	England XI	H	Testimonial - Dennis Mortimer	1 - 4		
May	17	West Bromwich Albion	H	Benefit - Bradford Fire Appeal	3 - 3		*

				1985-1986			
Jul	29	Hereford United	A	Pre Season Friendly	6 - 1		
Aug	3	Plymouth Argyle	A	Pre Season Tour (West Country)	4 - 1		
Aug	5	Liskeard	H	Pre Season Tour (West Country)	6 - 2		
Aug	6	Exeter City	A	Pre Season Tour (West Country)	3 - 1		
Aug	10	Sunderland	H	Pre Season Friendly	2 -1		
Oct	14	Hednesford	A	Testimonial - Billy Morris	4 - 0		
Nov	11	John Powell XI	A	Testimonial - John Powell	6 - 2	**53**	
Feb	15	Shrewsbury Town	A	Friendly	3 - 0	**54**	*
Apr	21	Atherstone Town	A	Testimonial - Brian Kendall	4 - 2		
May	5	Birmingham City Select XI	A	Testimonial - Kevan Broadhurst	2 - 2	**55**	
May	18	Mauritius Select XI	A	End of Season Tour (Indian Ocean)	4 - 0		
				1986-1987			
Jul	30	Burton Albion	A	Bass Charity Soccer Vase	2 - 2	**56**	
Aug	2	Celtic	A	Pre Season Friendly	0 - 1		
Aug	6	Pisa	A	Pre Season Tour (Italy)	0 - 0		
Aug	9	Lamporecchio	A	Pre Season Tour (Italy)	8 - 0		
Aug	13	Port Vale	A	Pre Season Friendly	1 - 0		
Aug	16	Leeds United	A	Pre Season Friendly	3 - 1		
Aug	18	Atherstone	H	Pre Season Friendly	9 - 0		
Jan	30	Sheffield United	A	Friendly	0 - 0	**57**	
May	26	Caribean Select XI	A	End of Season Tour (Jamaica)	2 - 0		
May	31	West Indies Select XI	A	End of Season Tour (Jamaica)	4 - 2		
				1987-1988			
Jul	26	BK Vargarna (Nortalje)	A	Pre Season Tour (Scandinavia)	5 - 1		
Jul	28	Gullringen GoIF	A	Pre Season Tour (Scandinavia)	2 - 2		
Jul	30	Enkopings	N	Pre Season Tour (Scandinavia)	2 - 0		
Aug	2	Varmbols GoIF	A	Pre Season Tour (Scandinavia)	8 - 0		
Aug	4	Nykopings BIS/IFK Eskilstuna	A	Pre Season Tour (Scandinavia)	4 - 2		
Aug	8	Coventry	H	Friendly	3 - 2		
Aug	10	Derby County	A	Testimonial - Gordon Guthrie	1 - 0		
Feb	8	AS Monaco	H	Friendly	3 - 0		
Apr	13	Birmingham City	H	Founders Centenary Match	5 - 2		
Apr	16	Blackburn	N	League Centenary Tournament Wembley	0 - 0	**58**	
Apr	17	Nottingham Forest	N	League Centenary Tournament Wembley	0 - 0	**59**	
May	11	Wolverhampton Wanderers	H	Testimonial - Nigel Spink	2 - 1		
				1988-1989			
Jul	30	Halesowen Town	A	Testimonial - Geoff Moss	2 - 1		
Aug	4	St Johnstone	A	Pre Season Tour (Scotland)	2 - 1		
Aug	6	St. Mirren	A	Pre Season Tour (Scotland)	0 - 1		
Aug	8	Greenock Morton & Athletic	A	Pre Season Tour (Scotland)	3 - 2		
Aug	10	West Bromwich Albion	N	Bass Charity Vase 3rd Place Play Off	3 - 1		
Aug	13	Notts County	A	Pre Season Friendly	2 - 3		
Aug	16	Gosport Borough	A	Pre Season Friendly	5 - 1		
Aug	19	Walsall	H	Testimonial - Allan Evans	4 - 2		
Aug	20	Hull City	A	Pre Season Friendly	1 - 1		
Nov	15	Barnstable Town	A	Opening Floodlights	6 - 0		
Dec	20	Israel	A	Friendly	0 - 1		
Mar	4	Trinidad and Tobago	A	Mid Season Tour (West Indies)	1 - 0		*
Mar	5	Tobago XI	A	Mid Season Tour (West Indies)	5 - 0		*
Apr	3	Banks' Brewery League XI	N	Friendly	4 - 1		
				1989-1990			
Jul	15	Servette Geneve	A	Pre Season Tour (Switzerland)	0 - 1		
Jul	16	Reinal Select (Regional Select XI Swiss)	A	Pre Season Tour (Switzerland)	0 -2		
Jul	18	Winterthur	A	Pre Season Tour (Switzerland)	4 - 4		
Jul	19	FC Solothurn	A	Pre Season Tour (Switzerland)	6 - 0		
Jul	21	Echallens	A	Pre Season Tour (Switzerland)	9 - 0		
Aug	3	Paget Rangers	A	Benefit - David Okorhi	7 - 0		
Aug	5	Hibernian	H	Pre Season Friendly	1 - 0		
Aug	9	Chester City	A	Pre Season Friendly	5 - 0		
Aug	12	Crewe Alexandra	A	Pre Season Friendly	3 - 4		
Aug	14	Watford	A	Testimonial - Ken Jackett	6 - 1		
Dec	20	Nettleham	A	Opening of Floodlights	5 - 1	**60**	*
May	9	Halesowen Town	A	Testimonials - Penn & Joinson	6 - 1		

53 This game was played at Aggborough Stadium home of Stourbridge.

54 This game was originally designated a Midland Intermediate League game

55 Aston Villa lost 4-5 on penalties

56 Aston Villa lost 4-5 on penalties

57 This match was abandoned at half time.

58 Aston Villa won 2-1 on penalties

59 Aston Villa lost 0-1 on penalties

60 This game was abandoned due to floodlight failure.

				1990-1991			
Jul	13	Ljusdals IF	A	Pre Season Tour (Scandinavia)	6 - 0		
Jul	15	Assyriska Foreningen	A	Pre Season Tour (Scandinavia)	5 - 1		
Jul	17	IFK Askersund	A	Pre Season Tour (Scandinavia)	11 - 1		
Jul	19	Sollentuna Alliansen	A	Pre Season Tour (Scandinavia)	1 - 0		
Jul	21	Krylbo IF	A	Pre Season Tour (Scandinavia)	4 - 0		
Aug	7	Bohemians	A	Friendly - Centenary	3 - 0		
Aug	10	Arsenal	N	Makita International Tournament	0 - 2		
Aug	11	Real Sociedad	N	Makita International Tournament	0 - 1		
Aug	18	Walsall	A	Bescot Stadium Opening	4 - 0		
Aug	20	Bristol City	A	Testimonial - Rob Newman	2 - 0		
Oct	13	Moscow Dynamo	H	Friendly	0 - 0		
Dec	17	Ryde Sports	A	Friendly	2 - 0		
Feb	15	Moscow Dynamo	N	Malborough Tournament in Hong Kong S/F	1 - 0		*
Feb	18	Hong Kong XI	N	Malbrough Tournament in Hong Kong Final	1 - 3	*61*	* 61 After Extra Time
May	14	Kuala Lumpur	A	End of Season Tour (Far East)	2 - 1		*
May	16	Sarawak	A	End of Season Tour (Far East)	4 - 0		*
May	20	Malaysian Select XI	A	End of Season Tour (Far East)	4 - 0		*
				1991-1992			
Jul	18	Hannover 96	A	Hannover Tournament - Gilde-Cup '91	2 - 0		
Jul	19	Gornik Zabrze	N	Hannover Tournament - Gilde-Cup '91	0 - 1		
Jul	21	TVS Ottersburg	A	Pre Season Tour (Germany)	3 - 0		
Jul	24	TuS Syke	A	Pre Season Tour (Germany)	2 - 1		
Jul	28	Borussia Monchengladbach	A	Pre Season Tour (Germany)	0 - 1		
Aug	1	Witney Town	A	Pre Season Friendly	5 - 0		
Aug	4	Shelbourne	A	Pre Season Friendly	4 - 0		
Aug	7	Plymouth Argyle	A	Tesimonial - Tommy Tynan	2 - 1		
Aug	9	Wolverhampton Wanderers	H	Testimonial - Paul Birch	2 - 3		
Aug	13	Gloucester City	A	Pre Season Friendly	2 - 1		
Oct	14	Hibernian	A	Testimonial - Alan Sneddon	2 - 4		
Mar	17	Bari	H	International Friendly	0 - 1		
Apr	14	Shelbourne	A	Friendly Challenge Match	1 - 1		
May	11	Cheltenham Town XI	A	Testimonial - Dave Lewis	3 - 4		
May	13	Worcester City XI	A	Testimonial - Martyn Bennett	5 - 1		
May	23	Sporting Lisbon	N	Friendly	0 - 3	*62*	62 This match was played in San Quen (Paris)
				1992-1993			
Jul	25	Bournemouth	A	Pre Season Friendly	2 - 2		
Jul	28	Shrewsbury Town	A	Pre Season Friendly	2 - 1		
Jul	30	PFV Bergmann Borsig	A	Pre Season Tour (Germany) - Friendly	5 - 0		
Aug	1	Dynamo Dresden	A	Pre Season Tour (Germany) - Friendly	3 - 1		
Aug	4	Peterborough	A	Tesimonial - Chris Turner	1 - 1		
Aug	7	Portsmouth	A	Pre Season Friendly	0 - 1		
Aug	9	Wolverhampton Wanderers	A	Testimonial-Stan Cullis + Opening Cullis Stand	2 - 2		
Sep	8	Birmingham City	H	Testimonial - Jimmy Dugdale	2 - 0		
Oct	8	Witney Town	A	Opening of Oakey Park	7 - 1		
Nov	14	Fiorentina	A	Friendly	2 - 1		
Mar	5	Drogheda United	A	Friendly	0 - 0		
May	10	Stoke City	H	Testimonial - Gordon Cowans	4 - 1		
May	12	Manchester United	N	Memorial Match-Mervyn Brown in Belfast	1 - 1		
May	16	Everton	N	Friendly - Mauritius	3 - 1	*63*	63 This game was played In the Mauritius National Stadium.
				1993-1994			
Jul	19	Yomiuri Nippon	A	Coca-Cola Cup (Tokyo)	2 - 1		
Jul	27	Hull City	A	Pre Season Friendly	2 - 0		
Aug	2	Port Vale	A	Testimonial - John Rudge	3 - 2		
Aug	4	Walsall	A	Pre Season Friendly	4 - 0		
Aug	7	Wigan	A	Pre Season Friendly	1 - 0		
May	9	West Bromwich Albion	A	Testimonial - Gary Robson	2 - 1		
May	16	Kidderminster Harriers	A	Testimonial - Paul Davies	3 - 2		
May	22	Liverpool @ Ellis Pk Johannesburg	N	United Bank International Festival	1 - 2		*
May	24	Manning Rangers @ Kings Pk., Durban	N	United Bank International Festival	1 - 0		*
May	29	Moroko Swallows @ Ellis Park, J'burg	N	United Bank International Festival	0 - 0		*
				1994-1995			
Jul	19	Falmouth Town	A	Pre Season Tour (West Country)	3 - 1		
Jul	23	Torpoint Athletic	A	Pre Season Tour (West Country)	9 - 1		
Aug	1	Oxford United	A	Testimonial - Ken Fish	3 - 3		

			1994-1995 (Contd.)				
Aug	5	Atletico Madrid	A	Trofeo Conception Arenal	0 - 0	**64**	
Aug	10	Coventry City	A	Steve Ogrizovic Testimonial	2 - 1		
Aug	12	Drogheda United	A	Pre Season Friendly	3 - 0		
Aug	13	Moor Green	A	Friendly	5 - 1		
Aug	15	Rapid Bucharest	N	Friendly	8 - 0	**65**	
Nov	15	Birmingham City	A	Opening of the new stand @ St.Andrews	1 - 1		
Dec	6	All Star XI	H	Memorial Match- Tony Barton	1 - 1		
May	9	Birmingham City	H	Testimonial - Paul McGrath	2 - 0		
May	21	Trinidad & Tobago XI	A	End of Season Tour (West Indies)	1 - 2		
May	24	Barbadian XI	A	End of Season Tour (West Indies)	1 - 3		
			1995-1996				
Aug	1	West Bromwich Albion	A	Pre Season Friendly	0 - 1		
Aug	5	Northampton Town	A	Pre Season Friendly	3 - 1		
Aug	8	Portsmouth	A	Pre Season Friendly	2 - 0		
Aug	12	Partizan Belgrade	H	Pre Season Friendly	2 - 0		
May	1	Birmingham City	A	Testimonial - John Frain	6 - 0		
			1996-1997				
Jul	30	Walsall	A	Pre Season Friendly	2 - 0		
Jul	31	Lincoln City	A	Pre Season Friendly	1 - 0		
Aug	3	Wrexham	A	Pre Season Friendly	2 - 2		
Aug	6	Oldham Athletic	A	Testimonial - Ian Olney	3 - 0		
May	13	San Jose Clash	A	End of Season Tour (USA)	1 - 1		
May	21	Los Angeles Galaxy	A	End of Season Tour (USA)	1 - 1		
			1997-1998				
Jul	18	Wycombe Wanderers	A	Pre Season Friendly	5 - 0		
Jul	22	Partick Thistle	A	Pre Season Tour (Scotland)	3 - 0		
Jul	26	Motherwell	A	Pre Season Tour (Scotland)	3 - 0		
Jul	29	Kidderminster Harriers	A	Testimonial - Graham Allner	5 - 1		
Jul	30	Birmingham City	A	Pre Season Friendly	0 - 0		
Aug	3	West Bromwich Albion	A	Testimonial - Ronnie Allen	2 - 1		
Feb	13	Tamworth	A	Friendly	3 - 0		
Mar	19	Oadby Town	A	Friendly	4 - 1		
May	5	Port Vale	A	Testimonial - Dean Glover	5 - 3		
			1998-1999				
Jul	28	Wycombe Wanderers	A	Pre Season Friendly	3 - 0		
Jul	31	Peterborough United	A	Pre Season Friendly	2 - 0		
Aug	7	Seville	A	La Linea Trophy	2 - 1		
Oct	5	Hednesford Town	A	Testimonial - Kevin Collins	4 - 0		
Dec	15	Hereford United	A	Testimonial - Chris Price	2 - 0		
May	11	Cardiff City - Carl Dale Select XI	A	Testimonial - Carl Dale	3 - 1		
			1999-2000				
Jul	16	Stevenage Borough	A	Pre Season Friendly	3 - 0		
Jul	23	Ajax	N	DLJ Direct Gotham Cup - New York	2 - 2	**66**	*
Jul	25	Fiorentina	N	DLJ Direct Gotham Cup - New York	0 - 4		
Aug	1	Feyenoord	A	Pre Season Friendly	0 - 0		
Aug	2	Kidderminster Harriers	A	Testimonial - Martin Weir	0 - 1		
Apr	25	Cheltenham Town	A	Testimonial - Chris Banks	6 - 1		
May	9	Swansea City	A	Testimonial - Martin Weir	3 - 0		
			2000-2001				
Jul	30	Wolverhampton Wanderers	A	Testimonial - Mike Stowell	2 - 0		
Aug	11	SL Benfica	A	Pre Season Friendly	2 - 2		
			2001-2002				
Aug	12	Racing Santander	A	Pre Season Friendly	2 - 0		
			2002-2003				
Aug	4	De Graafschap	A	Pre Season Friendly	2 - 2		
			2003-2004				
Jul	22	Turun Palloseura	A	Pre Season Tour (Scandinavia)	3 - 0		
Jul	24	Pitea	A	Pre Season Tour (Scandinavia)	8 - 0		
Jul	26	Umea	A	Pre Season Tour (Scandinavia)	4 - 0		
Jul	29	Bodens BK	A	Pre Season Tour (Scandinavia)	4 - 2		
Aug	2	Walsall	A	Pre Season Friendly	1 - 2		
Aug	5	Scunthorpe	A	Pre Season Friendly	5 - 0		
Aug	9	Leeds United	N	Dublin Tournamet	2 - 2		
Aug	10	St. Patricks	A	Dublin Tournamet	6 - 0		
Nov	12	Al Nasr	A	Friendly in Dubai	5 - 3		

64 The Villa won 3-1 on penalties.

65 This game was played at Walsall's Bescot Stadium.

* **66** Aston Villa won 3-2 on

2004-2005

Jul	21	Kungshamn/Smogen	A	Pre Season Tour (Sweden)	6 - 0
Jul	22	Kungsbacka Combined XI	A	Pre Season Tour (Sweden)	7 - 2
Jul	24	Jonkopings Sodra	A	Pre Season Tour (Sweden)	3 - 0
Jul	27	Orgryte	A	Pre Season Tour - Friendly	0 - 0
Jul	30	Walsall	A	Pre Season Friendly	1 - 2
Aug	3	Derby County	A	Pre Season Friendly	1 - 2
Aug	7	AZ Alkmaar	A	Pre Season Friendly	1 - 0

2005-2006

Jul	18	Wycombe Wanderers	A	Testimonial - Steve Brown	2 - 0
Jul	21	Gallstads	A	Pre Season Tour (Sweden)	14 - 0
Jul	23	Jonkopings Sodra	A	Pre Season Tour (Sweden)	1 - 1
Jul	26	GAIS	A	Pre Season Tour (Sweden)	3 - 3
Jul	30	Wolverhampton Wanderers	A	Pre Season Friendly	1 - 2
Aug	2	Walsall	A	Pre Season Friendly	3 - 0
Aug	5	Utrecht	A	Pre Season Friendly	2 - 1

2006-2007

Jul	21	Walsall	A	Pre Season Friendly	5 - 0
Jul	25	Hull City	A	Pre Season Friendly	2 - 0
Jul	29	Wolverhampton Wanderers	A	Pre Season Friendly	3 - 0
Aug	4	Hanover 96	A	Pre Season Tour (Germany & Holland)	0 - 0
Aug	8	Nijmegen Eendracht Combinatie	A	Pre Season Tour (Germany & Holland)	1 - 2
Aug	11	Groningen	A	Pre Season Tour (Germany & Holland)	2 - 2

2007-2008

Jul	25	Toronto	A	Pre Season Tour (North America)	4 - 2
Jul	28	Columbus Crew	A	Pre Season Tour (North America)	3 - 1
Aug	1	Stoke City	A	Pre Season Friendly	2 - 0
Aug	4	Internazionale	H	Pre Season Friendly	3 - 0

2008-2009

Jul	10	FC WIL 1900	A	Pre Season Tour (Switzerland)	6 - 0	
Jul	12	Zurich	A	Pre Season Tour (Switzerland)	1 - 2	
Jul	15	Lincoln City	A	Pre Season Friendly	1 - 3	
Jul	22	Walsall	A	Pre Season Friendly	3 - 2	
Aug	2	Reading	A	Pre Season Friendly	1 - 1	
Aug	6	Real Balompedica Linense	A	Pre Season Tour (Spain)	1 - 1	67
Aug	8	UD Marbella	A	Pre Season Tour (Spain)	2 - 0	68

2009-2010

Jul	18	Peterborough United	A	Pre Season Friendly	3 - 0	
Jul	21	Colchester United	A	Pre Season Friendly	2 - 2	
Jul	25	Malaga	A	Peace Cup	0 - 1	
Jul	29	Atlante (Mexico)	N	Peace Cup	3 - 1	
Jul	31	Porto	N	Peace Cup Semi-Final	2 - 1	
Aug	2	Juventus	N	Peace Cup Final	0 - 0	69
Aug	4	Oxford United	A	Pre Season Friendly	0 - 2	70
Aug	8	Fiorentina	H	Pre Season Friendly	1 - 0	

2010-2011

Jul	18	Basingstoke Town	A	Pre Season Friendly	1 - 2	71
Jul	19	Peterborough United	A	Pre Season Friendly	3 - 2	
Jul	24	Bohemian FC	A	Pre Season Friendly	1 - 2	
Jul	27	Walsall	A	Pre Season Friendly	2 - 1	
Jul	30	Feyenoord	N	Guadiana Cup	3 - 1	
Aug	1	Benfica	A	Guadiana Cup	1 - 4	
Aug	6	Valencia	H	Pre Season Friendly	0 - 0	

2011-12

Jul	21	Walsall	A	Pre Season Friendly	3 - 1
Jul	27	Blackburn Rovers	N	Barclays Asia Trophy - Semi Final	1 - 0
Jul	30	Chelsea	N	Barclays Asia Trophy - Final	0 - 2
Aug	3	Derby County	A	Pre Season Friendly	0 - 2
Aug	6	Sporting Braga	A	Pre Season Friendly	1 - 1

67 This match was designated as a behind closed doors friendly but as so many fans turned up the crowd was admitted.

68 See 67

69 Aston Villa won 4-3 on penalties

70 Aston Villa fielded a weakened team.

71 Aston Villa fielded a weakened team.

The above record of matches is as complete as detailed research has revealed.
The following type of matches have not been included: Those played 'behind closed doors' (not seen by the general public), matches generally recognised as non-First team games, 'non-serious' games, e.g. those versus 'All Star X1's', versus Celebrities, etc.
* Refers to games that have been covered in the text section.

Yore Publications

Was formed by Dave Twydell in 1991, and during the last twenty plus years, a large number and variety of football books have been published.

We specialise in Football League club histories (arguably the leading publisher in this field), currently over 30 titles, plus several updated reprints and Scottish clubs. Recent titles have included: Doncaster Rovers, Brentford and Chester City, plus - from Scotland - Motherwell and Partick Thistle. These are all large, quality books of c.300 pages containing detailed statistics, illustrations and the written history. We have also produced around twenty players' Who's Who books, covering both English and Scottish clubs.

With a keen interest in non-League football, the 'Gone But Not Forgotten' series of books, two per annum, is approaching its twentieth year. Each addition covers, in reasonable detail, around six clubs that have folded or grounds that are no more.

Finally some of our unusual 'specials' include: 'Through The Turnstiles' (A history through attendances), 'Ultimate Directory of English and Scottish Football Grounds' (every past and present league ground in England and Scotland), 'Denied F.C.' clubs attempts to gain membership of the Football league, etc.

For a full and detailed list of all our publications, see our website:
www.yore.demon.co.uk or write to:
Yore Publications, 12 The Furrows, Harefield, Middlesex (England)